ABUNDANCE

ABUNDANCE

Nature in Recovery

Karen Lloyd

BLOOMSBURY WILDLIFE
LONDON · OXFORD · NEW YORK · NEW DELHI · SYDNEY

BLOOMSBURY WILDLIFE
Bloomsbury Publishing Plc
50 Bedford Square, London, WC1B 3DP, UK
29 Earlsfort Terrace, Dublin 2, Ireland

BLOOMSBURY, BLOOMSBURY WILDLIFE and the Diana logo are trademarks
of Bloomsbury Publishing Plc

First published in the United Kingdom 2021

ISBN: HB: 978-1-4729-8908-6; Audio download: 978-1-4729-8905-5;
ePub: 978-1-4729-8909-3; ePDF: 978-1-4729-9388-5

2 4 6 8 10 9 7 5 3 1

Typeset in Bembo Std by Deanta Global Publishing Services, Chennai, India
Printed and bound in Great Britain by CPI Group (UK) Ltd, Croydon CR0 4YY

MIX
Paper from
responsible sources
FSC® C020471

To find out more about our authors and books visit www.bloomsbury.com
and sign up for our newsletters.

For our sons and daughters,
and for theirs.

Contents

'The future is an infinite succession of presents, and to live now as we think human beings should live, in defiance of all that is bad around us, is itself a marvelous victory.'

Howard Zinn

'How is it that you live, and what is it you do?'

William Wordsworth

A Primer for Abundance

A willow warbler flies inside a house by the sea. I don't know why the warbler decided – if that is what it did – to enter the human-made world. Perhaps its attention had been locked on to a day-flying moth that had, unobserved by me, swithered through the door I'd left wide open to let the heat out and the outside in. Or maybe there'd been a sparrowhawk locked on to the willow warbler, and maybe the hawk had twisted from the wall of the house at breakneck speed as the willow warbler went where the hawk wasn't able to follow. Perhaps the hawk swivelled back towards the foraging grounds of the oak woods at the back of the house where it was able to pursue other small birds in different, less human-entangled ways.

I'm speculating here. I'm speculating about the sparrowhawk and whether or not this was the driving force that drove the greenish-yellowish-whitish warbler in through the open door. But there's no speculation about the way the willow warbler sets about doing what every bird that finds itself inserted into the built environment will do in situations like these: the warbler begins to batter itself against the window. And of course, there's no speculation about my attention and the way it has locked on to the battering of the bird – and how I want the battering to stop.

Sometimes the warbler (which is similar in size to a blue tit but of slighter build) allows itself to drop onto the white-painted windowsill to rest momentarily. When it does this, I see how the bird's breath is the breathing of battering and panic. The warbler is panicked because of its inability to pass through the glass to the outside. It has no ability or perception of how to remove itself from the world of window frames and glass.

By now I'm standing to attend to the problem, and I know what needs to be done. But here on the sill, among all the flailing of the greenish wings, and the vibrating of the tiny chest as the bird's heart adjusts itself to what panic is, I focus my attention on the subtle green stripe that interrupts the warbler's eye – the kind of flourish a calligrapher might make with the flick of a brush tip. From there, the green carries on over the head and the wings and over the back of the bird. Above the stripe, there's a yellowish parallel stripe and in the warbler's eye a mote of light from the sunshine that floods through the glass. The warbler's whitish chest is more difficult to see because the bird is orientated away from me and towards the outside. In glimpses I catch the yellow edge of the underwing, its rim illuminated in the way the early-morning light sometimes catches the contours of the hills on the island across the inlet.

I lean towards the bird with my hands outstretched because what I want is for the battering to stop. And so easily, so accommodatingly, the warbler allows itself to be gathered inside them. Within the world of my fingers and thumbs, the wings become still and the panic stills, too. What I don't know is whether a bird stilled by hands is stilled inside or whether the panic merely becomes internalised as the body, by necessity, stills. No doubt I'll never know but, for a few moments more, I hold the bird inside my hands.

I'm thinking about abundance and how many ways there are to see, and when I read a book on the British artist Mary Newcomb, I find a painting called 'A football match seen through a hole in an oak leaf eaten by a caterpillar'. When I first look at this painting, I don't understand why this title or why this image of a leaf gnawed by blue-black hairy caterpillars (four of which hang from threads above the leaf like circus performers suspended by ropes) have anything to do with football. After some time my eye eventually distinguishes a tiny football net and a pink-shirted player off to one side of the leaf and another pink-shirted player on the other. These miniature manifestations of the human world behave as a guide that helps my eye find the small hole in the middle of the leaf through which, now I've begun to understand some of the ways this artist sees, more of the football players become visible. A couple of them hold their arms high, and in the air above their heads is the tiny sphere of the football itself.

When my eye tunes in to another person's way of seeing, I begin to see the world differently.

The hole in the leaf is a way for both artist and viewer to consider the *thingliness* of the subjects under observation; a lens through which we are invited to view the world, its various perspectives and distances. If I look at the middle distance through a hole eaten into a leaf, what might I see that I wouldn't otherwise? I want to bend closer towards the natural world – to pay it close attention because attention to the natural world has not been abundant in the Anthropocene (the current geological age during which human activity is the dominating influence on our climate and environment). The word 'attention' is derived from the Latin 'to stretch towards'. I want to bend or stretch not only towards all the holes in all the leaves but also towards the holes humans have created during the Anthropocene. I need to work out what I've not been looking at but should have been. I want to pay attention.

In the field of ornithology, birders talk about 'getting your eye in'. It means to become skilful because you have practised the visual and auditory and the factual fields of birds. I look up the expression online at home, and my eye is caught by an article further down the screen about how to flush something out of your eye. What do we need to see, and what do we need to flush out? An overwhelming

amount of biodiversity has been flushed away because of
our collective actions. Sometimes this flushing might
manifest in tears. I might weep because of all the losses;
this weeping won't do me or the world any good. When
my sons leave home, there is a logic to the tears I weep.
For both of us, it is a rite of passage; part of the necessary
act of being in the world. Everything is connected. When
Callum first left home, my tears fell for two days. Then I
put on the biohazard suit, opened the door and went in to
tackle his room.

When I turn on the news or read a newspaper, I am
assailed by all the losses in the natural world. The natural
world is being flushed out. In the natural world, there are no
rites of passage to cope with this. Sometimes, frequently in
fact – I am overwhelmed by all the losses and the reporting
of all the losses, and what I want to do is get my eye in, in a
different way. I want to use my binocular vision to look at
and think about abundance and what that might mean in the
Anthropocene. I want to take my binoculars into the field
and see if it is still possible to see abundance – or something
like it. And if I come across it, I want to know what kinds of
looking were employed to keep that abundance in place or
help build it up again, or that challenged the inevitability of
loss. If I push or pull on my binoculars' thumbscrew – the
focus wheel that helps me get my eye in – will it be abundance
or loss that comes more into view?

Another of Mary Newcomb's paintings is called 'The
demoiselles (a warm July evening Bradford-on-Avon)'. In
this painting, an abundance of banded demoiselles (a species
described by the British Dragonfly Society as 'a large *metallic*
damselfly') is zipping over the surface of a waterway that
reflects the blue sky and the landscape. There must be a
bridge upon which the artist stood to observe and draw the
damselflies because on the right-hand side of the painting a
reflected purplish-brownish strut appears and above this (or
below it, in the field of reflection) the tracery of ironwork

railings. For a long while my attention snagged on the airborne banded demoiselles that are huge because they were *this close* to the artist's field of vision. Beneath them, clustered on the margins and the green spears of emergent irises along the rim of the water, I see regiments of other demoiselles whose wings are also poised in the imminence of flight.

Although I think I'm looking intently at the painting, there's something I fail to see until one day, suddenly, here she is. The reflection of a woman has been painted in the pool of slow-flowing water (the preferred habitat of banded demoiselles – especially when bordered by banks of verdant foliage). She is there among the also-reflected bright-green confetti of the newly emergent leaves of the tree that is just out of the picture and above her head. This woman, too, is poised – poised in the act of observing. Her face has become stilled from the act of being caught by the world of the banded demoiselles. And even though her eyes are no more than two tiny dashes of paint, when I turn the painting upside down, I notice how the woman's attention is locked on to one of the pairs of flying demoiselles. I suppose this upside-down woman reflected in the water is Mary Newcomb. By painting herself in this partly hidden way, the artist invites us to keep looking. To look only once, she might be saying, is not enough. To understand, we need to come closer, to get our eye in. In the book, Newcomb questions whether she sees the world or the world the artist sees. From this, I think about how artists and poets allow the rest of us to become reacquainted with the familiar; how in each new response, they reinvent the world for us. I think above all, this is a form of generosity because it helps us to see differently.

This woman is also me. I'm walking along the banks of a river. My eldest son has moved away. He has been away to

university, returned home and moved away again to a small
city in the north of England. We visit him, my husband and
younger son and I, and we walk from Callum's home on the
outskirts, following the riverside path alongside the wide,
slow-flowing river. It's early summer and the riverbanks are
brimming. Coronets of cow parsley surge upwardly and,
among the greenery, ragged robin builds towering pink
assemblies of itself. Mary Newcomb would have been
perfectly at home.

My two sons are walking ahead of me, their father just
behind them, and as usual in these coming-togethers, the
conversation is animated. The young men are telling each
other stories and laughing, and I can tell how their father is
enjoying their being together again. I enjoy getting my eye
in to the way my sons are with each other, and with us. At
the same time, I'm noticing the abundance of banded
demoiselles zipping their damselfly histograms over the path
and the banks of the river. I only know of banded demoiselles
because of the damselflies in Newcomb's painting; they are
not a species found in my ecological part of the world
where our shorter rivers boulder their way around tight
curves, indeterminate slow deeps and sudden drops. I begin
to accommodate myself to the new ecologies of unknown
rivers and the nascent ecology of being a mother part-way
through the work of releasing her sons into the world.

Trapped behind glass, the willow warbler cannot distinguish
one kind of seeing from another, and this is understandable.
It is my impulse to set the warbler free because I want the
battering and panic to stop. I wonder exactly what we
humans have been looking at since our attention became
distracted.

In 1992, almost 2,000 of the world's leading scientists
presented us with another way of looking at the world. In

'World Scientists' Warning to Humanity', they informed us that the current trajectory of global warming was unsustainable. In 2020 Caspar Henderson wrote: 'More than half of all the carbon emissions in human history have been produced since [American singer-songwriter] Taylor Swift was born [in 1989], a little over a month after the fall of the Berlin Wall. About a quarter have been released since Swift released her first album in October 2006.' Or, to put this another way: since my sons were aged thirteen and six in Tony Blair's final year of being Prime Minister of the UK; since the population of the United States reached 300 million and that of the UK reached 60.62 million; since the population of the world reached 6.594 billion. In the fourteen years since, the population of the world has risen to 7.8 billion.

The lens we are not looking through is smeary with neglect. We have not been looking at the middle ground or the further away (time; distance; the rate of loss) nor the closer at hand (what is no longer here that always was). From the 1960s onwards, because of over-intensification of farming and human encroachment on the natural world, the biodiversity-loss shit really began to hit the fan. We know this – of course we do – but the swing of our world hasn't allowed us to stop. Some of us see what is happening but have little ability to act. Others see something else entirely because maintaining the juggernaut of the free market and globalisation is the priority. For them, the natural world does little but get in the way.

The philosopher Timothy Morton describes 'hyperobjects' as objects of such vast scale that they defeat more traditional ideas of what a 'thing' is – whether that is the world, or the biosphere, climate breakdown, evolution or capitalism. A 'hyperobject', then, is something that is simply too vast and unwieldy for us to begin to grasp or deal with. Morton says that for us to begin to process hyperobjects, there needs to be new ways of thinking about the world, about our politics,

our art, our ethics. That we need to reinvent the ways in
which we think. My friend Susan says that when a job is too
big, you have to 'eat the elephant'. How do we begin to eat
the elephant? A bit at a time, of course. But what I don't
know is whether there is still time for us to go so slowly. The
human race continues to either batter against and be
panicked by or not sufficiently panicked and not batter
against the systems whose regimes we operate within and
that hold us in thrall. I want us to reach towards the
hyperobject, to shake hands with it. I want us to open the
conversation.

In 2009, the Castle Museum in Norwich held an exhibition
called *Mary Newcomb's Odd Universe*. It so happened my
sister-in-law was one of the curatorial team and, thanks to
her, I discovered the universe of Mary Newcomb, who had
died the previous year.

Newcomb was an outsider in two senses of the word.
She was an untrained artist whose work was unusual and
idiosyncratic, and – to borrow a phrase from that other
rural outsider, John Clare – much of her work was found in
the fields. Newcomb lived on the Suffolk–Norfolk border,
and her painted world is concerned with her deeply rural
way of life there, with fields, orchards, country shows, the
seaside and the inhabitants of all of these places – both
human and animal. When I think about Newcomb's work,
I see an artist leaning towards the world by peering through
holes in leaves and studying the habitats of bullfinches, bees,
hoverflies and butterflies. I see a woman tuning in to how
the bullfinch exists, partly at least, in a world of thorns, a
private world that humans have little ability to enter,
that we may only enter by pausing and looking closely.
When I lean towards Newcomb's world, I see how humans
are part of the weft and weave of her universe on the

Suffolk–Norfolk border. A man rides towards her on a bicycle but is only half there because of the hill in the road between the artist looking and the man riding. A woman watches comets in a cowshed accompanied by cows. A woman has passed through a field and left an after-image behind her; it is this after-image that Newcomb paints. I wonder if this is another kind of self-portrait in which Newcomb invites us to question what other sorts of after-images we leave behind ourselves in the fields of our world after we have passed through.

I find something that John Berger said, about how looking at an original painting closes the distance of time between the act of painting and the act of looking at it. When I look at Newcomb's world from the perspective of the Anthropocene, I wonder if, during the latter years of her life, she had any sense of the rate of flushing away of many species that became unable to exist because of me and because of us, that are unable to speak for themselves. Had she understood that so many habitats and species lived on the cusp of change, that things were ebbing away? That the fields were less abundant because of how we continued to look – or not look at – our natural world?

When John Clare wandered far from his home village as a young boy, he also walked out of his knowledge: 'I eagerly wandered on and rambled among the firs the whole day till I got out of my knowledge when the very wildflowers and birds seemed to forget me and I imagined they were the inhabitants of new countries.' Although enclosures had been underway for centuries, in Clare's lifetime (between 1793 and 1864), further Acts of Enclosure swept away the feudal village and its demesne, together with the commons, or open-field system of agriculture. By the mid-twentieth century, the world that Newcomb inhabited was witnessing the systematic flushing away of hedgerows and the wrecking of ancient East Anglian field systems under the wheels of ever bigger machines.

More recently the artist Carry Akroyd documented the
presence of those machines in a series of screenprints – or
serigraphs – she made during the 1980s. In Akroyd's
images, the landscape is dominated by the new tenants of
agribusiness. The cab windows of combine harvesters are
blacked out like celebrity limos, removing any shred of
humanising occupation. There are machines for spraying
chemicals on the fields and machines for tearing up the
past. There are the hedgerows and field systems, like ridge
and furrow, that had existed in the landscape since the
Middle Ages. In many of Akroyd's prints, other kinds of
machines also intrude; stealth spy planes or fighter-bombers
surge through the sky, pursuing their own particular way
of looking at and not looking at the land below. In the
book '*natures powers and spells*': *Landscape Change, John Clare
and Me*, Akroyd journeys through the landscape of modern-
day Northamptonshire. She encounters both the landscape
and the poems of John Clare as a lens for witnessing the
process of agricultural intensification. In a print called
'Remember', the historical landscape (which is also a
remembering of the landscape of Akroyd's childhood)
clashes against the new. The uncertain rectangles of old
field boundaries butt up against the industrial tramlines
from a crop-spraying machine, the landscape moribund, all
the old boundary hedges grubbed out. The words of Clare's
poem 'Langley Bush' are distributed throughout the print,
the final lines subsumed beneath a bank of road construction
machines.

> By Langley Bush I roam, but the bush hath left its hill;
> On Cowper Hill I stray, 'tis a desert strange and chill;
> And spreading Lea Close Oak ere decay has penned its will,
> To the axe of the spoiler and self-interest fell a prey;
> And Crossberry Way and old Round Oak's narrow lane
> With its hollow trees like pulpits, I shall never see again;
> Inclosure like a Buonoparte let not a thing remain,

It levelled every bush and tree and levelled every hill
And hung the moles for traitors – though the brook is
    running still,
It runs a naked brook, cold and chill.

Some of our ecological friends saw the effects of intensification of the farmed landscape decades ago, but the
effects were not quite as visible back then. So, we carried
on in our collective acts of looking and failing to see. As
biodiversity crashed around us – the British Isles has one
of the most seriously depleted landscapes in the
world – very late, we began to understand that without
the world outside – the biosphere – humans would be
unable to exist. Very late in our world, we began to see
that more rather than fewer odd or different or idiosyncratic ways of seeing the natural world are required. If this
is the case, shouldn't the natural world be placed firmly at
the centre of everything? The natural world itself doesn't
have an opinion on this.

   Some of us think we have seen the future, and because of
what scientists and the weather and the disappearance of
species are telling us, the way our thinking has shaped itself
has led us to fear that maybe our kids don't have much of a
future. The weather in my head makes it impossible to think
about the fact that my kids might not have much of a future;
I cope with this by not seeing too far ahead. Yet I want to
know what God – if a god is looking down on all these
different ways of being and of seeing and not seeing in the
world – might think about how my kids might not have
much of a future. And I'd like to know what he (assuming –
if he exists – he is, in fact, a he and not a she) thinks about
all that business of dominion over the fishes of the sea and
the birds of the air and over all the trees and all the seeds of
all the trees, and what he thinks about some of the ways we
humans have entangled ourselves unhelpfully in the ways of
the natural world.

In the photo-documentary series titled *Spill*, photographer Daniel Beltrá exposes some of the effects of the
Deepwater Horizon oil spill in the Gulf of Mexico. The
final photograph in the book, titled 'Oil Spill #20', is an
image of eight American brown pelicans rescued from the
Gulf. The pelicans have been cleaned but will have to endure
the cleaning again – and yet again. The way they have
shuffled hopelessly inside the crate has resulted in the once-
white floor cloth being scrabbled into a series of folds that
remind me of draped fabrics in Renaissance paintings. The
drapes lead the eye in towards the birds. Inside the crate and
inside the photograph on the no-longer white fabric that is
utterly saturated with oil from the pelicans' feathers and
their filthy oil-anointed feet, the disposition of the pelicans
is that of a pieta, although without the central protagonist.
Instead, *all* the pelicans in the photograph have been plunged
into that oily, unnatural viscosity. *All* the pelicans and *all* the
other seabirds affected in this and every other oil spill or the
intentional dumping of oil at sea have been sacrificed to
economic carelessness.

Beltrá's photograph is an alarming confrontation with
loss and with how far we have – or haven't – come. And, oh
god, when I look at the pelicans in the photograph, I see
how utterly they are fallen.

During the Deepwater oil spill, when BP's chief executive
Tony Hayward was criticised for 'wanting his life back', he
duly apologised, saying: 'My first priority is doing all we can
to restore the lives of the people of the Gulf region and their
families – to restore their lives, not mine.' He also said to Sky
News: 'I think the environmental impact of this disaster is
likely to have been very, very modest.'

Beltrá's image stays with me. As I imagine the stink of
the oil that the birds and their rescuers endured, I begin to
think about the photograph differently. Because to act to
save birds and other species from ruination caused by
humans is not only a profound sense of engagement with

our imagination but illustrates that human agency is also the dynamic of repair. And I know which version of humanity I prefer.

In midwinter, the UK's resident population of starlings are joined by influxes of starlings from Europe, and great starling murmurations begin to materialise in our skies. One of my favourite places to watch this phenomenon is Great Asby Common in Cumbria's easternmost dales. Under anvil-edged Orton Scar, I look west towards the sunset and the profile of the Cumbrian mountains. In twos or threes or sixes or sevens or hundreds, starlings fly in from all points of the compass, and as they do so, I find myself considering what kinds of communication they use to determine that *this* is the place. Murmurations appear to be a constant phenomenon occurring in a specific place, but sometimes, at least here in Cumbria, they change location; here one week, gone the next. To be a starling intent on joining all the other starlings and finding safety in numbers is to have identified the precise location for a murmuration. And when I watch these little starling aggregations coming together, what I notice above all is the absolute sense of purpose with which they gather for the benefit of the whole.

The murmuration accumulates in the space between the edge of the scar and the tenebrous conifer plantation into which the birds will eventually drop and roost. The murmuration turns on its axis, transfiguring into a smirr of dark confetti. Wobbling and indeterminate, it rotates towards me and all the other starling watchers who have gathered on this bitterly cold afternoon. It shimmers darkly against the orange and pink intensity of the sky, then fractures into two. One cluster accelerates and flexes into a parascending arc, and the other veers away to the east before swivelling and returning again. Reinforcements arrive continually; nothing is absolute, and everything shifts as the murmuration continues to expand.

It's then I see the mothership. A starling rhomboid materialises over the scar, the leading edge hauling perhaps a million birds in its wake. Above my head, the smaller flock is assimilated inside the greater, like X-wing starfighters returning to the Millennium Falcon. In such close proximity, the sound of all those wings is the sound of re-entry.

Out of nowhere, a peregrine shoots towards the flock: Superman, arms fastened against his sides. The peregrine attempts to pierce the flock but the flock compresses into a darkening galaxy; a black hole of birds. When the starlings react like this, the peregrine cannot make headway. The murmuration swirls and drops away, and now two more peregrines enter the scene. Seen through the mass of the starlings they are fractal versions of peregrines who patrol distractedly around the edges of the murmuration as if undecided what to do next. Meanwhile, on this side of the flock, Superman tilts and arcs away.

When the peregrine articulates itself towards the murmuration and attempts to pierce the flock, and the starlings compress themselves into an even tighter ball of birds, an image comes to me of a microscopically engineered IVF needle pressing against the wall of a human egg. When the point of the needle and its payload of sperm presses against the egg's wall, the wall compresses inwardly under the pressure applied by the needle. I think of all the pressures we are applying to ourselves in the centre of the Anthropocene.

In 1986 a computer programmer called Craig Reynolds designed a program to help develop the use of digital animation. This artificial life system 'Boids' ('bird-oid object'; 'boid', New York slang for bird) was designed to simulate birds' flocking behaviours. Manifest on the computer screen, the 'Boids' are a dynamic flock of pointy arrows that function according to three kinds of stimuli: separation, alignment and cohesion. Most of the time, the arrows flock together. 'Boids' like to be close to their neighbours; think starlings. Aligned like this, they flow in sinuous waves around the lacuna of the computer screen. When the simulated obstacles of red dots are introduced (think peregrine) rather than contract into a black hole of birds, the 'Boids' split and separate to move around and past the object because the obstacles themselves are static. But like starlings, these computer-generated flocks reunite when the obstacle has been successfully negotiated.

In the Boids' world, this is known as 'emergent behaviour'. I wonder what kinds of emergent behaviour humans might programme into our ways of being to allow us to move away from all that battering and panic. Maybe there just isn't enough panic yet. Maybe the battering needs to continue. Maybe we mostly need to follow the trajectory of the flock, but then where does that leave people like me, who would like their sons and their daughters to have a future? Do I become an obstacle that the rest wish would quietly go away?

Scientists have shown how a globally ordered state may emerge from within a set of simple behavioural rules inside a murmuration. The three-dimensional position and velocity fluctuations of individuals within the murmuration are correlated to each other and the value scales within the size of the flock. The scientists discovered that change in the behavioural state of one individual is affected by that of *all* the other individuals within the flock, no matter how large the group may be. They call this 'scale-free correlation' and in this correlation – or alignment – each individual is provided with an effective range of perception that is far larger than the individual range of each individual. This scale-free correlation enables the flock to behave as a critical system that can respond maximally to environmental 'perturbations'. For perturbations, think peregrine. For perturbations faced by entire ecosystems and the human race, think global heating and biodiversity loss.

To be inside a murmuration is to be controlled by the magnetising imperative of turn, loop, compress, expand. Looking up into the eighteenth-century skies above his vicarage in Selborne, Gilbert White observed the different ways that birds propel themselves along; 'starlings, as it were', he wrote, 'swim along'. You can swim with, or you can swim against. You watch or intuit your neighbour's decisions. You follow suit. When a single starling swims against the flow of the flock, the flock isn't going to stop and question why that one bird might have chosen to behave like this. How many need to swim against for the scale of the change to be noticed?

I wonder about my sons' experience of the natural world during their early years and primary education. Now they are young men, over dinner one evening, I ask them to try to remember what kinds of activities they did at school that focused on the world outside. At first, what they remember is nothing. I remind them of the hedgehogs they made from self-hardening clay and matchsticks during an autumn term as a way of exploring hibernation. Simultaneously, those hedgehogs were fashioned by all the small hands across the entire country, because this is how the national curriculum works. Was this it, I asked? Nothing else came to their minds.

At the same time, the computer had entered the sphere of the classroom, and of course, it was here to stay. When we arrived at nursery each morning, my only-just-three-year-old Fergus wanted to be in front of the screens. He leaned towards the computer screens, where there was a guaranteed

queue of little boys who also preferred to lean towards the
screens. The little girls, meanwhile, were elsewhere – making
and painting and doing. What does this say about how boys'
and girls' brains are wired or about how, as educators, we
prepare for those differentiating ways of being in the world?
I talked to the nursery teacher about the use of computers. I
expressed my concern that I didn't feel it appropriate for a
three-year-old to be in front of screens; there would be
plenty of time for that ahead. The teacher said: 'Computers
are part of the national curriculum.'

Screens present us all with a choice; simultaneously, they
are a way of engaging with and dropping away from the
world outside. The screen is the glass we can see and don't
see, a way for us to reach towards and disassociate ourselves
from the real. How many times, I wonder, were my children
encouraged to look through the screen of the classroom
window at the world outside? Meanwhile, I attempted to
inhabit the role of nature-nerd by dragging my kids out into
the fields and the lanes and the hills of our world to SHOW
THEM THINGS! My sons believed I had lost it. They
showed this in the way they looked at me when we were
out in fields.

If we are sufficiently clear, as I think by now we are, that
the problems of global warming and biodiversity loss are
perpetuated through our disconnection from the natural
world, then I question the value of an education system that
reinforces this disconnection or at least does little reparative
work. Is it not clear that the positioning of the natural world
at the centre of all our seeing is what might lead towards the
kinds of changes we urgently need to begin making, and
upon which all future generations depend? Where in our
national curriculum is the mandate to invest in our children's
understanding of the natural world as fundamentally as the
rest of the curriculum is invested in?

My friend Gill is a reception class teacher. She takes
her class of four- and five-year-olds to the woods, where

the children lie down on a parachute and look up into
the canopy of the trees. What they see above them are the
tremendous towering trunks of beech trees, ash trees,
sycamore, oak, an understorey of holly, hawthorns and
saplings. When the children look up into the trees' canopy,
Gill asks them to describe what they see. What they see is
the tangled and complicated clutter of the natural world.
Because of Gill, they break the complication down using
experience and thought and philosophy and language.

Screens do, of course, hold a place in this discourse; they
can help to mediate experiences that would otherwise be
denied to our children and ourselves. I think about the
British artist David Hockney's films of May blossom on
Yorkshire's lanes, which he made by setting up eighteen
cameras on the roof of his vehicle to record the blossom
bending under the breeze that the passing vehicle itself made
manifest. When later I stood and watched the film, albeit in
the dementedly busy Hockney exhibition at the Royal
Academy, it felt as if I was seeing hawthorn blossom for the
very first time. And judging by the mesmerised expressions
on the faces of other visitors, it was as if they were too.

When we are asked to look closely like this, the mundane
is elevated to a different layer of consciousness, as if in
showing the world better, or in close up, it's somehow more
beautiful; a lot more beautiful. In this way, the process of
looking becomes a profound engagement with beauty itself.

Of course, when my sons were at school, I wanted them
to learn to read and write and be numerate so they could
make their way through the world. These days what I mostly
want is for them to have a future.

ᕀ ᕀᕀ

As a schoolgirl, the comic *Bunty* provided me with a moral
framework upon which I could hang my thinking around
right and wrong, bullies and friendship, work and personal

endeavour. In *Bunty*, the bullies always get their comeuppance; right always prevailed over wrong. In the free market, the lines between right and wrong have become distorted and blurred; we are all implicated, are all at fault. Expressed as a proportion of Gross Domestic Product, spending on nature by political regimes in the UK has declined by 42 per cent since 2008. At the time of writing, ten of the twelve years since then have been led by a Conservative administration. In *Forests: The Shadow of Civilization*, written some thirty years ago, Robert Pogue Harrison wrote: 'Today we are witnessing the consequences of those one-sided declarations of the right of a single species to disregard the natural rights of every other species.' Most one-sided declarations are at present concerned with the rights of humans. The philosopher Bruno Latour suggests that 'political questions have also become questions of nature'. In the political sphere, the species and habitats upon whom we all depend utterly are at present utterly voiceless. I want to give them a voice. I want to align my thinking with the thinking of others whose actions give voice to the voiceless by assisting them to remain in the world.

But change is happening. In 2020, the suburb of Curridabat in Costa Rica's capital, San José, granted citizenship rights to pollinators, to birds and bees and native plants and trees, transforming the suburb into a pioneering haven for wildlife. Curridabat's mayor Edgar Mora said: 'Pollinators are the consultants of the natural world, supreme reproducers and they don't charge for it. The plan to convert every street into a biocorridor and every neighbourhood into an ecosystem required a relationship with them.' Now known as *Ciudad Dulce*, or Sweet City, Curridabat's urban planning has been entirely reimagined around its non-human inhabitants. Green spaces are now being treated as infrastructure, with accompanying ecosystem services harnessed by local government and offered to residents. Using geolocation mapping, the elderly and children are targeted to ensure that more vulnerable members of society benefit from reduced air pollution and the cooling effects the trees provide. The suburb is now a widespread network of green spaces and biocorridors through which pollinators travel and thrive.

Is it too great a leap of our collective imagination to take up this notion of citizenship for species that cannot speak for themselves? Can we take up the idea and run with it through the world – like runners holding the Olympic flame? If we run through the world holding torches to bathe the natural world in light – the life-support system that gives and keeps on giving without demanding anything in return – wouldn't that help us to see? The natural world urgently needs to be placed at the centre of everything we do, at the centre of all our seeing.

The woman walking the riverbank with its familiar ecology of sons and its unfamiliar ecology of damselflies becomes the 'I' of the story. The me whose sons are grown and, because of this, is increasingly able to think about the further away. I begin to look for stories about particular ways of seeing, about particular ways of paying attention. I want to discover places and people who have decided that loss is not inevitable because of the way they have looked at and thought about the world. I want to find some of their stories, to make sense of their unfamiliar ecologies. I lean towards the idea of abundance and whether it can still be found in the world. And, if I find it, I wonder what that abundance might look like.

I lean towards the willow warbler on the windowsill. I reach out my hands. For a moment, though, I pause because when might I next be in such close proximity with a wild bird or have the opportunity to look this closely, to become entangled with a creature in whose presence I am blessed by abundance? Can a single animal or bird or insect or field or tree be a way of becoming entangled with abundance? How many of those altruistic citizens of the natural world do we need to encounter to find ourselves entangled? Or should the question be more about when we meet them? When we find them in the fields, or in the ecologies of unfamiliar rivers, or in the tangled branches of the trees above our heads, or unexpectedly in a house beside the sea, is the task more about thinking how exactly it is that we see?

A tiny peep. This is all I have left of the willow warbler. By opening a gap between my thumbs and my fingers, I have a couple of seconds to take an even closer look at the greenish head and the miniature blaze of light and life kindled in the eye of the bird. I see that sometimes its eye is concerned with the inside of my hands and sometimes with the world outside them. But the warbler needs to be free. For the few steps I take to carry the bird outside, my hands are concerned with the buoyant sum of a migrant whose being has fostered an analogue of heat and light and habitat and food. Its tiny keel and skull are instruments for tracking continental shift, are tuned in – locked on – to the swing of the world, are barometers of altitude, sun and storms, the wind, the rain.

I open my hands. For a moment, the willow warbler sits and looks and considers the open nature of the world. It clocks the outsideness and flies.

To Receive the Wolf

A lone wolf passes through the night streets of a suburban town, trotting along the white line in the centre of the road and crossing diagonally towards the bright lights of a corner shop. At that moment a cyclist appears, and the wolf moves in front of the cyclist. The cyclist must have seen the wolf because how could he *not* see it as it heads directly towards him? The cyclist brakes and the bike stops, and let's assume that even the cyclist's breath stops as the wolf lopes towards him in its long, easy gait. The wolf passes just a few metres away from the front wheel of the bike, and maybe the wolf's nose twitches as it detects the scent of the cyclist, who may or may not be sweaty (although let's face it, there are not many hills for cyclists to struggle with in the Netherlands). The cyclist is almost certainly frozen in the strangeness of the moment, yet no doubt he is of but passing interest to the wolf. And maybe the wolf accommodates the presence of the cyclist as the worlds of the wild and the suburban collide, and the wolf takes a sideways glance and, for a moment only, let's just suppose that the eyes of the cyclist and the wolf meet.

I'm watching the film clip of this moment and wonder in what ways the wolf measures the human world – the bright street lights, the corner shop, the houses and gardens, shrubs and trees. Its not-quite-right habitats for wolves, the numerous unfamiliar scents that assail the wolf's senses of cyclists, rubbish bins, cats, drains.

When the street lights run out, the wolf disappears because what the wolf really needs is somewhere dark and quiet where it can settle down, unassailed.

Like a travelling medicine show, the lone wolf appears in the small town of Bennekom for one night only; *Canis lupus lupus* is travelling back into the heart of one of the

most densely populated countries in Europe. Seventeen
million people live in the Netherlands, where wolves were
last counted among its fauna 150 years ago. Gradually,
though, the *idea* of wolves' presence begins to occupy space
in the minds of the people of the Netherlands and, with so
many people in such a small country, it's no wonder there
are sightings. The wolf steps out of history and into the
modern world.

The wolf is invading our human spaces. It is visiting our
corner shops. Should we be afraid? Or does the wolf bring
wolf medicine along with its presence? The restoration of
habitat and trophic cascade rustling quietly in its wake. Or
should the wolf be wiped out again before it gains a
foothold, puts down roots, starts a wolf family? To provide
fewer opportunities for late-night cyclists to be confronted.
To prevent the wolf from becoming commonplace in the
collective imagination of a country. How ready are we for
the wolf?

A couple of days later, 30 kilometres to the south-east, in
the small town of Veenendaal, a wolf that may or may not
be the same animal paces along the pavement of a suburban
street. At first glance and in this domestic setting, it looks
like an Alsatian dog on the loose, but it's not. The wolf runs
past tidy bungalows, cars on driveways, picket fences, a
garden with a model windmill, strandlines of autumn leaves
linking one street light to the next. The wolf is shadowed by
a car that keeps pace, and someone inside it is filming the
wolf on their phone and, although she's speaking in Dutch,
I can tell by the inflection in her voice that the young
female passenger is saying: 'Is it? It is, isn't it? A wolf? That's
not a dog! Yes – it is. It's a wolf!'

There are numerous reported sightings of a lone wolf
here and there throughout the day. This is the world of the
young, inexperienced wolf, an animal that must endeavour
to work out its place in the world, to accommodate itself
into the human landscape. But in accommodating being

seen, the wolf has not yet worked out – may never work out – that its presence causes ripples to flow through the world, like shock waves from an earthquake felt hundreds of kilometres from the epicentre. The youngster has yet to learn of the gulf of separation between the human world and its own. And now I'm wondering about this and thinking that when a wolf tracks along a suburban street, it isn't the wild that draws the line.

I'm watching another film. A wolf emerges from the undergrowth of a forest, pauses in the middle of a forest track and looks directly at the camera. As the camera holder zooms in on the wolf, the image is wobbly, unsteady. The wolf's eyes, meanwhile, keep the person holding the camera fixed in their steady gaze, registering nothing more than a moment's attentiveness – of one animal taking stock of another. In that moment caught on film, we humans are a species towards which the wolf appears utterly indifferent. Seconds pass, then the wolf resumes its leisurely pace and wanders back into the forest. The whole incident takes no more than eight or nine seconds. The film replays four maybe five times, and each time I lean forward in my seat as if to come closer or as though to find meaning in the presence of the wolf.

What really happens in the wolf's mind when it encounters humans in the forest or in suburban avenues or, for that matter, when it runs past the front wheel of the bicycle? What exactly is it that the wolf sees?

I'm standing at the edge of a forest clearing late at night in the Veluwe forest in the Netherlands. Fourteen of us have walked about a kilometre from the car park, head torches on red so that, rather than intrude, the light infuses hazy spheres around us as we walk. We've put on hats, jackets and gloves but there's no need; it's mid-September and mild. As

I walk, I look down at the ground, not trusting myself to
negotiate stray tree roots in the way I would in daylight.
Either side of the footpath, the earth has been churned into
pits and mounds where wild boar have rummaged for
tubers and acorns.

After perhaps ten or fifteen minutes, we assemble in a line
at the edge of a clearing. With the forest to our backs and an
indeterminate space in front of us, one by one our head
torches are extinguished. It doesn't take long for my eyes to
adapt to the lack of light, yet light there is. The space above
us is pitch dark, and the lack of clouds has rendered the
constellations brilliant. The Milky Way is an etiolated,
vaporous entity that braids one forest-lined hemisphere to
the next.

The clearing in the forest has silence – of a sort – but
occasional aeroplanes rumble overhead, engines thrust into
gear for the approach to Schiphol, wing- and tail-lights
flashing. We talk in low voices, joshing about how we must
be mad when we could have stayed in the restaurant
drinking mint tea or beers. There are ten volunteers from
the 'Wolves in the Netherlands' project, the two project
leaders Ellen van Norren and Glenn Lelieveld, me and
Jennifer Hartlauf. Jennifer is an expert on the golden jackal
but, fiddle as she does with her digital megaphone, she can't
get the damn thing working. There's technology for you:
never available when you need it most. A couple of us shine
our head torches on the contraption and Jennifer fiddles
some more before abandoning the idea.

'Well,' she says, 'I guess there's nothing else for it.'

In the darkness, I can see spirals of auburn curls
corkscrewing from beneath her woolly hat as she places her
hands on either side of her mouth and inhales deeply. She
arches her back and tilts her head towards the stars. What
emerges is a shriek, or a wail, as if someone had set a banshee
free in the forest. A needling animal cry travels out into the
night, stunning the rest of us into silence. There's something

strangely human about the call too, which is funny, given that a human created it. A human imitates a wild animal, the authentic call of which resembles the sound of a human mimicking a wild animal. We know this because we also heard it earlier today. And if I hadn't known that Jennifer could do this, if by chance I'd been walking in the forest at night because that was something I liked to do, and if I'd heard what arose into the darkness but didn't know what it was, I think I might have been more than a little unnerved. And even though it's only Jennifer generating the sound, a charge of something uncanny, not to say primeval, surges through my bloodstream.

In replicating the call of a predatory species, has the human put herself inside the animal's skin? You can study the animal. You can learn and become familiar with the way it looks, the animal's habits and the food it likes. But studying the detail of its specific call? And learning to call in the same way? What if Jennifer's golden jackal call is the preamble, a way of preparing the forest for the idea of another species about to arrive?

You study the call of a jackal, and you practise until you have it – just the right amount of yap and yowl, pitch and tone. You learn the specificities of the sequence and the length of each moment in it so that, if push comes to shove and your technology fails you, you can re-enter (for a moment or two at any rate) a world you used to be closer to. Is it like love, this attention? Like a love lost that, when re-engaged, it becomes clear that you hadn't lost it at all but had merely become preoccupied with other things?

We wait in silence for three minutes. This is the protocol. This is the three minutes in which the blood in my veins settles. We remain in the night-forest listening attentively in case anything should return the invitation, and if nothing does, the call is made again – and again. I have learned that this is called bio-acoustic surveying. We are speculatively surveying for the golden jackal in a country where there has only ever been one confirmed sighting and one more possible sighting. Nothing happens. Of course not. Given the odds, how could it? But golden jackals are travelling. They are travelling out from their habituated territories in the Balkans in the south of Europe and the Dalmatian coast in Croatia. They're moving north through Germany, Hungary, France and into Austria (where Jennifer lives and works), and now here we are, granting the jackal at least the notion of welcome to an entirely new country. I begin to think of the jackals as migrants. Are they travelling further and further from their home territories simply because it is no longer possible to stay?

Most of our group have spent the day in a room with around a hundred other folk at a golden jackal and wolf symposium co-hosted by Wolven in Nederland and the Aeres Hogeschool in Wageningen. I'm learning that this is how things are done here in the Netherlands. You have the notion of an animal making its return after a long absence (like the wolf) or appearing in your country for the very first time (like the golden jackal), and what you do is gather a bunch of ecologists and animal scientists, volunteers and enthusiasts – not forgetting the government advisors – and together the bunch of you listen to presentations and think and question. What comes under scrutiny is not the whys and wherefores of the species' return, but their habits and habitats, the kinds of food they eat, and how to tell a golden jackal from a fox. And you discuss how you might begin to prepare a country for the return of a carnivore. There's speculation about potential human reactions, positive as well as not so positive. Yet a sense of perspective is maintained all the time and the bigger picture kept in close focus.

Jennifer shows images to help distinguish that the jackal is larger, rangier than the fox, that its fur is more golden, its back and the edges of its ears stippled with grey. In front of a screen of images – golden jackal versus fox – and a hundred delegates, Jennifer adopts the position and releases that absurd, ear-splitting wail. When she finishes, she says: 'And the bio-acoustic protocol is, we wait for three minutes.' But, being unaware of the bio-acoustic protocol, the dogs outside in the university's veterinary kennels begin to howl. They'd heard what you hear when one wild animal communicates with another and joined in the conversation. The howling of the dogs provoked considerable mirth. I laughed. Everyone laughed. We all paid attention to the dogs and their uncomplicated response. We gave the dogs their moment.

I really liked the wolf and jackal people. Here they were, rationally considering the complications and opportunities that accompany the reappearance of carnivores and having a laugh on the side. As well as philosophising about the return of a species and all that this meant – the images of wolves shot or walking on the wildflower margin of a farmer's field or waiting on the central reservation of a busy road, lorries and cars blurred by speed in opposition to the wolf's static nature – these people also knew how to lighten up. If I had to assign myself to a tribe, this could well be the one I'd choose. You couldn't say they were interested in these matters because it gave them status, that they had a platform and were damn well going to use it.

At the lunch break, Ellen introduced me to Peter Venema. Peter had long, straight silver hair parted in the middle, and he wore black trousers, a black jumper, black clogs. Peter is the chief conservation advisor enlisted to help the Netherlands government consider the return of the wolf. I mentioned that I'd heard the expression 'to receive the wolf' the previous year during another visit to Holland, and how much I liked this idea. That time, I was in the hawthorn dune forest of the Kennemerland National Park on the hunt for reintroduced bison and the bison project co-ordinator, Yvonne Kemp, had told me the government were holding meetings specifically to consider the best ways to receive the wolf. This idea was revolutionary to me. The Netherlands' government were not interested in hysteria or histrionics; they just wanted a pragmatic way of thinking about and dealing with a wild animal making its way through the world.

Yvonne also told me that wolves had already arrived, though the presence of those early wolves was not made public.

'The wolves were doing it for themselves,' she said. 'One of those pioneer wolves was found dead at the side of a busy road. When they examined the body, the scientists discovered that it had been shot, the body moved to make it look as if it had been hit by a car.'

It would be stupid to pretend that wolves are not without predators of their own.

The group that gathered that day gave valuable context to the overriding reaction from farmers and others in the UK on ideas around the restoration of apex predators, such as the lynx and the wolf. In comparison to the Netherlands, conversations in my country felt far removed from this more rational approach, so *unenlightened*. Ready to wheel out the histrionics before any consideration of value, in the UK, the same voices are always dominating the narrative. Were we not an island nation, of course, the animals would be arriving under their own steam, and from this, it's just possible that levels of national hysteria might not have become so deeply entrenched. But then what?

You could say that, in mimicking the jackal's call, Jennifer had climbed inside the animal's skin. What kind of space exists here, I wonder, for inserting animal myths into the vacuum of their absence? The central messages of most if not all those myths are negative. The wolf as a killer of humans, cattle and sheep still underpins the justification for not only having rubbed out a species but for not wasting our time in the effort of thinking differently. At a friend's house one evening, I met a lovely, intelligent woman with whom I'd had a perfectly reasonable, argumentative back-and-forth on politics, but when I'd mentioned meeting Paul Lister at Alladale in the Scottish Highlands, who thinks differently and wants to return wolves to an enclosed ecosystem, the woman looked aghast. 'Wolves?' she'd said. 'I don't think we want that!'

In the UK, we have obliterated even the thought of return. After however many thousands of years of evolution, is this really the point at which we have arrived? And where did it come from, this notion that causing the last of anything is good, and that preventing its return is courageous? How then should we think of an endling – the very last individual of a species – like Martha, the passenger pigeon living out its restricted final days in a zoo, the last one of what had literally been billions? Should we think of them as powerless and ruined? Or as heroic, overflowing with the tenets of our failures towards their cultural, imaginative and ecological significance? At the first hint of reintroduction, our land managers and our governments roll out the rhetoric on why there is no longer any room – no *appetite*, you might say – for returning a wolf, a lynx or a beaver. But that is complicit in denying a species its ability to restore a world in which we have forgotten how to live. A Last Wolf here. A Last Wolf there. The effortlessness of tuning out the ecological reality of the natural world. This is the crux of the issue. We can talk about anything as long as we don't also have to live with it. Instead, we impose ourselves as apex predator, and look where that has got us. No one suggested we got rid of ourselves, yet that, the scientists say, won't take much longer because of the hash we've made. Talk about shooting yourself in the foot.

In the forest, Jennifer fills her lungs with air and becomes jackal again. We wait for the three minutes. This time, something returns the call. From deep inside the forest, the open-throated roar of a red deer stag booms into the night. A moment later, it comes again. It's the start of the autumn rut, and the stag might want to know what this unfamiliar call is and to whom it belongs. When the roar comes a third time, it's clear that the stag has moved closer. It has moved into the blank space of the clearing in front of us. You could say that it has taken centre stage.

This is all highly unfamiliar territory to me: the forest I don't yet know the name of *and* being in a forest late at night. Or wolves returning to our towns and, yes, to our pavements and corner shops! Or the golden jackal spreading its range across Europe – the certainty of it, the shifting filament of a species on the move. I'm unfamiliar, too, with hanging out with a bunch of wolf and jackal people for whom the possibility of the presence of carnivores has also stunned them into silence, into the paying of a certain kind of attention.

The stag roars again.

Imagine it like this. The stag walks out of the forest onto the periphery of the clearing. It takes a few measured steps at a time and, with each one, a foreleg is raised high, like a prancing pony, then stamps a cloven hoof into the soft ground. And those antlers – they're so huge and heavy and so branched that if they were somehow separated from the head of the stag, you'd probably need a removal firm to shift them.

I wonder if by roaring like this, the stag is expressing high dudgeon at such an unnatural imposition into the world it believes it controls. After all, there are no top predators here. And yet …

Far away, across the open space that might or might not be a meadow, the forest appears to rise along a contour as if there's a low hill over which it flows. I'm still thinking about the stag when a pair of lights appears in that far edge of forest beneath what might be but probably isn't a hill. The lights are fugitive and momentary, and I can't make any sense of them. Do they belong to other late-night forest walkers? Or what about that retro American soft-top that had growled into the car park when we were getting ready, a man at the wheel and a bunch of hoodied youngsters, one of them sitting up on the top of the back seat, silhouetted? Even though I'd tried to control it, my inner health-and-safety officer had kicked into gear and the finger in my coat pocket had begun to wag before the car turned a wide circle, growled out of the car park and took off along the road, its engine gunning like a fishing boat in a harbour.

The lights among the trees are moving at the wrong pace for car headlights. They seem to sweep and burn, wending their way so slowly, so uncommonly. Now two lights: a slow-moving lorry? Now three. Now unified into one, like lights brought to bear on an incident. But then the lights don't so much sweep as linger and brighten, lose luminescence and dissolve. A few moments later, they return. If the lights are torches, then the hands that hold them are extraordinarily steady. Was something unnatural happening here? I recognised a sense of growing unease. What if there were folk out there lamping, as it's called at home? Locating foxes to shoot by the torchlight refracting in their eyes. It was pitch dark, and if there were people out there with shotguns, they wouldn't have a clue about us.

By now, our attention had fallen away from what may have been audible or present in the forest and towards this strange fugitive light that was stealing into the world like the first light that ever was. Slowly, the light began to burst above the treeline, orange and hot, and someone said, 'OK, so what on earth is it?' and then the hot orange swelled again and finally, simultaneously, our collective synapses snagged.

A waning gibbous moon, its declining edges convex; a fat seedpod about to burst. The texture of the penumbra was visible, the gradual division between light and shadow. By now the moon had cleared the tree line. Someone said: 'It's incredible.' Someone else said: 'Well, I have never seen anything quite like this.' And then silence fell over us again and, higher still, plane lights flashed silently, and the clearing before us was infused with an orangey-red phosphorescence born of the moon's strange light as if a diffuse spotlight was infiltrating the landscape. It felt portentous, mysterious, as if something was about to begin. Like the beginning of all things. The darkness before light, and now here the light was, with its incipient, struggling glow.

In a way, it was a kind of spotlight. The clearing had become a space or atrium into which it was possible for us to once again position the wolves and the jackals and anything else from the natural world that made our lives richer, more complicated. Position them now, the wolves, like printed card animals in a miniature Victorian play theatre. Give the stage a forest backdrop. Add the rising moon too if it helps, so that, like the one in front of me in the Netherlands, the forest in your hypothetical theatre is lit by this strange, seminal light. To one side there's a little wooden house and in front of this a duck pond. Surrounding everything, the forest. Now take hold of the tab attached to your wolf and push and pull back and forth. See how that feels. You might want to manoeuvre your wolf forwards a touch so that, as the moon rises and the light begins to emit that strange, unearthly glow, the wolf's head becomes visible, peering from behind the trunk of a pine tree. You might want to raise the theatre lighting incrementally until the glint in the wolf's eye becomes the point, the *punctum*, and when you see it, you make the decision to inch your card animal out from the shadows.

The orchestra begins to play. A flute is the bird, an oboe the duck. Go on, push the duck around and around on its little pond in front of the wooden house. A clarinet introduces the cat, and now this imagined cat circumnavigates the edge of the pond, its gaze fixed on the duck, the two of them circling like gears. Then the young boy comes out of the little house, and the string section is Peter. When I was a child, Prokofiev's *Peter and the Wolf* was one of our family's few records. From my usual position on the carpet, what this 'symphonic fairy tale for children' provided me with was pictures. Pictures that came into my head as I listened to it over and over again. Pictures of the little wooden house in the forest and the duck on the pond, and Peter – who was not much older than me – and his grandfather. And, of course, the wolf. Three French horns are the nasty, calculating wolf. The wolf, we know, will soon attempt to predate on young Peter, who is, so far, obligingly unaware. So it begins, this misaligning of truth, this mythic reinterpretation. The wolf comes out of the forest, and the picture we receive is that all it wants to do is eat our children.

Into your cardboard theatre bring a second and a third and now a fourth wolf; you have created a pack. And in the pack, these sociable adult animals share the responsibility for caring for their youngsters. Now feel the weight of responsibility we must attach to the animals we have lived without for so long and have, in our long distraction, forgotten how it might be possible to live *with* them. We have forgotten their value, in among the mess they sometimes create. The wolf rendered savage for the sake of upholding myths left over from a time when, during a long dark winter, stories and legends really mattered. How exactly did the tales we tell ourselves become so clouded, so diffuse, our thinking so scattered?

We allow ourselves to become distracted. The modern world crashes in. But the problem is that the crashing is non-stop, a slow-speed car crash of loss. And the things we lose slowly – the wolves, the cranes that once were just a fact of life in the British Isles, the beavers and their beavery wild wetlands cascading with species that come travelling back in the wake of the wild – we have become so dissociated from the species we have lost, we have dispensed with the memory of them utterly. At what point did it begin to form, this void inside us that caused us to forget how to see?

The wolf that loped along the suburban pavement in Veenendaal ran past the house of Glenn Lelieveld. Glenn and I were drinking coffee in a break between talks at the jackal symposium. 'Yeah, when I watched the film, I couldn't believe it. I thought – that's my house! A wolf ran past my house and I was there at the time and I didn't see it! I can tell you, I was gutted!'

There's another clip of a wolf running through a field at the edge of an industrial zone. In the background, just beyond the buildings, is the grey North Sea. There's a wind farm, a factory, a single train track towards which the lone wolf runs. Think of wolves and you think of forests and mountains, not this inauspicious, human-entangled industrial zone. Someone is filming the wolf using an extended zoom, and the wolf is running inland away from the coast. Everything is grey, the film grainy. Wind buffets the microphone and there's fine rain in the air. Were the film in black and white you could be forgiven for thinking a scene from Tarkovsky's *Stalker* was unfolding.

The film was of the first wolf to enter the Netherlands in more than 150 years. It had crossed into the Netherlands from Germany some 50 kilometres to the east, which is no distance at all for a wolf. Watching the clip, I see the wolf in the thick of it all, among our green power, our transport, our mess. A cyclist turns into the road to the wind farm less than 10 metres away from the wolf. A truck has stopped at the side of the rail track and someone gets out. I wonder if they've noticed the wolf. The person filming talks to his companion, but I can't discern what is being said. I think of how a friend of mine once said that wolves don't walk or run so much as float above the ground, and here comes this lone wolf, floating above the winter field.

As the film continues, the wolf pauses, looks around and moves on. A car pulls up at the junction at the same time as the wolf crosses it, and the car waits for the wolf presumably because the person inside it knows exactly what they are seeing. When it has cleared the junction, the wolf begins to run, but not in the confident lope of a wild thing in its element; the wolf appears distracted, bewildered even by our modernity. As I watch, what I see is how the wolf might have just been delivered through a portal from another age into a place and time where nothing is as it should be. Perhaps that's not so far from the truth.

As it runs towards another road junction, the wolf constantly looks around, slowing down, looking again, but it continues loping forwards in its intangible, doubtful fashion. I can't help but feel for the wolf, an animal lost at sea among tarmac and steel, street lights and power lines. I suppose this is the nature of pioneering, of wandering into the unknown, into a place where our clichéd expectations are blown to smithereens. The wolf just entered the post-modern age.

In the restaurant the evening after the symposium, Glenn tells me more about the film of the wolf in the forest, the one that had me on the edge of my seat earlier. Because that particular session had been delivered in Dutch, I'd not been able to follow the whole story, and my preconceptions had proved utterly wrong. What I'd thought was a wolf in a forest was indeed a wolf in a forest, although the encounter was not in the Netherlands as I'd presumed, but in Romania, and the clip had been appropriated by a pharmaceutical company marketing anti-tick-bite cream in a TV campaign. Glenn explained, 'The advert used the words, "There's something even more dangerous out there in the forest."' And so the wolves known to have taken up residence and to have produced young in the Veluwe National Park – a popular holiday and recreational area that also contains astronomical quantities of ticks – were stereotyped in that disassociated, generic way.

The advert made both Glenn and Ellen nervous. From the first wolf's entry into their country, they've both worked hard to keep hysteria levels from rising. The anti-tick-bite cream advert compromised their efforts – through the expedient of flogging a product. 'We'd made so much progress with the media,' Ellen said. Glenn added, 'Most wolf sightings come from the public, and we've always responded by saying: "Look, there's no danger; it's just a situation," and the press really got behind us on that. So this advert was a real blow.'

The morning after the symposium, I'm walking in the Veluwe National Park with 'Wolves in the Netherlands' volunteers Carolien Koldyk and Jaap van Leeuwen. It's so early that the sun is still low to the horizon, and when we walk through forest clearings, the streaming light obscures my vision. The project knows that the first pack of returned wolves have produced a litter of cubs in the forest here this summer. I'm excited. I want to see a wolf, of course I do, but the previous evening, Ellen's response to my question of how likely this would be had brought me crashing down to earth.

'We don't go out looking for wolves,' she'd told me. 'It's not a zoo. The wolves have to be allowed to get on with being wolves. We have to give them their privacy and respect that they don't want to be disturbed.'

Most sightings of wolves in the Netherlands are unanticipated, made by unsuspecting members of the public. Sometimes they upload their clips to YouTube, showing wolves travelling outside the anticipated sphere of the wolf – the one near the corner shop and the one running past the gardens in Bennekom. One of the wolf volunteers (oh, how I long to be a wolf volunteer), a woman of my own age called Anne – and who, like me, had grown-up kids – lived in the Veluwe with her forester husband. When she had gone out to her car one morning, she had found scraps of wild boar skin and hair on the lane outside their property and a bloody trail leading back between the trees.

In the Veluwe, the forest cover is uncompromisingly thick. The day begins to warm and I'm glad to have left my jacket in the car. We are looking for wolf scat, hair samples, footprints, and to do this, we walk on sandy paths, Jaap navigating with GPS. Jaap has an endpoint in mind – a dew pond some kilometres away, where he'd recently installed a motion-activated camera. Some of the forest paths are blocked with simple wooden barriers.

'We can't go this way,' he'd say, pointing at the sign. 'It's a "Wildlife Resting Area".'

I like this idea of providing space for wildlife to live undisturbed. In the small islands of the British archipelago, isn't that another fundamental problem we have also yet to engage with: our right, our *demand*, to have access everywhere?

Carolien tells me of a plan she is developing with another volunteer, a woman who visits farmers to talk about wolves and sheep and fences – and installs them, if necessary. The two women have found a site where they plan to open the first wolf-rehabilitation centre – in an abandoned golf club. Now there's a cultural shift for you.

We find a red deer wallow and pause to investigate. It's just a damp, muddy depression off to one side of the path, and there are plenty of deer prints.

'If you come across a wallow just after the stags have been,' Jaap said, 'you really know it; they stink to heaven!'

'Red deer love potion,' I replied.

We walk through the forest and along its edge adjacent to open meadows of golden grasses. At the side of one particular meadow Jaap tells me this is where, when he'd not been looking for wolves, he'd happened upon the first new-generation family. He takes out his phone and plays the film. He says there were three young wolves in the meadow.

'Wait a minute; you'll see them.'

In the clip, three female red deer saunter through the meadow. Something has clearly caught their attention. Then the heads of three young wolves emerge from the grass. The young wolves stand up, intrigued by the deer. Or should that be *electrified* by? One of the wolves moves as though to follow, then thinks better of it. The deer keep walking and looking at the young wolves, their demeanour saying simply: 'At your age and size, you have no chance, mate.'

It's getting hotter now. I let the others carry on as I crouch down to retie my bootlace, and when I've done it, something catches my eye. Out in another shady meadow and walking sedately towards the next bank of forest is an animal. It is grey and sandy, and it keeps moving towards the trees, and I think 'that is not a deer'. It moves all wrong to be a deer. The sunlight streams into my eyes and my fringe falls across them, and I can't be sure, but then I *am* sure because deer just don't move like that and this animal is, well, like a large dog. And then it's gone. I try calling in a stage whisper to the others, but they don't hear so I pick myself up and run to catch them up, and when I tell them what I've just seen they shrug calmly and Jaap says: 'Yes, it's very possible – that's another wildlife resting area.' There's no fuss. No excitement. Just: yes, that's possible.

Once they'd been given protected status by the EU in 1992, wolves began their exponential return through Europe. In the same year, they began to travel out from Italy and crossed the Alps into France. At the turn of the twenty-first century, they began to walk out from Poland and into Germany. For the first time in more than 200 years, wolves were seen in Denmark. Increasing numbers of abandoned farms across depopulating areas of Europe provided wolf habitat and plenty of food in the shape of deer. In Germany, military training areas unwittingly provided stepping stones from one habitat to another. (I came across one photograph of a wolf pup scrutinising an advancing tank.) Wolves were seen seen walking along the suburban avenues of German cities. The wolf was beginning to slip out of oblivion.

At the golden jackal symposium, Peter Venema had told me it was only ever a matter of time before the wolf arrived back in the Netherlands.

'We had plenty of time to prepare,' he says. 'We knew from our monitoring work that the wolves would eventually cross the border from Germany.'

'So, tell me,' I ask, 'what did those preparations look like?'

And Peter explains: 'We began to meet with the government, with policy makers and stakeholders, NGOs, farmers and hunters, and we began to ask questions. We considered philosophically what the return of the wolf meant for us. We wanted to share knowledge and understanding and assess how we could minimise human–wolf conflict.' Peter notices my widening eyes. 'What?' he asks. I pause.

'So, have I understood this right? You're telling me that your government was involved in philosophical discussions about what the return of the wolf meant for the Netherlands as a country?'

'Well, yes,' he says. 'What other way could we have done it?'

When you plan for the return of the wolf, you ask questions. There's no 'us versus them', farmers versus scientists. Knowledge is pooled, and a wolf roadmap is constructed – not to facilitate the travelling of wolves, of course, but to facilitate finding ways to accept and discuss and build and support. So, when it is understood that a lone wolf killed two sheep, support in the form of compensation is forthcoming. Some of the wolf volunteers, like one of the women I'd been in conversation with at the volunteer meal, acted on their own initiative. There's no need to have an NGO label to hang your name badge on; just visit farmers with land near places where wolves have been seen and ask how concerned they are about the possible effects of wolves on their sheep, then offer to put up fences. Wolves are understood not to jump fences; the pragmatic solution is arrived at merely with a sensible conversation. And in the conversational to and fro, an agreement is reached that a volunteer will carry out the work if the farmer provides the materials for the fences. The deal is done.

Conversations are frequently held with stakeholders to find out how it's all going. Banks of wolf data are gathered, and those philosophical questions continue to be asked about what specifically the presence of the wolf means.

'There is an old Russian saying,' Glenn said during the evening meal with the 'Wolves in the Netherlands' volunteers ahead of bio-acoustic surveying, 'that where the wolf lives, the forest grows.'

Consider the situation from all sides. Keep hold of the bigger picture. Tune out the interference and the white noise. Tune in to the ways and means in which the landscape communicates. Pay attention to what it needs to perform its work efficiently. Understand the nature of trophic cascade, where the presence of a single apex species drives – no, *nurtures* – healthy and fully functioning ecosystems.

What do you need for the return of the wolf? Do you need a wind-blown industrial coastline? Wind turbines? Rail tracks? Road junctions? From the domesticity of your suburban home, you watch videos of wolves moving through the human world: the wolf following the white line of the road; the wolf that looks quite at home running past the model windmill in the garden; the wolf running towards the cyclist near the corner shop who no doubt only intended to fetch the papers and a pint of milk. And this is all very novel, these wolves caught on film, colonising our human spaces. But the films might help us ask questions about what on earth has happened to the divide between the wild and the human. Indeed the films might also act as points of embarkation from where we can begin to philosophically consider whether, in stepping from its world into ours, the wolf has committed an act of transgression.

If you live on a wolf-free island, you might think you are safe from the possibility of wolves appearing. But in the winter of 2018, wolves crossed the sea ice and arrived sans fanfare on the Baltic's Ålund islands, midway between Finland and Sweden. Here the populous mostly became divided: for or against the wolf. However if you live on a UK island, you can forget about the possibility of sea ice; no matter how long or how hard you look, the wolf won't be approaching your shores or your pavements or your corner shop any time soon.

Take hold of your card wolves. Remember them? Now push them right out into centre stage. Fade up the lights – but not too bright. Understand that the wolf doesn't always need the forest. What it needs is the possibility of quiet and dark and the ability to find shelter. If you encounter the wolf in your town, the wolf isn't interested in real estate. The wolf is just passing through on its journey to find the right kind of quiet habitat that you, were you a wolf, would seek out to make your home in.

I want us to consider the nature of those card theatres for a moment. They are a Victorian invention, an imaginative fancy in which the proxy director – child or adult – can reiterate long-established stories and basic tropes of good over evil. It is interesting, then, to understand that across the UK, equally Victorian constructs remain as the primary shaping forces that dominate much of our thinking on land use and species. This reductive way of thinking presupposes that humans are entirely separate from nature. It alienates us from more productive narratives on how to think and to live. In the UK, we repeatedly told ourselves until the myth stuck fast that the wolf disappeared because it needed to disappear. We have forgotten that buried in those outmoded stories we keep telling ourselves is the concept that the wolf is a far more nuanced bedfellow – not in the bedsheets, in the cottage or in the forest, where the wolf assumes human identity for its own animalistic needs, but in the world at large. I want us to rip up the image – rip up those flimsy card arguments – and reimagine the wolf for exactly what it is: a sometimes complicated, sometimes problematic character, yes, but also the quiet benefactor whose generosities are to be uncovered in the philosophical, in the sensible, in the considered. Above all, in acts of human agency and imagination.

Circumspect Dancing
in Fields

I'm in Monfragüe National Park in Extremadura, Southern Spain and I'm looking across a deep gorge at the crags of Peña Falcon. Peña Falcon is a pyramidic rock extrusion that leans somewhat like a ship atilt in the wind. At first, I notice how the sun catches the south-facing aspect of the crag in a wash of lemon light. Many of the slabs are smeared with something lime green that I think must be lichen. Occasional shrubs colonise the rocks, and the north-facing slope is shadowed, wintry, though it's 21 degrees already; typical for November in Extremadura.

I'm glad of the railing; there must be a hundred feet between me and the still green water down in the gorge. My instinct is to call it a river, but there's nothing riparian about it; a rime of exposed rock shows the discrepancy between drawdown and rainfall. Once, this was the River Tajo, and once, the height between road and river would have been greater, the aspect more vibrant as the river plundered its way through the gorge. But that's all in the past, what with progress and the demand for electricity, and it's hard to argue with any of that.

The locals still like to tell stories about the coming of the Embalse del Torrejón-Tajo. How, when the dam was completed in the 1960s, no one bothered to inform the keeper of an isolated electricity substation. In the middle of the night, he was woken by the sound of – nothing whatsoever – as the backed-up water choked the night-song of the river once and for all.

I'm in Monfragüe to see vultures. I have never seen vultures before, and my expectations are, well, blown out

of the water. It takes a little while, though, to get my
eye in.

I've come to Extremadura because I've heard about the
abundant wildlife here, and I want to see something of how
abundance might manifest itself in a landscape unfamiliar
to me. I'm staying with renowned guide Martin Kelsey
together with a small bunch of birders. After breakfast, we
pile into the van, and Martin drives us to Monfragüe
National Park, skirting the medieval town of Trujillo on its
plug of volcanic rock above the plain, then we swing north
through Mediterranean cork and holm oak forests. This is
the 'dehesa' – the vast 'agrosylvopastoral' system where the
oaks are cultivated and managed rotationally for fuel and for
cork, underplanted by wheat and where an abundance
of acorns provides food for the famous Iberico pigs, and
where sheep, goats and cattle graze. Some 50 per cent of
Extremadura is dehesa. It is a system that benefits humans
and provides food and fuel and merino wool, which until
recently Spaniards referred to as Spain's 'white gold'. All this,
and there's plenty of room for wildlife.

Acorns are also a staple for the thousands of cranes that
migrate south to overwinter in Extremadura, though these
days the cranes are spoilt for choice – what with the region's
prodigious rice paddies and cornfields. The irrigated paddies
are stuffed full of incidental wetland foodstuffs for wading
birds – invertebrates, reptiles, roots and plants. The common
cranes are the field clean-up gangs gleaning cornfields after
harvest. I like this version of field clean-up gangs. When
Martin tells us this, I picture the trashy aftermath of a
Glastonbury Festival.

When I think about managing land on this scale under
a system that benefits people *and* wildlife, it speaks of a
very different way of paying attention than what I'm used

to at home. In Britain, in a disturbingly brief period of sixty years, abundance has almost universally shrivelled away. Some 70 per cent of biodiversity has been destroyed, nearly all of it through dangerously unthinking incentivisation payments to farmers. We know this now. We've known it for some time – but when those systems are flagged up as 'progress', most of us, especially those duly incentivised, choose not to look ahead at the consequences while doggedly pursuing our annihilating practices. Over a mug of tea in his kitchen, I'd spoken with a farmer about a ground-nesting bird, the curlew. I asked him whether he ever saw them these days. Observed by his son and mates who helped run the farm and didn't know what a curlew was, the farmer answered, 'When we're mowing, we're not looking.' I'm interested to know when and why many farmers and land managers – who frequently refer to themselves as 'Guardians of the Countryside' – began to stop looking? And when and how they allowed themselves to be tipped into blindness over the fundamental relationship between humans and land and the natural world. The landscapes of Extremadura and the UK are both managed landscapes; the difference is that, in the UK, we have chosen to prioritise economic means of production over a fully functioning landscape.

Martin parks the van at the top of a steep incline and we begin the climb up onto the ridge of the Sierra de las Corchuelas. I take my time, occasionally pausing on the narrow path under wild olives and oaks to peer out as this unfamiliar landscape unfolds. The rolling hills and valleys of dehesa extend all the way to the southern horizon, yet among all that expanse only a couple of habitations intrude.

Pliny said a squirrel could travel from Spain's northernmost coast to the Mediterranean coast without touching the ground. When I look out at the dehesa, I can't help but think of all that was at home in my small island nation before humanity got going with its axes and saws, farms, concrete, and steel.

I approach the ridge with Jez, another of our group. The others have already reached the top and are looking north through binoculars. That's when the first vulture slips into view – brown and grey and massive – drifting above our heads.

'Look up!', Jez calls to them as it flies langorously above their heads. As we reach the ridge, it's impossible not to be confronted by these giant birds in the air beneath, above and in front of us. If a white-tailed eagle is a flying barn door, then a griffon vulture is the whole flaming wall. And here they are, sliding about in the sky, weird and unexpectedly elegant.

On the ridge are the remains of an Arabic castle, a leftover from the days of the Moors. Inside the squat tower, plastered against the roof are weird clay tunnels like conceptual ceramic sculptures – the nests of red-rumped swallows. Further along, we climb up to a modern viewing platform that has 360-degree views of the landscape. For a passing vulture, the distance between where we gather on the ridge and the crag of Peña Falcon was nothing more than a moment's glide.

Martin points out the differences between a griffon and a black vulture. The black vulture is one of the giants of the avian world, with a wingspan of up to three metres. The griffons – of which there are far more, around 7–800 pairs – have a wingspan of 2.8 metres.

When a griffon soars above the ridge, I see the motionless fuselage of the body and the wings barely disturbing the air as the head articulates and the bird studies the land below. What I also see is the vulture as a conjurer making magic out of the air in his cloth of brown and gold.

The Ancient Greeks believed that all vultures were female, that they bred by parthenogenesis (reproducing asexually), and that reproduction took place with the arrival of specific winds; the *Boreas* from the north, the *Eurus* from the east, and the most ferocious of them all, the *Notos*, the humid wind from the south. The etymology of 'vulture' might derive from the Latin *vellere*, to fleece or to rip. Meanwhile, the sixth-century Spanish scholar Isidorus offers another explanation, one that is played out in the air around me: the 'slow flight' or *volatus tardus*.

The Greeks also believed that griffon vultures were the servants of the gods who carried the souls of the dead into the endless universe. Craning my neck to watch a kettle of vultures ascend to prodigious heights above Monfragüe, I can understand this.

When Leonardo da Vinci wanted to understand the mechanics of flight, he wrote an instruction to himself, 'You will make an anatomy of the wings of a bird together with the muscles of the breast which are the movers of these wings. And you will do the same for man, to show the possibility that there is in man who desires to sustain himself amid the air by the beating of wings.' When I read this, inevitably, I picture Icarus, that mythical ill-fated attempt to inhabit the empire of the sky; the hubris of human desire, what we want to possess that we cannot.

With my feet firmly planted on the ground, I am beguiled by the vulture's slow flight. I notice the way these giant birds slip around the sky so effortlessly, so silently. But as I study them rising into the stratosphere, what I really want to know is what it's like to ascend 700 metres in a cauldron of thermals – along with a gang of your mates – making no declarative statements, just rising and rising higher still – 'kettling', birders call it – until you've gained all the perspective you need, and from where it's merely a matter of gliding slowly out over miles of landscape accompanied by

however many of your pals discern you have found
something and follow in the slipstream out over the dehesa.

Another vulture slips past, and I think of that questing eye
homing in over more than a thousand hectares of land; the
vision of an avian superhero burning through the atmosphere.

'Let's head down into the gorge,' Martin says, and we
wander back down to the van passing the capacious mouth
of a cave around which crag martins dart and swoop. When
I stop to study the cave, frustrated that the entrance is
gated and locked (Martin has told us of Bronze Age
paintings of men and animals on its walls), I notice a
stationary vulture on a lip of rock above the cave's mouth.
Studying the bird through the binoculars, I see how the
vulture's neck is barely feathered with bare skin visible
through baby-down plumage. This, of course, is an
adaptation that allows vultures to poke their heads inside a
carcass without the risk of dirt or infection accumulating.
Then there's the thick hooked cleaver of its bill, and the
head turned aside as if in disdain. The image I see isn't the
picture of a vulture I grew up accustomed to – an
unsavoury animal at best, but more Laurence Olivier got
up as Richard III, the ruff of white feathers around the
base of the neck and the bronzed wing shoulders raised
somewhat, all resembling the velvet puff of a Hollywood
costume department. There's another vulture in a slightly
more elevated position on the crag and now what I see is
John Cleese' ludicrous French guard on the castle
battlements in *Monty Python and the Holy Grail*. I'm
supposed to be birdwatching, and all I can do is amuse
myself with the kind of ludicrous notions that nature
sometimes delivers; the unbidden pictures that arise – from
what exactly? The need to compare this with that. To make
allegiances between images and ideas. To render the
metaphysical, the supra-human in form and word.

More prosaically, I also see that the vulture is a creature
of ecological fortitude whose habits have been forged

through evolutionary processes. Through deep time, in other words. But our recent experience of the world tells us that should we choose to pull or push in the wrong way – manage it all to hell in other words; it can all come tumbling down.

I'm studying this vulture high-rise across the dam. I see it as less tenement, more yuppie flats. There's none of the hardscrabble malarkey of a British coastal seabird colony, where one wrong move and you're out on your ear, shoved unceremonially back into your own few square centimetres of cliff; the precariousness of it all. There are none of the acrid stenches of a gannetry or a sea-cliff colony of razorbills and shags.

By late morning the thermals have really got going. The birds exploit the warm rising air so that it's as if the sky is opaque with vultures. The griffon's wings, I notice, are held flat, and the black vulture's wingtips are flexed slightly downwards. They slide past Peña Falcon, join the kettle up high or glide elegantly back towards the cliff. When a vulture lands among more of its kind, there's no pushing or shoving, just a tacit greeting; an 'alright?' asked of a passing acquaintance. And they give each other space, these mighty birds. Rather than scrutinising the land and what opportunities it might offer, they resemble spectators at an event, taking it all in, and yes, you could say they are *unruffled*.

In his notebooks, Leonardo wrote, 'A bird is an instrument working according to a mathematical law'. The laws of physics apply here too, of course, which is straying uncomfortably close to subjects that have always felt alien to me. To maintain altitude, the birds must sit tight within the part of the thermal in which the air rises faster than the birds themselves are sinking. Therefore, when I look up, what I'm seeing is the texture of temperature and how the air itself works; the spiralling vultures help me see it. What I also see is the manifestation of a species whose behaviours and adaptations act on the human mind – *this* human mind – which is something far more resonant than physics alone.

In ancient Rome, it was believed that a kettle of vultures revealed the most auspicious site for an ensuing battle. We know well enough that the natural world is embattled. In Monfragüe and elsewhere in Extremadura, even among the region's celebrated abundance, mathematics is still at work. It manifests, of course, in the actions undertaken by humans and the effects of these upon the natural world.

It's November the following year, and I'm back in Extremadura with my friend, the poet Karen Izod. Karen and I have been drawn back by the abundance of birds in the fields. It's the week before the Festival of the Cranes, and we're at the Crane Centre with Martin Kelsey. Martin translates as we study the display boards with diagrams of crane migration routes.

'The cranes travel 4,000 kilometres from northern Europe to Extremadura. Some of the cranes are satellite tagged. A juvenile crane, given the name Lordez, was identified as recently arrived from Estonia alongside her parents. Other cranes travel from Sweden, Norway, Lithuania, Finland.'

'The cranes gather in huge numbers at stop-over feeding places to renew their strength for the onward journey – at Lake Hornborga in Sweden, and then again ahead of the Pyrenees on the French side. When they eventually fly over this vast chain of mountains, some cranes have been recorded flying at speeds of 155 kilometres per hour. Having successfully navigated the flight path over the Pyrenees, the cranes gather again at Laguna de Gallocanta, a lake on the Spanish side.'

The population of cranes overwintering in the Iberian Peninsula now numbers some 270,000 individual birds. Recent years have seen 200,000 cranes overwintering in Extremadura alone. Every November Martin volunteers to help with the crane count. He tells us how his left elbow still aches from the repetitive strain caused by clicking the lever of his mechanical counter 11,739 times in one day. He clicked as the cranes fed or flew across the sky or stood on the skyline silhouetted by the setting sun. In the winter of 2017, a record-breaking 132,000 common cranes were counted by the volunteers in Martin's part of Extremadura alone.

The calls of the common crane are the running music that binds autumn and winter and stitches the fields and the sky to each other. A guttural purr rises to a trumpeted catch of air, the breath corkscrewing through the tracheal passage and building to a crescendo before dying away. All in a matter of seconds. All on repeat. When we drive by or walk through the land there are so many cranes aloft you could say the sky was full. We watch cranes travelling in skeins or in family parties or in long lines that stretch from horizon to horizon. The sky is a blue resounding echo chamber, an archive of the contact calls of cranes. The crane's call is an ache, like something just beyond the line of vision, or a memory you can't quite get to – or get past.

Xeno-canto is a digital field of sound curated by birdwatchers around the world. When I'm back home and need to be reminded of a specific bird call, I'll pay a visit to this digital audio field. There are thirteen pages for *Grus grus*, the common crane, each page headed by a map, and tabs for breeding or non-breeding ranges, on-passage stopping places, and one tab Xeno-canto calls 'uncertain places'. I want to remind myself of the strangely affecting call of the common crane, so I select a random page and scan it. I read the birdwatchers' field notes and sit at my computer assimilating the cranes' calls I hear with the kinds of habitats and conditions each was recorded in.

'A big flock passing overhead.' 'In the beginning of the night.' 'Small family groups were calling.' 'On a mountain pass during a heavy snowfall.' 'Bird seen – yes; playback used – no.' 'Hundreds of birds in a dormitory.' 'Call of flock passing above Bieszczady.' I'm lost in the woods of the digital field, and I'm reading about crane recorders in Poland, Finland, Hungary, Sweden and Tunisia. On the next page, I'm lost in Gujarat, Ethiopia and Italy where the symbiosis of cranes and recorders spans the known and the unknown. From wintering lands and breeding lands and uncertain lands, birds are recorded passing over mountain ranges or as they watch over their young from nests in the boreal forests. I'm wondering if there are places that cranes pass through or feed or breed or rest unseen and whether all this looking and listening disrupts the anonymity of birds.

I choose at random and read the accompanying notes: 'The cranes are gleaning in the cornfields at the edge of the pine forest. They're calling continuously, both in-flight and on the ground.' Another entry is written in Spanish, which necessitates the use of Google Translate: 'Cranes in a flooded channel thick with vegetation. There have been circumstances this year; the winter has been rainy, and the cranes delayed their departure to the point of coinciding with the arrival of the first nightingales.' But I see that instead of 'circumstance', the software has suggested '*circumspect dances*'. And I like this because it makes me think of how the dance of cranes establishes or re-establishes pair bonds as they walk side by side in stately circumspection, throwing their heads back and calling as though to consult the sky on the matter. And I imagine one crane dancing a glissade and another curtseying in response, or a pair of cranes shaking their wings and bowing to one another, like the romantic protagonists in a Jane Austen novel.

In Extremadura, we get back in the car and Martin drives us a short distance from the Crane Centre and we park in the dehesa, then set off walking led onwards by a pair of hoopoes that alternately skim the ground and loop high into the branches of holm oaks as if the air were elastic. When we come close to them, off they go calling their jubilant exhortations while we pace out our leaden human steps. There's something about how the trees are spaced one from another in the dehesa, how you can see for miles even though you are inside a forest. I imagine this is what it was like when humans first walked the African savannah, in the places where our primary relationships with landscapes were forged.

At the edge of the dehesa is a bird hide – a long wooden affair raised on stilts with a flight of steps to the door. Inside, all of the wooden benches had been ripped out, redundant anchor points marking where they'd been screwed to the floor. Martin says drily, 'Maybe someone was desperate for firewood.'

We open the window slots and lean our elbows on the wooden sills. Heat shimmers over distant mountains. Beyond a shelterbelt of scrub and trees, there are grain silos and the long grey roofs of industrial buildings.

A hot wind pushes inside. Gradually, as our attention stills, the birds begin to materialise. A common snipe and a couple of wood sandpipers, needling scrapes of wetland. Lapwings in their Robin Hood caps. The bright centre of

the world in the eyes of lapwings. The oily aurora of
lapwing wings. Pied beauties, tied to the worlds of earth
and air. They lift together all foppish, wafting aloft in aerial
waves. The *leap with a flicker in it*, Old English has it. The
lapwings come to earth again, crest feathers shifting
purposefully among the stubble. The lapwings lead my eye
to the black-winged stilt stalking the water. Long red legs,
black wings, white chest, pert bill, dark eye. If Audrey
Hepburn was a bird …

A single crane on the far edge of the field, a Victorian
matriarch, all feathery grey bustle and a little mop-cap of red
on the top of the head. A family of cranes pass overhead – a
pair and a single 'piper' or juvenile. I watch the crane in the
field as it watches the trajectory of the family. A juvenile
crane is perceptibly smaller than the parents it flies alongside,
and the call is higher in tone – hence the sobriquet.

A marsh harrier hovers into view.

'Look at the shallow 'v', or dihedral of the wings in flight,'
Martin says.

The harrier quarters the stubble rows, sunlight swilling
gold across her shoulders and back and wings. When the
harrier reaches the terminus of the field, it flips and swings
around to begin quartering all over again. Finally, she drops
onto a target hidden from us among the stubble.

Now my attention is snagged by something else. Beyond
the field boundary are ranks of regimented and uniform
green bushes radiating towards us like bearings on an ancient
map.

'What's all the greenery,' I ask, indicating the distant rows.

'That wasn't here last time I came,' Martin says. 'This is
new – olive plantations. But they're not great for birds –
when they plant olives, the ground underneath becomes
incredibly dry; there's not much on offer for birds.'

And I remembered in Madrid where Karen and I had
selected so many olives to accompany our beers a few
evenings before. Big fat green olives and small plush black

ones and olives stuffed with chilli or tuna. And when we'd
finished selecting, we carried our paper plates full of
slippery olives and our glasses of beer to a couple of high
stools. And because it was Friday night, the place was
packed, and we'd sat and enjoyed our authentic Spanish
olives and beers – of course, we had – without much
thought at all about where they came from, or what the
effect of this many olives might bring to bear on the
abundance of birds. What the new olive plantations
represent is the push and pull between humans and
abundance, between progress and not. And there is
significant financial gain to be made from olives. Martin
went on to tell us that when a local landowner converted
some of his land to olives and installed irrigation systems
without planning permission, a fine of a quarter of a
million was imposed. Had the landowner removed the
olives? Given the monetary inducements on offer, Martin
said, they might have been more incentivised to continue
regardless.

Inside the hide, we're chatting about the birds we've
seen that day. The pair of hoopoes that flared like Inca gods
onto a field of ploughed red earth then vanished like a
magic trick. And like any successful trick I'd been
incredulous that a bird of such intense gold, black and
white plumage could disappear in front of my eyes. And
shortly after this, Martin declared, 'Black-winged kite!',
and he pointed through the windscreen, and there it was,
rocketing down the road in front of us, rising, hovering – a
ghostly hawk – diving down and a moment later swooping
into the topmost branch of a leafless tree. The spotless
starlings that flung themselves past us whistling as we stood
at the edge of another field. The red avadavat. A finch: a
bird of India here in Extremadura. A red signal threading
itself through the spines of the bush at the side of the dusty
track. Red chest, red back, brown wing, brown belly, red
eye, brown tail, red feet, red head. The wing feathers

embroidered with tiny white dots like an Indian cloth. On high steppe grazing land where a warm wind pulsed among the grasses, little bustards bobbed up intermittently, enticingly. I could see their soft brown backs and paler breast feathers and all at once they lifted out of the grass and careened a short distance before the collective synapses synchronised. The flock parascended down again as if choreographed, white underwings flickering here, here, over here, waning like cooling sparks. The great bustards, distant, turkey-like, though statelier. And later, one flew across the road in front of the car, massive, quick and open-beaked, as though incredulous to its own purposes.

I was beginning to make sense of the abundance in Extremadura. It was with us from morning until night, in the early morning rituals of azure-winged magpies streaking across fields all fleet and blue against etiolated winter grasses. In the great grey shrike, *Lanius excubitor* – the butcher bird – busy in scrub, skewering its latest catch. And there was abundance too in how I noticed the hoopoe's snazzy crest when raised – its sumptuous gold and black and white plumage and how, when lowered, the crest resembles the engineered profile of a geologist's hammer.

The human world is littered with signs. Because we cannot predict what lies ahead, signs indicate that we need to watch out – for sharp bends, for kids on bikes, or for that pedestrian who just stepped out onto the road.

On my way to Madrid that second November, I'd looked down from the plane onto wind turbines constructed on the prows of sandstone karsts braided one to the next by white roads, like veins in red marble. And I'd considered then how birds have evolved to experience the sky as a place without objects, how migrating birds acquire different kinds of sensory apparatus through their long evolution.

Wind turbines, meanwhile, arrive in the blink of an evolutionary eye. The crane following its internal compass flies with its vision limited to the sideways and downwards fields of space. Being a crane, then, is like being the kid on the bike looking sideways to see how fast the world spins and downwards to see how quickly the wheels spin. This particular way of seeing means a crane travelling at speeds of up to 155 km per hour, looking down at the ground to navigate and sideways at her family, cannot see the blades of a wind turbine until it's too late.

Wind turbines tend to be placed far away from centres of human population. When the developers of wind farms plan ahead, they are mostly not preparing for the migratory flight paths or feeding habits or general flying around of birds. The wind farm placed on the migratory route of geese and swans along the coast of Cumbria, or the wind turbines assembled on the Scottish border despite information gathered during the consultancy period that had confirmed the planned location was on the direct migratory flight path of geese. I'm thinking of the conversation I had with an officer from a major NGO on the effects of wind farms on migratory birds, who told me that the duty for monitoring bird strikes rested with the energy company concerned, and that, yes, this was an unsatisfactory state of affairs, but no, I should not repeat this conversation. I'm thinking here of the numbers of seabirds – 150,000, I'd read in one study – that are killed in collisions with turbines in the North Sea each year. And I'm thinking of the 10,000 new wind turbines planned for the North Sea as a vital component of the Climate Change Committee's plan to help the UK transition to net-zero carbon.

The birds displaced because there's not much in the way of food for birds amongst olives or the thousands of birds killed by turbines – are any of these acceptable collateral? Are the numbers of bird losses equal to the gains of clean energy? (Maths again ...) And if it is possible to predict our energy needs, can we also anticipate the proximity of birds whose sensory evolution has told them that there's nothing at all in the way? That the sky and the route ahead is the same as it's always been for thousands of years? How long would it take the cranes passing over the Pyrenees or the vultures and raptors passing through the wind farms in Tarifa and all the other birds on passage north and south to evolve to accommodate the blades? Can we wait long enough to find out, or are the wind farms and their cargoes of hurtling cranes just too far away to see?

I need to remember the fields of Extremadura in the hope that this paying of attention will pin the abundance of cranes and marsh harriers and Spanish sparrows and cattle egrets and even the passing red avadavat into the map of my experience. And yes, of course, the digital field has much to offer. Without it, I would less easily become lost amid the archives of birds' sounds. I would less easily follow the birders' paths who commit birds' calls to the collective memory through their tenacity and perseverance out there in the physical field. And even though the digital field is a wondrous thing because through it and from anywhere I can tune in to image and sound as a way of paying attention to species and place, I am also deeply circumspect.

I am circumspect about the digital field because with the rate and speed of loss of species in my country – in many, many countries – I worry there will come a day when this is all that remains – a screen with a flicker in it, where cranes and pipers track across the digital sky and vultures carry the souls of their long-dead selves into the maybe eternal universe of the screen. Where even the unfamiliar personage of the digital red avadavat invites us to recall those numinous ideas of fascination and awe and joy as it stitches the thorny branches of the pixelated bushes with the dancing red thread of bright plumage. What's left when a field is reduced to a portal into a world without joy, without life, without hope?

Did anyone back up the hard drive before the data – the species themselves – become lost?

Some of what I need to do is to accept the idea that green energy is not necessarily clean: there will always be collateral damage – even if it is still too far away for me to see. Or maybe some of what I need to do is to look more closely, as the wind farm watchers in Tarifa in Spain and certain places in Portugal do, who signal to wind farm operatives when a raptor or another large bird is approaching so the worker can switch off a particular turbine until the bird and the moment have both passed. In the business, this is referred to as 'shutdown on demand'. I'm not sure how you do this at night, or in the North Sea, which is a sardine tin of seabirds and birds on passage, but it's a start.

In a way electricity is like those thermals the vultures use to gain lift and find food; it is mostly invisible to the human eye. Nevertheless, electricity is progress, and green energy is more progress still. Even though there will always be a cost, I have chosen to be more upfront with myself about this. I still want electricity. I still want to eat olives.

I wonder what Leonardo might have to say about all this progress. After all, his was a mind consumed by the idea of progress and the building of a world in which the lot of humans was expanded, improved, engineered, calculated, exacted, energised, and above all, wondrous. I imagine he might write down some instructions for us, something along the lines of:

You will make a diagram of all the wind farms and all the birds' migratory routes and the feeding areas and the general flying areas. And when you have done all this, you will map the one onto the other, and you will consider, above all, the marvellous, wondrous world of flight that you will never ever replicate (despite my many drawings and diagrams). And you will agree to limit the demands you place upon this world, and yes, you will even need to limit the numbers of yourselves because your demand generally outstrips natural capacity and because otherwise, what lies ahead, for you and the natural world, is an abyss.

Both Trump and Putin have declared that wind farms are a bad thing because they account for the unnecessary deaths of countless numbers of birds, even though these men are not known for their strength of feeling for the conservation of species or habitats. Theirs are the arguments of political expediency and an ideology that is irrevocably hooked on oil and gas. 52 per cent of Russian budgetary revenues come from oil and gas, and 70 per cent of export earnings. Meanwhile, and because of Trump and Putin's hunger for oil and gas and because of our continuing hunger for oil and gas, more than 200 gigatons is lost from the Greenland ice cap each year. Because of this, the wind farms must win through, but at the same time, we need to continue unpacking those questions about the true costs of our too many selves on the life of our too small, too fragile planet; how in the face of modernity, reason frequently fails.

꙳ ꙳ ꙳

I digress. I must digress. I am hungry for warmth and for light. I am hungry for olives and for travel and transport, and I'm also hungry for abundance. Without abundance, my appetites are unable to be filled. I am greedy for olives and for abundance. Abundance might be the glimpse through the rear-view mirror of what we are hurtling rapidly away from, or it might be that other kind of abundance, the sort I can find even now in the fields of Extremadura.

I have scoured the land for birds and been rewarded. The fields are the various painted grounds upon which birds have flown or fed or stalked or risen from or dropped into. Rice paddies, steppe country, dehesa, cornfields, a mountain. And I want to remember the last evening in Extremadura when our small group of birders walked, hot and tired, at the end of a day replete with birds.

Martin has a grin on his face. He's not saying a word. We stand at the edge of an unremarkable stubble field as the sky segues from high blue to tangerine, and the sun slips slowly towards the horizon. We're listening to the calls of cranes, but we can't see them because they're roosting in an adjacent field on the far side of a tall bank of willow.

I'm beginning to wonder what on earth we're doing, standing about at the edge of this field when a single bird materialises above the rim of the horizon, a distant flicker of black against the vivid sky. And the bird swings in towards the field and I think perhaps this has something to do with Martin's grin. In it comes, flying closer so that, as it approaches, I can see how the bird tilts and tips on air, see the shallow 'V' of its wings, and the broad chisel of its tail flexing. It moves towards us then shifts direction, and when it does, for a split second, I see the bird head on – a thin, drawn line that then configures the rest of the bird into being – a marsh harrier. And we're watching this one bird when another harrier approaches the proscenium of the field, flying along the shadowed boundary of the willows. And a third harrier flies in, and now the first marsh harrier swings eastwards quartering a row of stubble, and it comes so close I can see the white mantle of a female's head and the precision engineering of the yellow bill.

The harriers fly over the stubble rows without sound. A visual field flickers and pulses between the birds and me, radiating information now that I know what it is that we have been waiting for. And despite all Extremadura's distracting abundance, my attention is fully caught; the camera's focus ring is locked on to the subject. The field that was blank has begun to be filled. The brush has been loaded, and more harriers come in twos and threes to paint themselves into the canvas of the field, wafting in from the unknown. And another harrier flickers across the remaining quadrant of the face of the sun.

When twelve harriers are floating above the field, my ability to speak is lost. Thirteen, fourteen, fifteen. And the harriers' wingtips and primaries are flowed through by the warm Extremaduran air as the birds themselves flow through the field. Sixteen, seventeen. The sky intensifies into carmine, rose and citrine, and the remnants of vapour trails orientate themselves towards the horizon. Twenty-two, twenty-three, twenty-four. The flight of the first harrier stalls and the legs drop into position as the wings arch above the bird's head. The harrier uses these devices of lift to hover precisely above its chosen location in the stubble. Then the wings remain high but pulsing above the body, and the harrier folds herself neatly into the stubble like a piece of folded paper concealed in an envelope. How many of these avian letters are slipped away here each evening? And of course, we would not have found these secrets without Martin and his index finger and his by now only niggling shoulder and his paying of close attention. Twenty-eight, twenty-nine, thirty. Thirty-four harriers floating or wafting or folding themselves inside the stubble rows. I'm sorry that the rest of my life is a form of distraction because this now is a way of paying attention to the awe found in certain fields. From their margins, I am immersed. I slip the image of the harriers inside myself so that, when I am no longer in Extremadura, I will still remember them. How, one by one, they drop so softly, so unobtrusively, towards the earth without asking anything other than to be afforded the measure of a relationship where what humans provide is a humble, dependable habitat, a modest system, a symbiosis of human and animal, in which the harriers take what they need; this and nothing more. In this way, in this now, the harriers fold themselves silently into the velvet certainty of the coming night.

Dust

The broken leg anchored the little bird on a slippery axis of slide and fall. It was a common whitethroat, no doubt recently fledged and beginning to make its way in the world, then here it was scrambling inside a plastic cake box.

I was with my friend Szabi in the garden of a house in Hortobágy in eastern Hungary. Above the entrance gates, a stork family had taken up residence on the top of a telegraph pole. Szabi was sketching the storks, and Albert, our genial host, dressed as usual in rock band T-shirt, his hair drawn back in a straggly grey ponytail, was attempting to ply us with whiskey. It was not yet 10am.

The family on the telephone pole nest were all crammed in. By midsummer, the juveniles were almost fully grown. There was all this constant business going on up there, the adults on food delivery, the kids hanging around, raising a leg here, stretching or holding the pose, then lowering and raising again like ballet exercises at the barre. I paid attention to the storks' great preening sessions as they pulled out elongated wing primaries or worked through white breast feathers with huge intent, as if spring cleaning the car on a Sunday morning, all the while balanced on the edge of the nest. Compared to the whitethroat in the cake box, the juvenile storks were leviathans. I looked from one to the other, considering the precarious nature of it all.

'Five stork babies hatched,' Albert said, nodding at the nest, 'then a couple of days ago another juvenile arrived. It must have been lost, but the parents didn't mind – what's one more mouth to feed when you already have so many kids?' The nest had become so crammed with storks there was no longer any room for the male. He conducted his lone vigil from the tall chimney stack on the roof of the next house. I'd watch him from the window of my room in the evenings, a solitary silhouette against the darkening sky. I expect he was glad of the break.

Just a couple of minutes earlier, Albert's wife, Judit, had come swishing towards us in her customary long flowery skirt and flip-flops. She was carrying something very carefully. She sat down next to me and, opening her fingers slightly, said: 'Look.' And there was the tiny whitethroat, rescued from a kitten, one of its legs trailing badly.

'Oh dear,' I said. 'That's not good.'

'Damn kitten!' Judit whispered as she poured the bird tenderly into my hands. 'I'll fetch a box.'

The little body pulsed with warmth and the wings occasionally fluttered like a restless nerve under skin. Judit came swishing back, the Siamese kitten jumping as high as it was able against the low branches of an oleander, clawing at something. Judit tutted at the kitten and placed the plastic cake box on the table. She folded a couple of sheets of kitchen paper in half and half again, smoothing each one along the fold and carefully tucking then levelling them inside the box and placing the box on the garden table.

'There,' she said. I noticed the care she took, how it was the same when she folded towels and pillowcases and embroidered cloths, smoothing them into tidy piles as we talked at breakfast, while she stood beside the gigantic ceramic woodstove, its green tiles glimmering in the early-morning light.

When I'd manoeuvred the bird into the box and closed the lid, I felt like the jailer of a condemned prisoner. And indeed I was. But what now? I didn't want the bird in the box. Of course I didn't. I wanted to rewind time, to unbreak the leg and for the little bird to be off foraging caterpillars and keeping out of the way of kittens. All things considered, though, would it have been kinder to let the kitten have its way?

The whitethroat's wings frazzled against the transparent plastic and the leg ... well, the leg continued to drag about behind the bird, anchoring the centre of gravity. In a matter of seconds, the kitchen paper was in disarray. The body was strangely still between these feverish outbursts, but the little head circumnavigated the sky in minuscule animatronic movements that exposed the bird's white throat. By now the four of us were peering at the bird, alternately cooing and tut-tutting. I held the box up and saw how every individual feather overlapped the next, how the eyes were bright and wide, the delicate bill slightly apart as if the bird was uttering a single, prolonged, *oh!* The eye was ringed by a perfect pale circle, the crown slate grey. The back and wings were softest brown, woven with ginger seams, and each primary feather was edged with bands of pale cream. Where the darker wing coverts pressed against the body, they were overlapped by the plumulaceous down of the breast feathers.

My hands still resonated with their recent freight – a creature that was perfectly adapted to synthesise flies and caterpillars and beetles into the agitated monotony of a warbler's call, if not to avoid fatally attracted kittens. The bird's impulse to free itself was physical, small but urgent, like a phone on vibrate. Everything about the bird fitted. Everything was compact and complete – except for the twisted leg; a delicate twig, snapped.

I didn't know which migration route the parent whitethroats had flown to arrive here in a garden in eastern Hungary, or how their journey might differ from that of the whitethroats back home in England. But I did know how the parent whitethroats would have sensed the incremental shift in daylight and set out quite suddenly, buoyed on warm air currents over Africa, syphoning north over the desert and

the Med along with thousands more, encountering storms
and hunters' mist nets and the uncertain territories of Sicily,
Italy or Albania, where anything incoming is considered fair
game by some. All this and now look: here we were,
responsible for what to do with this little interruption in the
planet's hum.

'There's a rescue centre on the other side of town,' Judit
said. Now, what were the chances of that? Szabi and I were
to leave Hortobágy that morning, and so, of course, we
offered to drop the bird off. A little while later, we packed
the car while Judit cooed at the bird in the cake box as if it
were a sign or a small miracle. Szabi turned the car around,
and we drove out of the garden, waving back at Judit, who
flapped a tea towel at the kitten, as Albert raised the whiskey
bottle into the air and the stork family, still six of them,
continued clacking as we passed underneath.

Szabi and I had met through the Society of Wildlife Artists.
I was part of a team organising an event in 'curlew central',
or Wensleydale in Yorkshire, to raise awareness of ground-
nesting birds, curlews in particular. There was to be an
exhibition of wader art by members of the Society. I
remember unwrapping Szabi's painting in the Great Hall of
Bolton Castle, a large canvas with an intimate view of a
group of curlews on farmland. The light in the painting was
that extraordinary kind of light from day's end, low and
intense, illuminating yellow grass and bright green grass and
sky-reflecting puddled ground. This same light was reflected
from the shiny blue puddles onto the pale chests of the
curlews. In their midst was another, somewhat slighter bird
with the same colouring of the Eurasian curlew, that
particular mottled brown flecked with bands of cream. This
bird was a slender-billed curlew, one of the last to be seen
anywhere in the world.

In 1996 when Szabi worked for Birdlife Hungary, he'd received a tip-off: 'The guys said if you want to see it, you have to go now.' Szabi dropped everything and set off.

'My colleagues dropped me at the railway station. I had worked it out – if I travelled all night, I *might* get there in time to see it. It was a dream to see this – a dream for many birders, of course. I didn't sleep all night – at one point the plan nearly collapsed – but I made it to Hortobágy. From there it was eight kilometres to the fishpond where the bird had been seen. I tried to hitch – nothing doing. In the end, I got a lift for the final kilometre. And I didn't know the area at all. I was working on guesswork and intuition. Then I spotted other birders. After a short search, I found it. At last! That was a moment in my life.'

And in the painting, there the bird was, slighter than the Eurasian curlew and the bill shorter, feeding alongside its cousins and doing exactly what waders do: probing the soft wet earth with that ellipsis bill, detecting worms and invertebrates. You could say the bird looked perfectly at home. The subtle differences between the species are unmistakable to someone with Szabi's sharp eye. I'm sure I'd have failed to notice precisely what distinguished one from the other. And though the sighting was distant, he had taken photographs and made sketches as long as the slender-billed curlew obliged by staying present.

In 1994, there had been another confirmed slender-billed sighting, in Morocco, then in 2001, another in the Kiskunság area – the last seen anywhere in the world. That year, Szabi returned to the Kiskunság area, covering a vast distance on foot, but with no success. Later, he talked a museum curator into lending him a slender-billed curlew specimen and, duly accompanied, he had made an extinction pilgrimage. He drove the specimen to the same location in Kiskunság, set it down in the field and, paying attention to that absent endling bird, he painted. The slender-billed curlew in the painting is an amalgam of his sketches and photographs and the museum skin being set down in situ so that the light could inform the artist and the bird could look at home. In other words, Szabi wanted to get it exactly right. In so doing, in this act of painterly attention, he committed the slender-billed curlew to the natural-history archive of a country at a time when the species was about to be lost.

In the completed painting, what I noticed was that the slender-billed curlew fitted right in. It was in its element – literally – feeding on invertebrates in the puddled ground. It seemed to be entirely comfortable with its lot. There was no sense of vulnerability or the notion of the unbearable weight of being one of the very last of a species. And anyway, how could a bird have known? I'm aware of attaching very human sentiments to an extinct bird, but this dying away keeps happening all around us – a species on the verge of extinction appearing for the very last time on someone's local patch. In our time, on our watch.

A couple of days earlier, Szabi and I had been travelling in Kiskunság. We'd gone there to meet a team of conservationists working to prevent the local extinction of another species – the great bustard. As a national park, Kiskunság is untypical from a UK perspective. It is made up of a scatter of seven lots across the region, all interrupted by the fields of big agriculture. In the 4x4 with Great Bustard Conservation Project's Director, Lóránt Mikklós, or Mikki, we'd driven along field edges and across ancient tracks that connected one remote community to another in the days before roads. It was midsummer and, away from the fields of intensive agriculture, wildflowers bloomed riotously. Rollers were everywhere, bright blue and grey birds, streaming across our field of vision. One of them came to land at the side of the track, swaying back and forth on a little branch like a kid on a swing.

'The biggest issues for the bustard are the fragmentation of habitat and overhead electricity cables,' Mikki said, 'so we put the habitat right. We are a national park – we can dictate terms. We brought the various hunters' groups on board because bustards are susceptible to predation by fox and wild boar and golden jackal. Some people are not comfortable with this approach, but when one species vastly outweighs the other, we can't just stand by and let it all fall apart.'

I understood this well enough. There were similarities with curlews whose numbers have been decimated as a result of the switch from haymaking to silage, and the few that are left face the double whammy of predation. And as more than one conservationist had said to me over the years, without predator control most RSPB reserves would have nothing much to show.

'The overhead cables were a different matter – they're situated at exactly the height a bustard flies. The birds were disappearing like …' Mikki shrugged. 'So what we did – there are three electricity companies in Hungary. We asked them all to bury their cables in the project area. Of course, they all said no, so we began to lean on one company in particular. We said: "Look how people will see you if you are the first to do this." Within weeks they had committed.'

'And what does it cost to bury cable?' I asked.

'For one kilometre, 15 million forints. That's £40,000.'

I looked out of the 4x4 windows at that blend of natural and less natural landscapes, the field margins put back in, the strips of vegetation sewn across fields hectares wide, all hugger-mugger with agribusiness and those terrible roads. All this to allow the bustards to travel and breed and hang on.

'Then the other two companies – one was taken over by the Hungarian government. The Deputy Prime Minister came to visit; he was a pragmatist. "How do you define success?" he asked. We said: "We need to have fledgling

success for one year, and we build on that." Last year, the
winter was very hard and 500 bustards died. So we start
again. The government power company came on board. 75
per cent of the funds comes from the EU Life programme,
and 25 per cent from the companies. It's not big money to
them. That left only one company – and they didn't want to
be the one seen not to be doing.'

We were standing in a vast field adjacent to the River
Danube. On the far bank, a kilometre or two distant, the
brutalist tower blocks of a town.

'What's this place?' I asked.

'Dunaújváros – or "Danube New City",' Mikki said.
'Communist era. The ugliest town in Hungary.'

'One of,' Szabi responded.

We drove across vast open lands where sheep grazed,
watched over by swarthy shepherds, a few donkeys in among
the animals. Grey shrike zipped across the startling blue sky.

Mikki's phone jangled. He stopped the car.

'That was my colleague – he tells me one of the adult
bustards has stopped moving. Maybe this is not good. We go
and see.'

We swung off the road onto a track beside a canal. Mikki
turned on the dashboard's digital data tracker. The 4x4 was
a yellow line and the tagged bustard a red dot that we
began to move towards. A hot wind had brewed up out of
the afternoon, and it susurrated through the phragmites
fringing the water. We turned off the track onto open
ground where farm machines had deposited gigantic reels
of silage. The field, though, was mesmerised by bee-eaters
and swallows.

The phone rang again: 'No problem – he's moving again.'

And that was that. You lie down for an afternoon kip and
before you know it they're onto you. Such is the life of a
great bustard in the Anthropocene.

Eventually, Mikki spotted a small group of bustards –
perhaps a kilometre away or further – three of them

ponderously stalking the edge of a bank of vegetation. Mikki set up a telescope, and we took turns peering at those giant birds – some three feet tall and weighing in at 20 kilograms, brown and cream and merging perfectly with the land. The heat shimmered so that it was as if the birds were wandering through dilute mercury, occasionally ruffling their wings or inspecting a wash of ochre ground.

I wondered what the carbon footprint of a great bustard is, or whether anyone has done the maths. It is, of course, an alien concept. Perhaps no less ridiculous, though, than committing to burying electricity cable to preserve an endangered species – as well as your own public image.

In Hortobágy Bird Rescue Centre, the receptionist gave Szabi a form to fill in. I passed the box into the woman's hands. The way she lifted the box and peered inside and the way she leaned her head to the side and the edges of her mouth turned down told me there wasn't much hope for the whitethroat.

We were about to leave, but the woman said something to Szabi and gestured for us to follow her.

'She says we can see the centre without paying.' A thank you, perhaps, for delivering another injured bird. The woman held open a door with her free hand and ushered us through into a corridor lined with internal windows. I didn't look back at the whitethroat.

In the first window, a young man and woman were sitting opposite one another at a steel table, concentrating. They could have been playing chess, but the woman was holding a stork by compressing its wings to its body. Flat on its back and immobile, the stork's great red beak was skewed to one side, resting on the woman's arm. A tube ushered from the bill, connected to a gas tank at the side of the table. The way she held on to it, it was as if the woman didn't trust the stork one bit. As if at any moment, it might rise up and crash chaotically about the room, shaking out its cape of black and white feathers, its bill clattering in alarm as it smashed into the grey tiled walls or the steel shelves of boxes and bottles of medicines.

The stork was out cold, the one visible eye glassy. The woman's gaze shifted between looking at the place where the vet was inspecting the stork's leg, at the bird's head and then at us. Like a trick of the light, the stork's leg was missing below the knee joint. The lack of the leg was a neurological tripwire. When I had taken on board the fact of it being missing, my mind began frantically to attempt to reconstruct the lower limb. I badly needed the leg to be there, to imprint it back into existence in the same way I'd needed the whitethroat's straggling limb to be unbroken. And then I noticed, among all this, that the veterinary nurse appeared bored. She was holding an anaesthetised stork the size of a four-year-old child and apparently the whole business was tiresome. Perhaps that's just how it is at the bird rescue centre: the in-patient waiting list never finished, day after day after day until the tedium inevitably sets in.

The veterinary surgeon took a stainless-steel instrument from the table and investigated the cavity where the lower limb should have been. The skin was the colour and texture of uncooked chicken.

I have never been one of those people for whom watching medical procedures is a source of fascination, and looking through the window at stork surgery was uncomfortably like medical television – no, like the theatre of the absurd. It was more Gunther von Hagens than *24 Hours in A&E*. I moved on.

The next window revealed a couple of storks on a cement floor, each of them exuding a desolate air as if recovering from the mother of all hangovers. Both had one good leg, but the other was encased in a primitive prosthetic, like a mash-up between a red wellington boot and an instrument for clearing a blocked sink. The wellie-plunger thing didn't resemble anything remotely useful. It was as if the storks had been inserted into the devices, rather than fitted to them. What was going on here? Then I got it: the birds have their surgery and, like us, then the recovery begins. As a stork with one lower leg missing, what needs to happen is that the bird keeps still. Not to do so – well, I guess that once downed, a stork might not get up again. With the amputated leg inserted into the device, the bird is immobilised until the wound has healed sufficiently for the next phase. First of all, though, there's that massive hangover to get over.

In the next cubicle was a small bunch of storks, all of them sporting the kinds of apparatus you might see on the legs of war veterans or victims of land-mines. Yellow straps were attached above the storks' knee and suspended from these were an artificial lower leg made of red plastic and, at the bottom of this, a flappy red plastic foot. The storks in this room still had that air of desolation about them – who doesn't, post-surgery? – but they were all weight-bearing on those unfamiliar new limbs.

In the cubicle opposite were two marsh harriers perched on branches, both with one leg in a splint, the floor below them shit-spattered. Sad grey light filtered in through industrial wire mesh windows. The harriers had their backs to the light. One of them had an orb of dirty white where the eye should have been. I didn't know what it was, this white bulge, and I didn't want to look closer.

It was Dismaland for Birds; so much human-made mess! 'The Corridor of Demented Sideshows in the Fairground of Fatal Attraction'; a diorama of the battered, the broken, the imperfectly mended.

We came out of the building into a park with numerous caged enclosures and a path leading the way. In the first enclosure, kestrels. They were all brick-red and blue-winged, bug-eyed, the kind of disquieting gaze that burns directly into the soul. In the next was any number of owls. The little owls, those great questioners of the world of owls, ever surprised, ever amazed. They were perched on branches or on the ground, pressing their tiny bodies into the wire and scrutinising us rather than we them. There were Scops owls, the white facial disks rimmed with black and divided by a triangle of plumage extending from the beak to the little ear tufts above the head. Their amber eyes were extraordinary, burning orange, the pupil black. The Scops owl plumage resembled something fashioned from the bark of ancient, venerable trees. I longed to hold one, to push my hand inside that lavish depth of feathers.

'I've only seen this once before! When I was a kid! In the mountains! With my dad!' Another Szabi 'moment'. A bird more usually associated with taiga forest, the Ural owl's plumage is pale, verging on white, and shot through with elegant curving ellipses of black, the tail feathers banded with coffee and cream. The facial disk is enormous, the eyes dark and liquid. The Ural owl's configuration is that of a Russian doll. Next, the granddaddy of them all, the eagle owls, some with ear tufts laid flat to the head, others with the appearance of enormous, upward-sweeping eyebrows. The eagle owls stared at the middle distance through penetrating orange eyes. They appeared beyond being interested in the intermittent influx of visitors pressing our faces close to the wire. And who could blame them?

There were marsh harriers and peregrine falcons – those grey-backed ballistic missiles. There were red-footed falcons with their astonishing red bills and feet, the males like superheroes robed in grey cloaks and a grey hood from which those incredible red eyes startled. The most elegant of them all: the Saker falcon. My first sighting had been a few days before from the passenger seat of Mikki's 4x4 travelling along a track that was deeply rutted and bordered by mountainous banks of wildflowers. Szabi had pointed, suddenly declaring: 'Saker falcon!' And it was, diving through the hot air and flushing a pigeon from the undergrowth, the pair of birds rising up with the pigeon's wings clattering, the falcon scything and silent as they both disappeared beyond the flowers.

In the close proximity of the rescue centre, I was able to take in the river of brown and grey and white cascading down the breast and underwings, the striated earth colours of the back and wings, the black pupils rimmed with a bright phenomenal blue and the same blue pouring onto the tightly curved bill where it morphed into lapis and, at the very tip, into black. It was as if a committee of designers had planned how to make the most elegant creature, the coolest dispatcher of squirrels and birds.

In the centre of the park was the largest enclosure, its lower panels made of dark wood and above them, a high dome of black mesh. Szabi and I peered through small windows cut into the wood. The ground was a mass of small trees with a substrate of dense foliage. At either end was a tall larch pole supporting the roof mesh and, slung between these were cables from which emanated the regular pulse of electricity.

The enclosure was home to a horde of birds. There were storks, imperial eagles, golden eagles, buzzards, white-tailed eagles, marsh harriers. Some of the birds were busy preening, many were stationary. Groups of storks were gathered in little huddles, like the storks in Hieronymus Bosch's 'Garden of Earthly Delights'.

The ticking was relentless. Szabi read an information board and told me that the cables were live, though the voltage was at a safe, if *unpleasant*, level. 'Land on electricity infrastructure,' the birds were learning, 'and you won't like it one bit.'

The door into the enclosure opened and in walked a young man in a bright red rescue centre T-shirt. Securing the door behind him, he strode purposefully between stands of greenery towards the far end, hefting a furled green net attached to a wooden pole. A bunch of storks raised their wings unenthusiastically as he passed by, flapping out of the way like a gang of silly kids. The raptors, meanwhile, were unfazed. The man homed in on an imperial eagle. As if woken from torpor, the eagle attempted to take off, but it was too late. With a single flourish, the net shot skywards and brought the eagle down. The eagle flapped half-heartedly and, as it did so, I noticed the layering of colour in its greater and lesser wing coverts, the rich deep umber fused with the paler primaries. In a matter of seconds, the man had the huge bird disentangled and, taking hold of it by the ankles, he flipped it upside down with one hand and simultaneously furled the net with the other. The eagle flapped its wings distractedly as if really it couldn't be bothered with any of this carry-on. Together they left the enclosure, the man and the eagle, and I wondered what the next part of its recovery journey would involve.

Close to the next small window was a stork perched on a low horizontal branch. The long red bill was retracted into the white chest, and the black eye stripe was a line of ink that began at the bill and resumed briefly beyond the eye. Layers of white chest feathers shifted in the hot breeze. One of the stork's legs was shrouded in a thin layer of white dressings. No more than a metre away was an imperial eagle. The two birds eyed each other with cool indifference. The eagle held its wings slightly lifted from the body, and the tail feathers were compacted into a long curving wedge. The raptor's yellow talons wrapped around the branch. Together, the two birds were like a diorama of an Aesop's fable; let's call it 'The Eagle and the Stork'. I wondered what kind of moral imperative this unlikely birdy exchange might signify,

and which of the two might better the other should push
come to shove. The stork's bright red sword-length bill or
the raptor's precisely engineered hook?

Szabi had wanted to detour to take me to the exact location
where the very last slender-billed curlew in Hungary and
the world was seen. A couple of days earlier, we had driven
into the hinterland of Kiskunság. Every few minutes another
outsize grain lorry thundered past, and we had to squeeze
up against the grassy verge.

'How come the roads are so bad?' I asked, the car lurching
between one crater and the next.

'They were never designed for these heavy lorries,' Szabi
answered. 'And the companies are all external, big
agribusiness – mostly from the Netherlands.'

'I see they don't contribute to the road upkeep then,' I
said.

'You got it,' Szabi said as he manoeuvred the car around
yet another bomb hole.

We stood at the side of the road, looking at the dry,
bright-green summer grass where the field sloped towards
an orderly farm on a low horizon. I supposed it was a sort of
pilgrimage for Szabi. Needless to say, the puddles had gone,
likewise the birds, but there was this resonance between
being here at the exact place where the very last of a species
was seen and me unpacking the painting at an event to help
communicate the precarious nature of lowland curlews. It
was a kind of paying of witness to absence for both of us:
one species almost certainly gone, the other teetering
horribly close to the edge.

The place didn't feel like an extinction zone; it was just
an ordinary field in the countryside. It could have been any
field in any country. And these familiar-looking fields, of
course, are precisely the places from which unimaginable

numbers of farmland birds have haemorrhaged in the past sixty years. Those lorries were a litmus test of how.

$$\downarrow \quad \downarrow \downarrow$$

The slender-billed curlew is now believed to exist only in paintings and photographs. When Szabi hightailed across Hungary to see one of the very last, it was as an act of witness before the species disappeared forever. No one really understands what happened in the slender-billed curlews' vast and remote breeding territories of Siberia, though it is well documented that hunters shot the birds while they were on migration in their thousands. Even now though, and against all the odds, a few optimistic souls continue to believe that the species may yet be seen; they continue to issue requests for information on what just might turn out to be verified sightings. After all, what remains when hope is gone?

Let me bring back into focus for a moment the museum specimen that Szabi borrowed and painted in the evening light in Kiskunság. In a recent scientific study, thirty-five slender-billed curlew specimens were donated from museums worldwide, providing a very different kind of witness. The scientists were able to harvest stable isotopes from the specimens' feathers. Within their core, the isotopes held tiny traces from the environments in which the birds had hatched and grown. Traces of ingested food and water were locked into the birds' tissues during their first season: dust, in other words. The dust of species that may now only exist in glass cases, the world outside reflected through taxidermists' eyes.

When the scientists matched the samples from the specimens against large-scale data-bank maps, the resulting information allowed the scientists to place the slender-billed curlew into a specific band of latitude. And what the scientists discovered in this previously uncharted digital terrain was that all previous searches had been in the wrong places. The slender-billed curlew's nesting locations were further to the south than had previously been thought – in the steppes and forest-steppes of Kazakhstan and southern Russia, even in the Ural Mountains. Unlocked from the dust from the specimens' feathers, this brand-new information gave the ornithologists the chance to home in on the most viable areas of search. But nevertheless, how would you begin to look for a bird whose global total might be as few as fifty individuals? Needles. Haystacks.

The loss of the slender-billed curlew followed hard on the extinction of another in the same genus, *Numenius borealis*, the Eskimo curlew of the Americas. Some historians believe that it was flocks of Eskimo curlew flying with golden plover that Christopher Columbus and his crew followed to find landfall after sixty-five days at sea.

The Eskimo curlew was once the most populous shorebird across the entire American continent; they existed in their millions. But by the close of the nineteenth century, some two million were shot by hunters every year. Allied with increasing amounts of habitat loss, this once so vitally abundant species moved inexorably towards extinction. The last confirmed sightings of *Numenius borealis* was in 1962 on Galveston Island in Texas. A year later a single bird was seen in Barbados. Unconfirmed sightings have been reported as recently as 2006, and some say we should not treat the species as extinct until all remaining habitats have been surveyed and all incidental sightings cease to be reported.

What does it mean when a species is lost? At its most basic, it means no more adrenaline-fuelled dashes across the country or countries to see the very last one of a kind. It means having to pay attention before it becomes too late. In his foreword to Fred Boswell's novel, *Last of the Curlews*, W. S. Merwin wrote how we 'late arrivals' on

Earth retain the sense of an awareness that is considerably older than ours. That each migratory species provides us with a glimpse of creatures whose understanding of the turning Earth, its magnetic field, the sequencing of day and night, the seasons and weather, all intimate an alternately illumined consciousness.

And what about the idea that extinction occurs elsewhere – in the Amazon rainforest, on the plains of Africa or on polar ice caps? Mediated for us by natural-history filmmakers or newspapers or by *National Geographic*, something that takes place at a remove – a long, long way away from us, almost in a distant ecosystem. Not at the bottom of an unremarkable field in conventional agricultural land, the kind you or I might drive past on any day of the year. The only way we know that the slender-billed curlew is, in all likelihood extinct, is because a few people decided to take notice. And I wonder if noticing has somehow become a bit of a dirty word, getting in the way of our consumerist habits and our capitalist economies. Birds need what they need; few species can adapt and change.

The stork on the operating table and all the birds in the rescue centre are, for the most part, the victims of power companies that continue to deploy poor-quality and inadequate hardware, and fail to place baffles adjacent to the tops of their poles or pylons – or 'trees', as storks and eagles think of them. The problem of electricity infrastructure and bird deaths has been documented for more than a century, but it is only increasing. Electrocution is now the single biggest cause of mortality for some of Europe's most endangered species, including the Saker falcon and others that use high vantage points to survey the land below for food. Take a one-minute trawl on YouTube and you'll find videos of birds being fried – or, if they are smaller, exploding – as they short-circuit on power lines. Where would that scorched and otherwise ruined horde of birds be, if it weren't for the attention paid by the vets at the rescue centre?

Not all of the Hortobágy Rescue Centre birds will be released. For some, life was as good as it was going to get. Many that remain, however, will be able to breed successfully in the centre and their young will subsequently be released into the world. Maybe to the nest at the end of Judit and Albert's garden. Maybe to pick up an extra family member along the way; after all, it pays to be generous.

I no longer think of the birds in the freak-show cubicles or the park's cages as the fortunate receivers of rescue. They have become a legion of battered ambassadors that help to bridge the widening gap between our world and the numinous. And yes, they are a semi-ruined stash of birds, but through the bars and the cages, they are raising awareness.

When the French marine biologist Daniel Pauly identified what came to be called 'shifting baseline syndrome', we began to understand that every generation develops a particular awareness of their surroundings together with an assumption that what they see is normal. If we don't see those Eskimo curlews or the slender-billed curlew or the Eurasian curlew in our fields any more, over time, we lose sight of the knowledge that they once belonged here, that they were with us and part of who we were. The collateral damage is that we assume the landscapes they once moved through contain precisely what they always have and should contain. And so on, as time moves along, we believe that all is as it should be.

The loss of a species becomes a dying star. An unseen point of light still radiating faint pulses of hope.

Szabi and I headed towards the rescue centre gates. We didn't ask about the juvenile whitethroat. I doubt there was much they could do for such a tiny bird and, anyway, I wanted to forget the image of the bird flailing inside the plastic box. We walked past a few more cages: an ibis with a badly swollen eye; a bird I couldn't see very well huddled into the mass of its own feathers, one leg bandaged, blood seeping through. On our way out, we passed a zip wire with a seat suspended beneath a life-size plastic replica of a white-tailed sea eagle. Kids were taking it in turns, looking up at the bird that took to the skies and soared above their heads, if only for brief moments of time.

Mrs Janossy Goes Shopping for Cats

We picked them out of the long grass underneath the tree and zipped them into clear plastic bags. Four dainty hooves attached to fractured roe deer shin bones. A scatter of hares' feet. Boluses of hair and delicate bones. Feathers of sumptuous umber shot through with deltas of gold and cream. A matted cluster of dark grey feathers. The head of a heron – and nevertheless that only one eye still partially remained, it retained a heron's particular determined gaze. The strip of white under the chin was extraordinarily white, the black stripe on either side of the face damp and dull, the bill bone-hard. The emptied body of a marsh harrier, without the head. Raggedy fur attached to the hip joint of a deer. The tips of the ears of hares. A plethora of unidentified bones. More dainty roe deer hooves. More of those Renaissance brown feathers riven with seams of gold. The skull of a cat picked clean.

We'd drive to the nest site in the 4x4, and were off-grid, but our route showed up as a fine red line on the tablet attached to the dash. The red line was inscribed by the digital tracking system monitoring Imre Fatér's movements during the working day. Imre drove with one hand on the wheel, the other cradling the massive telephoto lens of the camera that lay across his lap as we juddered along. To either side were rectilinear blocks of sunflowers alternating with plantations of corn all awaiting the heavy machines. Elsewhere, vast acreages of pale stubble.

Half a field away – how far exactly was difficult to tell in this unfamiliar terrain – a pair of roe deer stepped together from a block of sunflowers and began to circumspectly forage among the stubble. Something disturbed them – us,

I think, and they turned on a coin and leaped back into the
sunflower forest like a scene from a medieval tapestry.

Imre drove unhurriedly, and despite all the windows
being down, there was little, if any, draught to provide respite
from the heat. The radio played Hungarian and Western pop
music and the red line tracked our route as we trundled past
another wall of sunflowers, leaving a nimbus of sand-
coloured dust in our wake.

Islanded in the middle of the next vast stubble field was
an area of woodland, and poking out from the branches was
a red roof, a chimney, a wall, a door, a pair of windows.

'An abandoned farm. The country is full of them. Now
it's all big agribusiness,' Imre said, waving his driving hand at
the landscape as the 4x4 lumbered past. 'Companies from
Austria and Holland. These days the small farmer is a thing
from the past. How do you say?'

'An anachronism?' I posed. Imre nodded slowly.

Another block of sunflowers, then a field boundary of tall
oaks. Imre steered through a gap in the trees and began to
plough across an ocean of stubble.

The satellite continued its fine red line as the 4x4 slowly
ate up the ground and we headed – where exactly? I was
utterly lost. All sense of direction gone – north, south, east
and west, all disintegrating under my inability to orientate
myself in this unfamiliar place. I was in Jászberény National
Park, though how it differed from the wider agricultural
land I had not yet understood. The one constant feature was
a translucent outline of distant hills that Szabi told me were
the North Hungarian mountains, and that Slovakia lay
beyond. He told me he'd been to the mountains once as a
kid on a family holiday. My own landscape psyche had a
very alternative set of needs; I couldn't imagine having only
one visit to these high places in half a lifetime. That brief
line of hills was a lodestone, the centre of my Hungarian
compass. It anchored me as we gimballed and gyred across
miles of earth. Even so, as the heat intensified, the hills

themselves became uncertain, shimmering through vaporous layers of ashen haze.

The phone in Imre's pocket began to jangle an irritating tune. He took it out, seamlessly swapping hands on the wheel while talking slowly, nodding and shrugging, and finally saying 'Szia' (goodbye), one of the few words of Hungarian I recognised. Imre's colleague on the other end of the phone had spent the day monitoring one of the project's imperial eagles through the satellite tracker, but the eagle had been stationary for what might have been too long. Imre sent the guy off to investigate.

My field notes are a stash of evidence of being jolted around incessantly, despite the dignified rate of travel. Some of the words were barely legible. Occasionally, a page would be filled with a single cryptic word resolving in a flourish of lost control – a ditch being crossed, or the parallel troughs gouged by heavy machinery on the move. The notes tell me the things we saw and some of the things that I wanted to know. Later, they reminded me of the questions I should have asked and hadn't. The satellite tracking system, meanwhile, smoothed the contours into that steadfast, singular red line.

Three egrets lifted from the stubble rows and journeyed away in a wavering path of white. A different kind of red line – red dragonflies knitting themselves radiantly across our route. Then Elvis came on the radio: 'I Can't Help Falling in Love with You'. The square prow of the 4x4 dropped into an irrigation ditch, flushing a female marsh harrier, her white head a flare enduring as an after-image. As the car climbed back out, we were flung around like crash test dummies, escorted by yet more dragonflies. Under a perfectly circular hole in the clouds, a single black stork moved in lazy circles, long legs trailing and the wings a fringed flying carpet. In the distance, another small woodland islanded on the endless plain.

Imre parked beside the wood adjacent to a block of corn tall enough to dwarf the vehicle. He climbed down, leaving the door open and the key in the ignition, triggering an alarm that beeped dementedly. That far away from civilisation, what I had expected was silence, but there we were, with Elvis filling the airwaves and the neurotic persistence of the alarm. The midday heat struck hard. The flies began their unassailable attack.

It was a relief to enter the shade of the wood where sunlight filtered onto the long grasses. I turned a slow circle, taking in the derelict farmhouse that had been entirely subsumed by the trees. It was the kind of place to which it was impossible not to ascribe stories. The house seemed tiny as though only small people could have lived inside. The doorway was closed, as if the occupants had just nipped out for a bit of shopping. Between the upper and lower floors was a narrow band of shingles greyed with age. Above this, a single window set square in the upper wall, the old white paint of the walls flaking. I walked around the side of the house and peered through a lopsided window frame. Light percolated down through the sheltering trees. Inside was an interior sprawl of boisterous ivy and elder, burdened by berries, rampaging and clambering, the corners filled with mountains of billowing briars that insinuated themselves inside the collapsed chimney opening. The traditional ceramic tiled cladding was long gone, and the stove lay aslant a fallen beam as if in the aftermath of an accident. Other roof beams lay collapsed across two adjacent walls, and the whole space had been invaded by an audacity of tendrils. I turned a corner, and there, almost completely buried under swathes of ivy and supporting part of the collapsed iron roof, was a barbican of stone. At first, I couldn't make out what it was – or had been. Then I got it – this stump, this resolute dolmen was nothing more than the remaining corner of a barn wall.

The house was an empty vessel; a place to fill with imagination. It was the house of Snow White or Rumpelstiltskin. The witch's house where Hansel and Gretel came and where Gretel − loyal sister − bettered the old cannibal. It felt like a wellspring of lost stories, of the long gone, the ruined, the disappeared. The ruined farm also articulated something, of course, of the hard, workaday lives of the small producers whose way of working had been utterly eclipsed by the progress of industrial farming. Inside the wood, the house was sheltered from the relentless summer heat of the open plains. It was sheltered, too, from the rain that had fallen mostly when needed and from the worst of the winter winds hammering south from the Ural Mountains. Maybe it was just as well the place had been abandoned; I couldn't imagine enduring here under the intensity of Anthropocene summers, landlocked, without air con. And no roads led here. Once the farming families had moved away, no wonder the place had collapsed. The place was simply surplus to requirements.

Szabi called to me. He'd found the sweep-well, or 'oofe' − the water supply. The mechanism was to one side, operated by pulling a rope attached to a long arm pivoting from a vertical beam. Together we leaned on the edge of the timber surround and peered down. The well had been built by people who knew their craft; rough blocks of stone laid in a perfect circle to a depth of some three metres. Small ferns unfurled in the mossy interior. The water remained as a darkly glowing mirror.

Imre came over. He was clutching great bunches of feathers in both hands, umber, shot through with gold. 'Last year,' he said, nodding towards the wooden box, 'I found a juvenile eagle down a well. I got it out OK; it was unharmed.' He shrugged, and Szabi shook his head from side to side and made that sound that means 'incredible'.

I asked Imre why he needed to collect the feathers. 'The shafts contain tiny droplets of blood, so if we analyse, we get a genetic fingerprint for each individual eagle. Then we know if pairs stay together or if they separate. Staying together is good; lots of changes – then the birds have lots of problems.'

Oak striplings pushed skywards underneath mature trees. Chaffinches sang unseen and a pair of turtle doves flew out from the trees over the endless fields. Beyond the woodland oasis was a fringe of relict trees, the grass knee-high, then a swathe of uncut grass that shifted under the hot breeze. Beyond this, the next viridian wall of corn obstructed the view.

'Did you notice the nest?' Imre asked, turning and indicating with his head for us to follow. We walked back to where we'd entered the wood. Elvis was over; now something in shouty Hungarian blared into the growing press of heat, the key alarm still beeping. I wanted to slam the door shut. Imre read my mind, switched off the radio and pushed the door closed. After that, the silence was sudden, and immediately disorienting. Without Imre or Szabi and the car, I had the sense I could have wandered for days out there without encountering anything resembling civilisation.

Imre pointed up into a robinia tree. It was difficult to make out between the extravagant swags of leaves, but directly above our heads was a nest. Or less of a nest and more as if someone had tipped the garden refuse into the tree. It had been constructed of layers of crumbling oak leaves and more recent additions of greenery that articulated in the breeze. Then I noticed the eagle: a juvenile, though difficult to discern among the branches and the dense summer foliage. I could see the undertail and the trouser feathers of the legs, but what was most apparent were the great yellow claws and shiny black talons gripping the branch adjacent to the nest. The bird was apparently immobile. Was it concerned by our presence? For all I knew, it was paying us acute attention.

Imre pointed again. A colony of sparrows was making regular sorties from the accreted layers of the nest. In and out they hurried. 'They make their home inside the eagle's nest,' Imre said. And there they were, the constant contact calls of these highly sociable birds, coming from inside the pile. Here we were again in the realm of story; the tiny sparrows literally underneath the feet of a giant raptor.

'In the breeding season, the adult eagles bring fresh nest material. They like to keep their houses clean.' And looking up at that cluttered pile, I had a sudden unexpected thought of home and of my adult sons' bedrooms. Maybe one day I will walk into their rooms and find the beds made, the mugs taken downstairs, the tea-stained rings wiped away, clothes picked off the floor, desks and computers grime-free. Until then, there's no alternative to working out the distinction between unconditional love and utter frustration.

'Always they bring more small branches – like this – with leaves still attached.' Imre picked a small branch from out of the long grass. 'They grip with their talons and ...' And he mimed snapping the branch in two.

Szabi and I began to help Imre collect the remnants of food and more luxurious feathers from the grass beneath the nest. Imre picked up eagle pellets and broke them apart to reveal small feathers from a long-eared owl. He told us how the eagles' diet has changed radically over the past thirty years. The eagles' usual staples of European hamster and souslik (ground squirrel) were in free-fall. I picked up an immature magpie feather and one from a long-eared owl.

'You've seen what they eat these days,' he said, indicating a pile of clear plastic bags of skulls and bones and hooves collected together on the ground. 'Now they eat hedgehogs and terrapins, owls, great bustard. The heaviest flying bird in the world,' he said, 'carted off to an eagle's nest. Grey partridges too. But agribusiness is not good for the grey partridge. When we had field margins, we had grey partridge. We had everything. We had wildflowers. Now this,' Imre indicated the miles of stubble and sunflowers, 'this; this is brutalist agriculture. Now it's all about big bucks – who pays, and how they pay.'

The eagle called out suddenly. The call was uncertain, delivered in intermittent single notes that seemed more crow than King of Birds. As we looked up, the youngster shifted position revealing the bronzed body and outer edges of its wings and shoulders. Slowly, the bird orientated its head and peered down at us as if it had only then understood that we were there, creating a disturbance beneath its home. It was plagued by flies. As the head swivelled towards us, I clocked its eyes, then, with a sudden rush of sound, it crashed out of the tree. But the damn foliage was in the way. There was just a glimpse of the tail and a snapshot of the sumptuous plumage as the young eagle racketed away into the world beyond the abandoned farm. From somewhere not very far away, an adult male eagle began to call.

'The maiden flight,' Imre said. 'You've seen the first one.'

'Really?' I asked.

'Really,' he replied and nodded his head, then waved his hand in the air as if following the young eagle's journey.

My first eastern imperial eagle. *Aquila heliaca*. The sighting may have been brief, but the image was ingrained even then. I tried to catch another glimpse, but the bird had already passed beyond our seeing.

Back in the 4x4 Imre thrust the gears into reverse and turned the car around with that by-now-familiar one-handed steering-wheel manoeuvre. The milky layer of cloud had dispersed, revealing a potent blue. We trundled back towards civilisation, the midsummer heat swelling in intensity. We turned onto a crossroads where a silver-haired man was fixing a puncture, his bike upside down among a profusion of wildflowers, then we went off-grid again, the red line showing our stately progress across the steppe.

Sometime later, Imre parked in the shade of a young plantation. We got out adjacent to a recently planted orchard of plum and oak and, away to one side, poplar and acacia. Once, Imre had explained, the land here belonged to a couple of small farms, but the farmers and the buildings were long gone. When the Helicon Eagle Project approached a couple of landowners about purchasing the land for eagle habitat creation, the owner of one lot had asked for over a million euros.

'He'd heard there was EU funding going, and he was more than happy to exploit the situation. We said, "No thanks." The other landowner, a very elderly lady, was a retired farmer; she wanted to *give* the land to us. Again, we said "No; we have to pay something." In the end, we agreed to pay her £160. Last time I saw her,' Imre said, 'she'd just turned 109.'

Imre unpacked a drone and set it on a bright-orange plastic sheet on the ground. The drone took to the sky with the buzz of a swarm of bees and zipped away over the tops of the young trees. Instantly it began to relay images back to the tablet in Imre's hands, the information arriving in stripes of information – a linear portrayal of the wild tangle around us.

'The trees have grown more than I expected,' Imre said. 'They're doing really well. Lots of fruit trees – and when the trees begin to bear fruit, the plan is to make fruit liqueurs to sell – another way to get the public onside!'

In the first half of the twentieth century, eagles, owls and other raptors were persecuted right across Hungary. Hunters were provided with information about the most effective ways to poison them; under Communism, anything that represented a threat to food availability seemed fair game. The eagles reacted by moving away. They began to move up into the hills – the very hills that anchored me into place that day. When Communism ended, and with the beginnings of the free market economy, attitudes towards wildlife slowly began to change. This time, the few remaining eagles moved back down onto the plain – though not enough to sustain the population naturally.

All of the imperial eagle territories that the project supports are centred on areas combining agricultural land with natural woodlands; often these are the kinds of abandoned farms we had visited earlier, or places that had been left fallow for years, like this one. Once purchased, the project sets about creating the right kind of infrastructure for eagle habitat. Here, the plantation included fruit trees.

'We make oases among all this agricultural desert. Right?' Imre said, and right on cue, an adult imperial eagle wheeled overhead, silhouetted and huge against sheer blue. A moment passed, and another raptor swivelled into the same airspace, slight, blanched and swift, the wingbeats quick and trim against the eagle's languid trajectory.

'It's a Saker falcon!' Szabi said, and as we shielded our eyes from the glare, we saw how the falcon was locked on to the eagle's every move, how the wings eclipsed instantly and the falcon dove and just as rapidly surged again onto a higher arc of flight. Seen together like this, compared to the eagle's broad wings, the falcon was a crossbow taught against the sky.

Almost transparent against the dazzle of blue sky, the falcon spun higher, locked on to the job of tracking and harrying the eagle from above.

The drone passed back and forth like a demented shuttle while stripes of images loaded onto the screen. 'It sends back six metres a second,' Imre told us as the two birds drew away and out of sight. The next time the drone buzzed across, there were the three of us on the screen. I pointed up and watched myself doing it on the screen. A second later, down the drone came, alighting in the centre of the orange sheet.

'You're a very good pilot,' I said.

'I'm not so sure,' Imre replied. 'Once I managed to land a drone smack in the Danube …'

Then Szabi put his hand to his ear. 'Listen,' he said, 'a Saker falcon calling.' Above us, a female falcon accompanied by a juvenile scythed across the searing blue; now we understood why the falcon had been so edgy, and so absorbed in the eagle's trajectory.

There were more visits to eagle nests, one in another line of oak trees. By now, my sense of disorientation had grown. I'm used to map-reading and getting myself out of a weather mess in the mountains, but this was unexpected. Once, distantly, I'd seen a factory chimney rising out of the plain, a striped red and white pin, and I noticed how I needed these anchors of orientation among all the unending steppe. On the journey to the next nest, something caught Imre's eye. He began to reverse the car. In an expanse of stubble, there was a juvenile eagle. Imre lifted the camera and fired away. At first, against that sea of earth and stubble, I couldn't locate it, but when I did, I noted how the coloration serves the imperial eagle so well, how they fuse seamlessly into the dark soil and the ochre vestiges of crops.

Imre pointed. Not very far away, poised on the branch of a dying tree, was an adult eagle. It was clearly keeping an eye. The juvenile mantled its wings over the prey. 'We'll move on,' Imre said. 'We don't want to disturb his dinner.'

Significant numbers of juvenile imperial eagles die in their first year; up to 60 per cent don't make it. Learning to feed themselves is vital. The ones that develop early, the tenacious youngsters who think they can cope alone, are far more likely to succumb. The ones that stay with their parents the longest are much more likely to survive. I liked this idea very much; me with my boys on the verge of leaving – or leaving again.

Next stop, a cafe on the outskirts of Jászberény advertised by a tubular red steel figure with a fixed smile and permanent wave. Inside the building was a heady thermosphere of fried food and pizza, so our office for the next couple of hours was a table on the veranda, though perhaps that's too much of a word for a row of uncleared tables hemmed in by ubiquitous Coca-Cola banners. After all that heat, when I saw the sign all I wanted to do was drink a Coke.

Imre wasn't happy about the sticky mess on the table. 'It's not good,' he said, brushing away crumbs with a napkin, but we stayed put, eating goulash, drinking Cokes and coffees, while Imre showed us image after image on the tablet.

This is how twenty-first-century conservation works – information is beamed through time and space to a tablet on a table that the waitress has by now cleaned, in a cafe on the edge of a town in central Hungary. Image after image and map after map rolled across the screen – layers of information captured, processed, analysed and presented as vital geographic and ecological data. Clusters of green dots indicated the locations of imperial eagles' nests. There were sub-pages for nests containing eggs and for those with juveniles. More pages for those where youngsters had successfully fledged – the maiden flight we'd witnessed would become another green dot on the system. Next, a set of crazy scribbles, the kind you make when your pen is running out of ink – the transcripts of satellite-tagged eagles. Then other scribbles recording every move the conservationists made across the steppe as they successfully brought the eagles back from the edge of extinction. Next, a spoor of blue dots – the locations where the project's sniffer dogs located dumps of poison or poisoned carcasses – then lists of suspects' addresses searched by police. The data is like archaeology, I thought; a way of sifting layers to reveal material from the past and present. What other kinds of systems, I wondered, log our world in quite such explicit and substantial ways?

Next Imre showed us drone footage of three eagle chicks in a nest. They were seven weeks old, only two weeks to go before fledging, and the youngsters were *very* interested in the drone. Interested and edgy. 'If a drone gets too close, the chicks shrink down – make themselves small as possible.' Then we watched footage of an adult bringing food to the nest – a roe deer carcass – the youngsters looking at the adult as if to say, '*Well, what do you expect us to do with this?*' Then Imre told a story of a bald eagle nest in the United States monitored by a webcam, and of how the camera had recorded an adult eagle bringing in a young cat – live on camera. Someone's kitty, limp, not quite dead. And I remembered the cat skull Imre had found under the first nest and how *other*, how out of place, it seemed inside the zip-lock bag. A missing cat? An adored cat? A cat that liked to lie out in the sun. A cat that was very interested in birds. *Doug – have you seen the cat?*

When I tracked down the footage on my laptop that night, what struck me was what a bizarre spectacle it was. The film quality was poor, and I couldn't tell whether it was the pixels fluctuating or the cat was still breathing a little as it was deposited at the feet of the two subadult juveniles, like an offering to the gods. For a minute or two, the young eagles had lowered their heads and inspected the kitten, perhaps sniffing or nudging it gently with their gigantic, hooked bills. A few more seconds, and they tucked right in. My domestic sensibilities kicked in. What if it had been my cat? The one I don't own, the one I won't own, although once upon a time I did. All the eagles had done is turn the tables on the domestic moggy. If I was flabbergasted by the footage of the young cat in the nest, I was in danger of meltdown when a few minutes later I read that it's estimated 27 million birds are killed each year by cats in the UK alone; some suggest it could perhaps be as many as 55 million birds per year. Imagine what that volume of birds would look like if we could see them all take to the air at once? And if we add into the mix the numbers of bird deaths directly attributable to human actions upon the land, then maybe it's not only cats we should be focusing on quite so closely.

In the cafe, Imre tells us that each breeding season someone wearing a harness and spiked shoes will climb each eagle tree and place each chick found in the nest inside a drawstring bag and lower it to the ringer waiting below. Satellite tags will be fitted to each youngster, and each of those tags will have already begun to translate itself into yet another cluster of dots on the map or will eventually show up as scribbly drawings that render lines of flight, feeding places and roost sites into data. As we reviewed the data on the veranda of the cafe on the edge of Jászberény, the scale of the work involved became apparent.

Then came another, more purposeful digital drawing; an eagle's expedition from its territory on the plain to right here in Jászberény, and there were the date and the time and the exact location of where the eagle came to call.

'The first eagle you saw,' Imre said, 'we named him Argo. All the birds we study, we give names – fantasy names – but there was one exception. The male from this territory was named after a respected ornithologist called Mr Janossy. Then someone discovered the bird was female, so quickly we changed to *Mrs* Janossy! This record shows Mrs Janossy – and she's coming to town.'

'A shopping trip,' I said.

Imre laughed and said, 'Yes; maybe shopping for cats!'

Another screen: the height of the tree, of the nest, the number of eggs alive, the number dead. Next, the number of chicks alive; the number dead. Then an aggregation of dots and Imre expanded the screen with his forefinger and thumb to show all the nests and all the known individuals in Hungary, in Romania, in Serbia.

'We look for the gaps in the map – that's where we go looking for new territories in spring. Now, here in Jászberény National Park, there are so many imperial eagles we're unlikely to find any gaps. Then the eagles will travel to find new places to live.' The nests are surveyed in June by the team and by volunteers using binoculars and scopes. 'If an eagle is sitting, she's on eggs. If she's standing, wings out, she's sheltering chicks.'

Cars and trucks came bowling along the road towards the town, the heat so intense that the vehicles moved through apparitions of rippling water. A horse carriage passed two or three times, its driver in traditional dress – long shorts, braces, white shirt, a trilby hat trimmed with pheasant feathers. Four greys pulled the carriage, noses pulled in by martingales, their powerful necks arched and dark grey manes swishing as they clopped along. Once or twice, tourists were on board.

Next, a screen that plotted the destinations visited by Mrs Janossy over the four years of her life so far, to Lithuania, Latvia, Poland, Austria and right over the heart of Budapest. There was a page with the scribble drawing of an adult bird making journeys to and from the nest, bringing in food. The drawing showed how the adult had taken to roosting in a tree a short distance away. 'To get away from the juvenile's constant begging,' Imre said. 'I get that,' I replied.

A map showing the locations where dumps of poisoned bait had been discovered, green and blue for the two human workers and red for the dog. A photograph of a white-tailed sea eagle, found in the classic position of a poisoned raptor – face down, wings spread, talons clenched into tight fists, pupils wide open. At the time of its death, this eagle was wearing a tracking device. Almost all the chemical agents used as a poison in Hungary are banned substances – mostly now deployed to control foxes and corvids. But poison does not choose. It sits and waits, passive for the time being, invisible inside the carcasses of baited animals. If a raptor is located within an hour of ingesting poison, and if a vet can administer an injection of atropine, the bird's life might just be saved.

Next, we saw pages of photographs of dead eagles, the mature birds recognisable by their darker plumage and the white patch on each shoulder. Some of the photos had been taken when they were only recently deceased, the plumage still glowing.

Someone delivered a box of rabbits to the kitchen door at the side of the cafe, each one neatly laid across the next like sardines in a tin. A pizza-delivery guy on a moped buzzed in and out, collecting pizzas in red and white boxes, leaving behind a greasy miasma of two-stroke engine oil as he buzzed away again.

'In Serbia,' Imre said, 'hunters poison golden jackals and hang the carcass in a tree. When they hunt in a pack, jackals can take a sheep. Usually, it's roe deer. But the farmers don't want their sheep taken and the hunters don't want their deer taken, so they put out poisoned bait. Then – so many white-tailed and imperial eagles and buzzards come to feed on the poisoned jackals – all the raptors that eat up all the carrion from the ground ...'

On the tablet, Imre pointed at a graphic of all the imperial eagle territories in Hungary. Two-thirds of the entire EU population breed in the country. In the 1970s, though, the numbers had crashed to fifteen or twenty pairs. Most of the birds had died from poisoning, but many had been electrocuted by live overhead cables. Starvation was an issue, too, and so was shooting. It was not a great time to be an eagle. A nationwide ban on poisoning was eventually instigated, but the ruling was ineffectual, and by 2011, poisoning was again the single biggest cause of eagle deaths in Hungary.

In 2012, funded by the EU Life Programme, the Hungarian Helicon Life Eagle Project began operations. In a type of collaboration rarely seen, 300 government investigators, 150 prosecutors, fifty court staff and judges were all involved. The Hunting Chamber of the Jászság region signed a co-operation agreement, and their members also signed up for alternative gamekeeping and conservation training. (I tried and failed to imagine this kind of co-operation between such diverse groups taking place in the UK.) The eagle project reports were made available to 60,000 hunters. A sniffer dog named Falco and his handler were trained at the national police headquarters and subsequently detected around 200 poisoned animals and bait dumps that would not otherwise have been exposed. A series of short films were shown on TV, and like this, the public became captivated by the dog's successes. The police, conservation groups, vets, zoos and filmmakers were all galvanised into support. Poisoning hotlines were set up, and an Anti-Poisoning Working Group was established. Some 2,500 people in other organisations made commitments to act against poisoning. The National Food Chain Safety Office was involved, and a veterinary network of twenty-five volunteer vets offered training on the treatment and care of poisoned raptors. Additionally, 230 volunteers took part in more than 3,000 days of nest guarding. After this, in the following year, thirty-three eagle chicks successfully fledged from twenty nests. In 2017, further funding was secured to allow the project's current manifestation, the Pannon Eagle Project, to continue the work.

'Tell me,' I asked Imre, 'what kind of value would you put on one imperial eagle after all this?'

He considered the question. 'Each one? About one million of your UK pounds.'

After lunch, Imre took us to the Eagle Centre on the outskirts of Jászberény. We'd not long hopped out of the 4x4 when the warden, Tibor, returned. Imre introduced us to him as he was lifting the tailgate of his van. Then he and Imre hefted a huge crate out onto the ground. Tibor had just responded to a call-out for a young sea eagle struck by a passing vehicle. Inside the crate the eagle appeared incredulous, its hooked gape wide open, its tongue pulsating under shallow breaths. The talons were bound together by copious amounts of webbing. Wearing giant handling gloves, Tibor reached inside and with one hand grasping the beak he hauled the eagle out. The bird was immense. Its vivid, flickering eye looked from one of us to the next; aliens from another planet. A wing drooped over Tibor's arm, the plumage rich, dark, veined with white.

Tibor carried the eagle into a caged enclosure. Keeping hold of the beak with one hand, he cut away the webbing. The bird flopped forwards onto the floor. Slowly, Tibor released his grip. The eagle half-flapped, half-lifted itself in a strange dance as though its feet were somehow disassociated from the rest of its body. It chasséd towards the front of the cage like a drunk at a disco, the bird's whole demeanour implicated in the trauma of accident and rescue.

The others wandered away. I stayed for a moment, talking to the eagle in a low voice from the other side of the wire. But what the eagle needed was peace.

Tibor's four-year-old son followed his dad everywhere, begging like a baby bird begs for food. He begged to be allowed to get the strimmer out from the shed. He begged to hold the baby little owl that screeched like a banshee in the small recovery room, its owl eyes huge and mad and orange. Tibor's son begged to hold the baby cat that might have been a wild cat or a hybrid that had been picked out of its cage for us to admire, yowling in fury as only cats and babies can. He begged to hold the swift pullus taken from a shoebox and the baby bee-eater from another. His eighteen-month-old curly blonde-haired sister, wearing only a pink and white striped vest and a nappy and with a pink dummy clamped between her teeth, clapped and shrieked with glee as the bee-eater, held tenderly in Tibor's fingers, warbled its wobbling, demented call. Through all this, his young son also begged to go fishing. And having noticed the fishing net and cricket stumps stashed in the corner of the room, he gathered them all up and clutching them as best he could, he continued in his father's wake, the net now upended and trailing along the ground.

Of all the places I visited with Imre as he managed the job of returning the eastern imperial eagle to its former abundance, it was the newly planted orchard that presented me with a way of pulling together a whole array of ways of seeing and thinking.

First, because of the elderly lady's initial intention to give the land away rather than use it as an opportunity to increase her personal wealth. And secondly, the project's response that, no, something must be paid. What this represented, then, was a transaction that honoured respect, its conclusion an opportunity from which many different kinds of wealth could flow. Measured against this, the alternative landowner's attempt to exploit the situation perhaps represented something like indifference to the loss of an iconic species. His decision was deeply situated in the demands of the free market economy.

There was, too, the drone's swift harvesting of data as it buzzed above the orchard transmitting an objective view of progress, despite the sheer noise of the thing displacing the otherwise stillness, save for the breeze in the leaves of the new trees. And above the drone, shifting through volumes of air, the imperial eagle continued asserting its place in the world, and higher still, the saker falcon, twisting on thermals, looking down upon us all.

Perspective allows us to work out our relationships with the natural world. The market economy and everything that follows in its wake is one kind of perspective; the economy of biodiversity is quite another. I wonder if, as a species, we had sooner begun to consider the damage we've wrought on our landscapes, we might have understood the massively diminished value of a landscape that has been drained of its previously momentous nature.

I have a series of photographs taken that day, a sequence revealing the minute and subtle variations in the two birds' behaviours: the eagle's commanding presence, the sheer amount of space it took up in the sky, its apparent lack of interest in the falcon. This, against the falcon's somewhat disassociated titanium shadow, the way the bird swerved so artfully, so *efficiently*, in the thermal above. In every photograph, the eagle's eye is orientated towards the ground as it notices whatever it needed to see to survive. For an imperial eagle, perhaps a Saker falcon is just a minor itch.

I don't know what the imperial eagle thought as it soared like a bronze banner above the orchard, its elongated, sinuous primary feathers taking the measure of the hot air, palpating the sky's invisible qualities, its great yellow talons furled underneath. Or indeed, the thoughts of the falcon, its taught bowstring sere as it arrowed across that blinding blue. What I imagine is that they regarded us with little other than slight judiciousness as they got on with the day-to-day business of provisioning and safeguarding and exploiting whatever situation presented itself in the ongoing necessities of their difficult lives. They would have no concept, no perspective, of how much we as humans give, or of how much we take away.

The last imperial eagle nest of the day was in a lone poplar at the side of a track at the edge of another vast field. To one side was a raised grassy bank and to the other a dry irrigation ditch.

We looked up through the foliage at what was a somewhat smaller nest than the others I'd seen that day. The juvenile eagle was perched a half metre or so away from the nest. It peered down at us with that, by now, familiar gaze that existed between alarm and disdain. The tree's open structure gave us a clear line of sight – of the massive, business-like raptor's bill edged with the fleshy gape, yellow as sunflowers. The eyes were encircled by yellow and there again were those massive yellow talons – talons that would need to work hard for a living. I noticed the coloured leg-ring below the bird's honey-coloured trousers, and Imre said there was a satellite tracker attached to the bird's back feathers, ready and waiting to begin relaying data.

Szabi came over. 'Look what I found,' he said, and held out a finger upon which perched a bright-green praying mantis, the hind legs sharply angled, the head and eyes perched on the end of the green stalk of the body and a pair of wiry antennae lifted above. Not far away a red-backed shrike ticked its irritated call from the hedge beyond the bank.

We wandered around near the tree, building our list of evidence. Knowing the routine by now, we packed everything away in those zip-lock plastic bags, Imre scribing the labels with dates and times and locations. The entire hind legs of a roe deer, the powerful joint still articulated, still covered in fur, devoid of muscle, the belly fur still attached to the hip joint. Handfuls of eagle feathers, some with the downy white barbules that trap air close to the bird's body and help to keep it warm. The leg bones of half a dozen hares. Deposits of yet more roe deer hooves, so neat and black, so *clean*. We didn't find any staring dead-eyed herons, or any more cat skulls — wild, domestic or in between. Only the dishevelled evidence left behind by a species making its way in the world, or rather *back* into a world from which it was almost completely lost.

We are all animals making our way through the world. We impose the impacts of our activities upon the land and sometimes these are discreet, if troublesome to herons and roe deer and yes, to some cats. Sometimes, they're the manifestations of big agribusiness and the economic precedents that allow them to do what they do. But consider the actions of the 106-year-old lady who wanted to give her land away rather than sell it because she understood the worth and the wealth and the place of one particular species among others. What is at work here is action as an economy of gifting, where everything circulates and where money isn't everything. What value should be placed on the eastern imperial eagle returned to its homelands on the Hungarian Steppe? I really don't think we can say.

Human Resilience Training

For me, part of being human means taking to the water. I'm resilient enough to swim from spring until autumn without a wetsuit. Wetsuits mean you can't feel the silky film of freshwater or saltwater on your skin. In water, I am in my element. I need it. When I swim in the lakes or the tarns or rivers, I carry home the trace of long immersion, the water's mossy amniotic scent. I have sensitive feet, and this is a trait of being Pisces. It shows on the days I forget to pack my swimming shoes and enter the water by slithering and slipping on the stones that hurt my feet, but that must be negotiated to reach the deeper water.

Pisces are sensitive souls in all kinds of ways. We are dreamers. I live with my head in the clouds even when my body is in the water. When I am not swimming, sometimes I dream about swimming. Sometimes I daydream about swimming and plan when I can next get away to swim. If I don't swim, I get depressed. Not medication-depressed, just ordinary depressed. When I was in my twenties, I swam every day. I got addicted to swimming, and on days when I didn't swim, my body itched to. I once swam with a friend who, in a bikini, swam in Lake Coniston after breaking the ice to make a swimming hole. I watched. I am not a swimmer in ice. Not yet.

Where does it all come from, this need to swim? This need to be carried by the only other element that can take our weight – as long as we know how to hold ourselves and accommodate it, to float or to swim. I could say that, by being immersed in water, we are returning to our amniotic time and to that idea of beginning again, like baptism, but there's nothing new in that. I was never baptised. At the age of eleven, I was suddenly horrified by the thought that my body could not be buried in consecrated ground. Instead, I would become an outcast. (Why it mattered, I never stopped to ask; I wouldn't be around to know the difference.) One Sunday, I left the house early and walked to the local vicarage. I knocked on the big wooden door. The vicar answered and I said that I'd come to be baptised. Instead of taking me into the church immediately and carrying out the procedure (which is what I'd imagined would happen – all over and done with in ten minutes flat), he asked me inside. He opened the Bible and said start reading here and see where you think you should stop. I didn't know where or when to stop. I read on. And on. He stopped me eventually and said: 'You can join in confirmation classes as well and then we can do both at the same time – baptism and confirmation!' Like two for the price of one. Like this was a good thing. I ran a mile. I tried to wash away all the embarrassment. To let it dissolve in the slipstream.

If I could begin again, would I make a better job of my life? Can I start again? Can I learn from my mistakes? Can we?

Sometimes in midsummer, when I swim in the lakes or the tarns, I swim with the tiny blue darts of common damselflies. If I swim early in the morning, the damsels among the reeds and the water lilies might still be dressed up in dew. Mercurial, illuminating the liminal, they sling transient, lissom nets of electromagnetic charge and purl azure stitches above the water lilies.

The whooper swan can see the Earth's magnetic field. The Earth's invisible-to-humans magnetic field is generated deep inside the Earth and, when it emerges, it stitches a net of blue that radiates around the blue planet. Inside the swan's eye is a protein called cryptochrome, or Cry4. Inside the bird's eye, Cry4 receives the blue light of the magnetic field. Cry4 is clustered in a part of the bird's retina that is sensitive to blue light. The process of seeing the magnetic field is called magnetoreception. The magnetic field spirals the Earth from north to south and is picked up by the eye of the whooper swan that has just set out on its autumn migration. As the swan heads south from the Icelandic breeding grounds, its eye receives the light we cannot see above the continents and the oceans, and it processes the net of blue for navigation. Cry4 is the arrow in the compass. It orientates the swan along a line of travel, maintaining it to within five degrees of correction.

Sometimes whooper swans travel very close to the surface of the ocean. They have been recorded leaving Iceland and arriving on the coast of southern Scotland in twelve hours straight. Hopefully, as they swing in from the north, they avoid the blades of offshore wind farms. And in the daylight or in the dark, when they land on the pools at Caerlaverock on the Solway coast, each already arrived swan family greets the next to arrive with trumpeting fanfares. Sometimes the swans stand on the water and beat their wings in an apparent act of recognition, and sometimes they arrive and ruffle their feathers as if to say: *Great. Now, where's the food?* And so it goes, all through the winter months, and when a full moon hangs in the dark like the backdrop of an opera and illuminates all the arriving-swan-family drama below, the raucousness continues long into the night. When I stay in the guest house overlooking the pools in the autumn and winter, sleep can be hard to find. I get up and stand at the window, peering out at the moon, and I see how it lights up the water and the earth around the water and the swans in the water and, each time I look, there are more and more swans.

I wonder about that net of blue. If I could see it, would it help to keep me orientated in my life or would it merely get in the way? Does it get in the way of the swans and the other migrating species who see it or sense it or use it? What is it like to follow the blue lines?

Damselflies, meanwhile, fly so fast that it's impossible to make out the translucent filigree of their wings. What you see, therefore, is just a fleeting image of tiny blue electrons that seem to propel themselves on a whim,

                    here

                                                        here
            over here.

Sometimes the damsels seem to be attracted to my head above the water because, unlike when I am in a swimming pool, I don't like submerging my head in cold water. My head is less resilient than the rest of me.

And here they come, zinging over the surface towards me,

            gathering in tangles of blue
        above my head.
                    Little aggregates of blue.
    Water-loving crystal switches of blue.
                        One fine twig of blue fused to the next.
        Where does one stick of blue begin, another end?

When damselflies mate, they knit themselves together in impossible stitches. The male displays his bright blue wings and abdomen to the female, and sometimes he zips above the water to show his prowess in zipping, as well he might. Of the Latin nomenclature, Zygoptera, or paired wings, I wonder if it might also mean 'they of the zipping over water'. The female, having been thus attracted to the idea of blue, and of wings, and of wings above water, offers her body to the male, who takes hold of her by the back of her neck using a pair of claspers at the end of his abdomen specifically designed for clasping. The female has special grooves in her anatomy that function as the receivers of claspers. She spirals her thorax upwards towards the male and, so joined, together they make the sign and the shape of a heart, though it is called a wheel. Sometimes damselfly mating is brief, and sometimes the damselflies are in it for the long haul; they and their heart-shaped wheel zip over the water, and sometimes over my head when I am swimming. Thus reconstructed, the damselflies zip too swiftly for me to keep up with – both visually and swimmingly.

Sometimes, in the lakes and the tarns where I like to swim, there is another kind of blue. The blue-green of algal bloom. The Environment Agency and the Lake District National Park tell us that this algal bloom is a *naturally occurring phenomenon*. That is true, in the same way that cholera is a naturally occurring phenomenon. They tell us this because they do not want us to worry. Algal blooms are made up of cyanobacteria, a kind of naturally occurring photosynthetic organism. It ranges, apparently, from unicellular and filamentous to colony-forming species. (I like those words: unicellular, filamentous. Sometimes I imagine my thinking has become filamentous.) Some types of blue-green algae produce toxins. You cannot tell whether it is toxic or not by looking at a Harmful Algal Bloom – toxic to me or to wildlife or to the dog over there that is now swimming through the water to fetch the stick I threw in before I'd even noticed the blue-green bloom.

One website tells me that 'In humans,' algal blooms 'have been known to cause rashes after skin contact and illnesses if swallowed.' I know this to be true because once, before any of us swimmers knew what an algal bloom was or what it might do, I swam through the blue-green scum. My skin began to burn, then it came up in large blotches of red, and some of them began to blister. I thought if I stayed in the cooling water, it would stop. It didn't. I had seen the blue-green water but had not known, and anyway, if I had known, apparently you can't tell only by looking. I got out of the water and drove to the doctor's surgery. He couldn't tell. He poked the blotches and asked how long I'd had them and more of those kinds of questions because in those days even doctors didn't know the right kind of questions to ask.

When the levels of the lakes fall because of the lack of rain, or when there has been another extended period of unusually hot weather, that's when the algae come out to play. To make us not know which one is which. Sometimes the algae are the result of human sewage build-up in the lake. This one is not nice to play in. And sometimes the algae occur because of agricultural fertilisers running off from the surrounding fields and fells that have built up over time. So yes, it is natural. Of a kind. According to scientists, cyanobacteria and the toxins they produce 'represent one of the most hazardous waterborne biological substances that produce a range of adverse health effects from mild skin irritations to severe stomach upsets and even fatal consequences.' And it doesn't end there. If the bloom lasts and continues to build, it blocks sunlight from the water, depriving fish and the plants that bloom in their own funny, unseen way on the bottom of the lakes and tarns, and aquatic insects too. If it all goes on too long, the plants can't obtain oxygen and can't assimilate the blue-green-grey filtered light of the sun.

Once in position, in the shape of a heart-shaped wheel, the male damselfly has another trick up his bendy sleeve: he scoops out any sperm deposited by other males. Sometimes, when the heart has eventually, inevitably been broken, the male follows the female avidly to guard her against the advances of other wheel-dreaming imperative blue males.

In a month, it's all over. The eggs are laid. The larvae pull themselves down the stems of mare's tail weed into the murk and the mud. Their hidden, translucent grasshopper-green bodies will feed on fish eggs and insects through two winters of me not swimming and not breaking the ice and two summers of me swimming. At summer's end, I will breast-stroke through the edges of the tarn, my arms making the shape of a heart over and over, wondering what happens to the no-longer-zipping blue bodies of damselflies.

I learned from my mother how to knit and to sew. From my father, I learned how to keep my feet on the ground and acquire an ability of sorts in practical things. In the garage, I watched him build or make or sand or paint or put up or screw one piece of wood to another. In the house, I knitted and sewed clothes and, in the garage, I helped my father to make houses for dolls. Some of those mother-father skills I carried into adulthood. Even so, if I assert my right to put up shelves, those same shelves may also assert their right to fall down again. I'm reluctant to begin again because, by now, I don't entirely trust my ability to make one thing fit well with another. This is the flaw known as mistrust.

Because she did not know how to do things differently, and because, during the Second World War, she had learned not to speak of difficult things, through my mother, I learned how to remain silent. As an adult and with my husband, I stayed tight-lipped when angry or broke my silence only by hoovering and banging around the house, and not speaking unless I had to for two or maybe three days in a row. This is the quality known as perseverance. It might be the result of being a sensitive Piscean or merely down to learning how things are done.

From both my parents, I learned how to shut myself away when the shouting started. Some days, when my instinct got the better of my sensitive side, I would be propelled by some unseen force out of my bedroom and down the stairs into the kitchen or the sitting room and, finding myself there, I tried to stop my parents from shouting at each other by shouting: 'PLEASE STOP THIS SHOUTING.'

During a morning bike ride recently, I came face to face with a huge and very expensive car that failed to stop when it was being driven out the gateway of a huge and luxurious house. Only managing to get one of my cycle shoes out of its clip, I crashed sideways onto the gravel. I felt justified at communicating my dislike of ending up on the road in a heap of bike and woman. But what made me feel even worse was that, initially, neither the young female driver nor her older male passenger got out of the car and, when at last they did and stood at either side of the car gawping at me, they did not apologise. In what by then was pretty much a full-on shouty voice, I suggested to them that on these narrow back roads – indeed, on any road – drivers are supposed to stop and check what's coming before pulling out. At that point, the man got back inside the car and shut the door, and I began to shout some more.

Do I show more resilience if I shout to communicate my anger at having become one with the gravel, or would I have shown more resilience if I'd apologised profusely for getting in their way? Is it resilient or not to find a pang of unsettling guilt creeping in later about the way I'd communicated my displeasure? I wanted to begin again.

BG (Before Gravel) as I'd cycled along on the back roads, I'd been thinking about resilience. What is it that makes us feel stronger or less strong? And in what kinds of ways – if any – can humans become resilient when all around us, the land and the planet are struggling? The Environment Agency are building concrete walls in my town that will hold back certain amounts of floodwater in the River Kent. Only a kilometre or so upstream, the Kent has just finished being three rivers – the Kent, the Mint and the Sprint. The Sprint is England's fastest-rising river. But the floodwalls will not, the engineers have said, hold back the effects of another Storm Desmond. How can you be resilient when the water rises through your floorboards because where you live the water table is saturated, and the rivers are overwhelmed by the amount of rain that, when it pours off the surrounding fells, resembles solid sheets of metal? How can you show resilience when you are feeling overwhelmed because this is the third or fourth time your home has flooded and you are, once again, homeless? When once again you have to find somewhere else to live? And how long this time until you can return, after the toxic bloom of chemicals, sewage, drain water and every kind of water is hosed down again and again, and the long drying out is done.

On 5 December 2015, the day of Storm Desmond, we looked out from our sitting-room windows and saw how the downhill road had morphed into a water-slalom that washed the gravel away from where the fellside spewed it out and across the road creating new shingle beds in the central reservation that remained for months.

On the opposite side of the road, the steps up to the house facing ours had become a terrifying water feature, like the pressure-release section of a too-full dam. The water smashed and bounced over itself and down the steps onto the road, and there it divided. It was biblical. Here, on the cusp of the hill in front of our house, the floodwaters split, one way draining north, the other south. It did not reach our front door. Not yet.

We listened to radio reports of roads and bridges being washed away and *Don't leave your house – stay inside – don't put the emergency services under even more pressure.* In our sitting room, a slow, bulging accumulation of water had inveigled its way inside the house's structure and had gathered in a big pregnant swag above the bay window. At any moment, the ceiling paper might have burst. I fetched a knife and a bucket and stood on a chair to stab a hole in the paper to relieve the pressure. It was a relief to ease the pressure. Later,

I joined the paper back together with glue and painted over it, but I know the flaw remains.

On my morning bike rides, I frequently cycle past a sign that hangs from a tree outside a house on the back road. The sign advertises something called Human Resilience Training. The morning my stately cycling progress had been so unceremonially disrupted, I had made a U-turn – checking first, of course, that nothing was coming – so that I could read the whole thing. We can, the sign said, be trained to resist. We can resist bullying and overload and depression. We can withdraw into the wilderness to teach ourselves resilience by meditating. We can retreat to realise our divine connection to the natural world and the universe. For some people, to do this means paying someone who is trained to teach them those things. If we are lucky, we are taught those things at the feet of our parents and our teachers.

I had already learned and deeply embedded the idea that silence is a weapon that leaves plenty of destruction trailing in its wake. But I am not resilient enough to wash it away, this learned and habituated imperative of silence. My children learned that my silence is a function of anger and a consequential inability to speak. They are ultimately forgiving – and don't do silence.

Sometimes I feel overwhelmed by the volume of rain that falls on Cumbria. Overwhelmed by the dozens of footbridges and road bridges that were still to be reinstated even four or five years after Storm Desmond. I am overwhelmed by the thought that because so many bridges needed to be rebuilt, the effort became overwhelming, and some repairs were prioritised while others never happened, even though all those bridges were important and some of them were vital. Some of those bridges are here in my community, and some are not. Have we been silenced in our acceptance of the not rebuilding of those bridges? Do the national newspapers show any interest? Our five-years-broken bridges and our roads are nothing now so much as old news.

What does resilience look like in relation to the broken bridge in your community? If you want to walk 200 metres to the shops or the post office but you can't because the bridge is still broken and instead you have to walk about a kilometre, what do you do? What are we supposed to do? Sit back and wait and drum our fingers on the table, making the sound of rain and think, *Well, there are plenty of other bridges that need fixing too* ... Where do you begin?

A few kilometres up the road, the village of Staveley is one of my cycling destinations. I can stop at the cafe and drink coffee and eat cakes. I can read a book while also affecting to lose weight by cycling and to work by eating cakes and reading. I can do all these things while sitting on the decking overlooking the River Kent and sometimes I can watch dippers dipping on stones in the middle of the river or buzzards floating overhead on those ever-so-tippy, apparently unevenly weighted buzzard wings. After yet another incident of unnaturally heavy rains, though, I sit inside, away from the windows. I don't want to let in the sight or the sound of the river, the way it won't be silenced. The way the water is always, always, more resilient than us.

During Storm Desmond, the village was divided when the bridge on the main street was destroyed by the volume and weight of water flowing beneath and around and eventually over it. But in the reckoning and the aftermath, this bridge was considered not to be urgent. The community waited. Then the community waited some more. But while they waited, they wrote letters. They were not silenced, and they did not do silence. They petitioned the local authority and implored them to understand that the bridge was vital to the village. The lack of it separated people from shops and businesses from people. But the county council went silent.

The community made a plan. The man from the post office and the man who rented out small business units got together and commissioned an engineering firm to redesign and rebuild their bridge. They went to the press, and they wrote to the local authority to let them know that they would be sending them the bill for the new bridge. And that was when the local authority broke their silence and came back to the table. After eighteen months of being broken, the bridge was rebuilt. There was a bridge-opening celebration. People dressed up, and the youngest kids in pushchairs were the first to travel over the new bridge, pushed by their parents. The older kids danced their way across, and then came the grandparents and the shopkeepers, and finally, of course, the cyclists – the whole fandango.

What I want to know is how we can build bridges so that those kids in the pushchairs and the dancing kids, and even the cyclists who sometimes get in the way, can have hope even through all the mess of climate chaos? I want to know what tricks we have secreted inside our unbending, unresponsive bodies – the kinds of tricks that I have read are all in there waiting to be allowed to function, were it not for the governments and the businesses and the economic precedents that just want to be left alone to function as they always have. To be stuck, desperately clinging on, one to another. To not admit even to each other that the wheel is broken. Not swimming but sinking. Is it too late to stab a hole and relieve at least some of the pressure? Is it too late to think again about why it is that the lakes and the rivers flood? To begin again? Can we start again? Can we learn how it might be possible – even ever so slowly – to fix one thing to another and build a meaningful landscape that is supported to function for its own sake as well as the sake of us? To not always have to give because you, the landscape, are beleaguered with giving?

I want to be able to see the light and navigate towards a place that is safer for my boys and eventually, for their children. And I want us to want the whole shebang of biodiversity. To understand, finally, actually, that all we have is the natural world, that there is nothing else apart from it and its damselflies skimming the water in heart-shaped wheels of blue and the whooper swans following the certainty of the Earth's magnetism through the light we cannot yet see.

If I want to learn about my deep connection to the natural world, I swim. You can swim in water, or you can swim through some days and drown through others. You can find deep pools to wallow in like a water-logged winter coat and, like Virginia Woolf, be weighed down by the big stones in your pockets and never be able to rise up again. Or you can swim through pools where the light gets in, even when you are not aware of the light getting in, only of swimming, your arms making heart-shaped loops as you propel yourself onwards and onwards through the water.

Beavergeddon

If you have never seen a beaver, and want to see a beaver, it helps to have some idea of size. What are we talking here compared, say, to the size of this small rucksack I'm hefting through the trees towards the river, I ask my companion, James Nairne. He thinks for a moment.

'About two rucksacks' worth,' he says. 'Yes, about that.' Then in a low voice, he says: 'We should really keep our voices down. Any sound and they'll be off.' I'm instantly aware of being a crashing, boorish person who has much to learn about the pursuit of *Castor fiber*, the European beaver. 'When we get to the river,' James whispers, 'watch out for something like a brown furry tea cosy moving through the water and a long line following in its wake. Not that I think we'll see any. We've not seen a single beaver here since the protection legislation came into force. But we need to keep checking, see if we can work out what's going on.'

On 1 May 2019, the Scottish government granted legal protection for beavers living in the wild. If you'd seen this as a news item, no doubt you'd take the protected status at face value. *Great! Our wild beavers finally have legal protection!* In the case of wild beavers, however, nothing could be further from the truth.

The rucksack I'm carrying is stuffed with gear. Camera with telephoto lens. Binoculars. Water bottle. Midge repellent, two kinds – it's early June in Perthshire; take no chances. James is a trustee and volunteer for the Scottish Wild Beaver Group. He'd invited me to stay so that I could learn something about the ways of the beaver and hopefully see one or two. A couple of months back, we'd talked on the phone and made plans. James suggested early June. In a typical year, with young kits to feed, beavers are more active in the early summer, easier to see. Just a few days before I was due to set off, James emailed. He described 'an absolute massacre'. Responding to invitations from Scottish Natural Heritage, 170 individuals in Perthshire alone had signed up to an accredited beaver shooter programme. If you wanted to shoot a beaver, even after 1 May, you could do so quite legitimately by attending a single training session, so long as the beavers that you wanted to shoot were on or adjacent to Prime Agricultural Land (known in the jargon as PAL).

'In the weeks leading up to protection,' James wrote, 'some of them went to town, killing as many beavers as possible.' And to strengthen the point, he included a link to an article in which it all became horribly clear. There were photographs of beavers shot with expanding bullets, of beavers shot in the head, their carcasses dumped on riverbanks *not* adjacent to PAL. There was film of a dying beaver on its back on the Firth of Tay, legs in the air as it was washed out to sea by the tide, filmed by a family on a day out at the beach.

James wrote: 'There are no beavers left where I'd planned to take you for our beaver watching. The dams are derelict. Someone has polished off all the beaver families in the area. The fact that it happened during the kit dependency period and after SNH installed, at taxpayers' expense, a "beaver deceiver" or flow device at the pond (a pipe inserted through the dam to maintain the flow of water and prevent localised flooding) makes it all the more galling. Do you still want to come?' And of course, I went.

On the first evening in Perthshire, James and I climb a short steep bank through the woods. At the top of it, James disappears around the expansive girth of a veteran beech. When I catch up, I am startled to find a man with his back wedged into a fold in the trunk. Beaver aficionado? Fisherman? Beaver hunter? James and the man nod to each other, and James whispers: 'Anything?' The man shakes his head and says: 'Not a single beaver since the first of May.' We stay a while, watching and listening as the gushing

River Earn hefts itself onwards, bouldering through a white-water curve. Dusk begins to gather itself around us, but there is something darker than just the failing light. A despondency, I sense, or an absence – as if James and the other beaver-watcher guy and perhaps even the river itself are bereft, are coming to terms with the loss of an integral part of the whole.

We drop off the bank and walk further along the lane, moving in between the trees, then push our way through ranks of Japanese knotweed. Japanese knotweed is invasive and unnatural. It has colonised vast swathes of our riverbanks, but it does not build dams. Nor does it undermine drainage channels on farmland. Instead, it shifts the riparian edgelands from wild, indigenous and sylvan to brooding.

At the edge of the river we sit, sheltered by tall bracken and the whippy stems of young ash. The river churns, fast and steady. In the absence of beavers, I find myself paying attention to the nature of the water itself – the self-replicating flow. The clicking notation as the Earn beats out its rhythms and pathways. How in midstream it roils around boulders, how it catches and douses that briar on the far bank time and again.

We have been watching – how long? Half an hour? An hour? My riverine meditation steals away any notion of time. James says he needs to collect the kids from his mum's place, get them into bed; he won't be long. Bats flicker above the corridor of water, following reiterated pathways through air that is damp and vitally alive, the sky smoothed by uniform grey cloud. A late, irate blackbird banks across the river and from the branch of an oak tree, tut-tuts its parochial concerns into the deepening dusk.

A sudden movement behind me. The beaver-watcher. I fail to understand how he could come this close without making a sound. Or how I failed to notice. He points across the river. 'There's an otter on the far bank, just beyond the bend. I think it knows we're here.' I keep looking, but I don't see the otter. 'No beavers though,' the man says and shakes his head. After a while, he slinks away again between the trees.

A while later, James returns. I hear him well enough as he tramps the damp path between the knotweed. We stay on, sitting and contemplating the river until it's too dark to see. Until the river melts into the bank and the bank melts into the woods.

I was paddling in the sea at the bottom of the jetty with my friend Sally. We were off to the Isle of Mull on holiday and were overnighting in Oban ahead of an early ferry. An hour or two earlier, when we arrived outside the guest house and opened the car doors, the heat had been like the blast when the aeroplane doors open, and you step down into a Mediterranean country. When he showed us to our rooms, the guest-house owner told us that the temperature peaked at 29 degrees that day. 'Enjoy it while it lasts,' he'd said.

Across the Firth of Lorn, Mull's mountains were blue and translucent, the setting sun imprinting fine lines of silver across the distant water. The summer season was in full swing. Visitors paraded along the harbour, the water was busy with boats, and tall ships migrated in for the season. We wandered through different zones of habitat: fish and chip zones, wafts of diesel fuel zones, music from pubs zones. When we found the jetty, we instinctively took off our shoes and walked into the incoming tide. It was utter bliss. In the water, rusty-red kelp forests flexed in a Mexican wave and crabs swiped themselves into shadows. A couple of young women and a guy walked down the jetty, and right away, we were into banter. Sally and I sloshed the water over our feet and joshed about *why don't you join us; it's so lovely!* They were newly arrived for a Scottish family gathering and hailed from Seattle. We chatted about the heat and how unexpected it was so far north. They told us about the wildfires on the coast of Puget Sound. Right now, they said, in the mountains and along the coast, more fires than ever were burning, and though the fires are a natural part of the cycle of things, these last few years, there've been far more of them, and they've been way more intense. They said that, with all the static weather, the smoke just keeps on accumulating. They told us that the smoke was so dense, there were fears for the health of people all around the Sound. But what's to be done?

One of the women suggested we introduce ourselves, so among the barnacles and the tide, me and Sally paddling and the others not, we shook each other's hands and traded names, me and Sally and sisters Sarah and Amy and Sarah's husband Beau, but still they declined to paddle.

Amy said: 'So much smoke hangs over the city and the coast, and well, the sun comes up right enough, you just can hardly see it.' And Beau said: 'I know, that's right. It's like a … like a smouldering disk.' He looked and sounded like a young Tom Hanks. I thought of what little I knew about the place where they live. The waterfront in *Sleepless in Seattle*. Tom Hanks leaning over the decking. Fireworks across the water.

While the others moved on to the common ground of families and GIs and wartime brides, Beau and I riffed on climate change and ecology and, before very long, that got us into beavers. Beaver wetlands, beaver biodiversity and not beaver biodiversity, and about the largest beaver dam ever found. At more than 900 metres long, the length of thirty football pitches, this thing was visible from space. It had been found by a climate scientist tracking melting permafrost in Canada's far north. But the dam was still not finished; a beaver's work is never done. Someone once calculated that the beavers had begun work on the dam more than forty years ago in 1975. When Beau and I had marvelled at it all, I talked about having been on the trail of beavers in Scotland and about tracking their habitats and their presence – or the lack of it – in Perthshire, and how there are two different kinds of beavers in Scotland. The 'legal' beavers in the officially reintroduced colony on the west coast at Knapdale, and the 'illegal' beavers that had 'escaped' or been 'released', depending upon your sympathies and point of view. How the first sighting of a beaver in the wild in Scotland was back in 2001 by a group canoeing in the lower reaches of the River Earn. That what they'd seen was unmistakable: the furry tea-cosy head, the streamlined body, the tail behind.

Our conversation segued into how some folk believe that the world's deserts might have begun due to the removal and extinction of beavers. Imagine that. Bring back the beaver to banish the sand and the heat. To give us, in our compressed island, the space for wetlands, so that the air might be full of dragonflies and birds. And that the temperatures might, eventually, after all that architecture and effort on the beavers' behalf, slowly return to normal.

Maybe twice a year, a couple of blokes turn up in the market square in my town. They have a homemade sign pinned to a wooden board, and they prop this against the war memorial. The sign says: 'Evolution is a Lie; a Dirty Inconvenient Lie.' I don't know what to make of this. The men look harmless enough. At least they don't have a microphone, which sometimes happens when folk of a similar persuasion come to town and think that loudness is the best way to communicate. Shout your way to God! I have never taken the time to talk with these people. Is that OK? Should I take the time? Is it OK to walk by and not engage with or challenge them? But where would that lead? Once I saw one of the sign-men and another man, the two of them locked in an evolution-denying/evolution-defending shouting match. I don't want that. What's the point in that?

The men with the sign make me feel a bit the same way I felt when I noticed that hardly any of our local swallows came back this year. Incredulous, upset, in denial. Yes, there were swallows elsewhere, but by the end of June, I'd not seen a single one above the house. They were later than ever, delayed by storms over North Africa and southern Europe. There was talk in the online bird forums that many hirundines did not survive migration. Imagine that: no swallows dandling from the telephone wires near the back garden. For the first time. There's a first time for everything. Even for the swallows not to come back. One swallow doesn't make a summer. Do no swallows make no summer? The law of diminishing returns. Evolution. What would the guys with the sign make of this?

My life is busy enough; I'm trying to hold on and not pay too much attention to the melting of the glaciers and the warming of the seas. Something in my neural pathways blocks me when I try (admittedly not very hard) to imagine what things will be like for my boys – for my two young adult sons – and for their one-day families. Will they have families? Is it OK to continue having families? What would the evolution-denier guys in the market square have to say about the swallows and all of the sons and all of the daughters? Maybe, like me, they are just way too scared to think.

In the years following Storm Desmond, I went in search of the kinds of stories we'd begun to tell ourselves about climate change in Cumbria. I looked at how some of our communities had been affected by this single and most significant act of climate disruption to strike the county and how, if they had, some of those communities had managed to obtain some sense of recovery. On 5 December 2015, in twenty-four hours, 15 trillion litres of rain fell on Cumbria, rendering

5,525 homes uninhabitable, countless homeless, and 557 bridges damaged or destroyed. Numerous roads were washed away, including the main arterial route through the centre of the Lake District. Not only did unprecedented amounts of rain undermine and lead to the collapse of the road, but at Dunmail Raise, the road through the mountains that connects the village of Grasmere to the town of Keswick, a section of mountainside collapsed onto the road, necessitating its closure for six months. This is how long it took for United Utilities to rebuild the slopes before anything else could begin to happen. Meanwhile, workers and schoolchildren endured a 270-kilometre round-trip commute.

On the first anniversary of Storm Desmond, the Royal Geographic Society held an event in the north of the county: 'Flooding: National Problem, Local Solutions'. Communities spoke about what they had done to begin finding resilience in the storm's aftermath. One of the speakers was from the town of Cockermouth, a place that knows only too well the potential of unprecedented amounts of rainfall for causing dangerous and long-term disruption. Serious floods took place there in 2005, 2008 and again in 2009. In 2009, 314 millimetres of rain – which to a layperson like me is easier to visualise as three metres – fell in twenty-four hours. I don't know how to imagine this amount of rain. I can only imagine Storm Desmond six years later because I saw it for myself.

In Cockermouth, when the River Derwent burst its banks in 2009, floodwater canalised the High Street to a depth of more than 2.5 metres – the height of first-floor windows. On the farms surrounding the town, whole fields were lost beneath accretions of gravel and stones swept in by the flood. A police officer died, swept away when a bridge collapsed on the west coast of Cumbria. Then, the damage was estimated at £276.5 million.

Soon afterwards, the pundits responded by saying it was a once-in-200-years event. Concrete flood defences were installed to protect the town at the cost of millions. A handful of years later, Storm Desmond hammered the north of England following six weeks of continual and unusually heavy rain, and Cockermouth's new flood defences were overtopped as the 'once-in-200-years' scenario played out again.

At the anniversary event, a speaker from the town talked about how resilience in her community meant co-ordinating action so that elderly or less-able people were not left alone and terrified – as had happened during the previous floods. The action group collected information on who lived where and what kinds of needs they might have. They had a plan, which made them feel as if there was an element of control, though with flooding, it can rarely be more than that.

I listened to the River Roe Catchment Group, a local group set up in the Eden Valley in the aftermath of devastating floods in 2005 and 2013. The villages of Highbridge and Stockdalewath had flooded disastrously, residents forced out of their homes. Repairs took over a year to complete. Instead of thinking like people, the Roe Catchment Group began to think like beavers. Part of the group's ideas about resilience was to install, among other things, twenty-five beaver-like dams. They toppled trees into the river and made stockades of brash to slow the flow. Beaver behaviour, in other words. The communities became the deceivers of rivers, deceiving the River Roe and its tributaries into thinking that beavers were at large. None of this was difficult. Nor did it cost millions. On 5 December 2015, when Storm Desmond came bowling over the north of the UK, their experiment was put on trial. The villages were on the edge of the storm, but neither of them flooded.

Beaver people call them analogue dams. We can install analogue dams in our rivers and watch how the architecture of beavers is the presiding architecture of our time. We can, if we choose, put beaver deceivers into beaver-made dams so that, where flooding might be considered a risk, the water levels can be maintained. Or, at the cost of £72 million and necessitating the removal of more than 500 mature riparian trees – as is happening here in my home town as I write – we can install more already-redundant concrete flood walls. And still, the floods will come. And still, the flood walls will be overtopped; we know this to be true because the engineers who have, in their non-beavery wisdom, designed the Kendal Flood Relief Management Scheme have said so. And what else is all this concrete but just another way of manufacturing millions of tonnes of CO_2 that will, among all the anarchic systems of a warming planet, help to deliver yet more once-in-200-years events? The designers of flood-prevention schemes and those who commission the work and those who believe that concrete is the god of flooding do not think or act like beavers. I doubt they ever *think* about beavers. They have not sat and watched or entered that long, unspoken conversation with the land to think about how the land responds to rain and how rain accumulates in rivers. How mountains without trees collapse under the weight of rain and spill their rocks onto the roads, and how whole communities are disrupted not just for months but for years after each catastrophic event.

But still, it was right that I should understand something about this concrete thinking. I got in touch with the Environment Agency and asked them some questions. The Environment Agency put me in touch with their PR company, so I wrote and asked them the same questions. When they replied, it was to say that answers about the scheme could be found on their website and, just to be helpful, they included a link. But my questions were not on the website, so I wrote again. They said there were too many questions. I sent ten fewer, but still, they did not respond. What was so terrifying about my questions? Maybe this is how the Environment Agency found its own kind of resilience against flooding.

I asked whether the need for the flood walls had increased since the vast new supermarket had been built on floodplain adjacent to the River Kent *after* Storm Desmond (the new supermarket that not many folk go to because now there are too many supermarkets for a town of this size). I asked why the two integral upstream flood attenuation schemes had been shelved when it was stated in the planning document that they should have been put in place first. Was it because the funding for Phase Three – the concrete flood walls – was to come from the European Union, and so the money had to be spent before Brexit was a done deal? The Union that gave subsidies to rural areas and to farmers, and the same Union that most farmers voted to leave?

I asked what the flood walls would do to prevent an influx of chemicals and oil and foul water and everything else that had inundated the town, not only swept in by the river of rain but from the local industrial zone and the walls of grey rain that slid off the surrounding hills. I asked how the walls would affect our wildlife – the family of otters that live in the river in the middle of town that sometimes dine on the rocks by the footbridge or groom themselves with an audience of passers-by. How will otters navigate the flood walls? And what about the colony of sand martins that will be locked out because the one suitable portion of sandy riverbank just north of the town will be replaced by a massive impoundment dam, or the kingfisher who, after all, cannot dig his kingfisher tunnel into concrete, or the birds that nest in the 550 mature trees that will need to be removed, or the insect biomass? How much biomass do 550 trees hold? And how many years will it take until the new trees are adequate to support this amount of biodiversity?

Sometimes, what the rivers need is just less rain. Sometimes, what they need is more rain. Sometimes, we can let the rivers get on with being rivers and concern ourselves with other things. Sometimes, though, our rivers are overwhelmed with it all, and sometimes the mountains are too, and because there are nowhere near enough trees to help hold them together, they collapse underneath the weight of the rain.

Sometimes the communities who have been sold the idea of concrete are overwhelmed when the water level begins to rise again through the floorboards of their homes. And here's the thing: most of the flooding of the houses and businesses that were inundated in Kendal during Storm Desmond was not caused by the river's floodwaters but by a water table that was already overloaded after six weeks of biblical rain. And no amount of concrete can stop that.

Rain needs rivers. Beavers need rivers. Humans need rivers. Farmers and crops need rivers. The planet needs rivers. The planet needs rivers that are fully functioning ecosystems, not rivers that are a bit of this, a bit less of that. The beaver was always a fully integrated part of British rivers until that is, we forgot how to see what beavers give as opposed to what we humans have taken away.

Before the beaver-protection legislation came into force, if you wanted to, you could shoot a beaver at close range – in the head with a shotgun or in the chest with an expanding bullet – without a licence. You could dump the body on the riverbank so that dog walkers and beaver-watchers could come across the results. If you want to, under the current legislation, if you have a licence, you can shoot a beaver that's doing its beavery thing adjacent to your PAL, even if it has dependent kits holed up in the lodge, and even though it may not actually be causing any problems on your PAL. If you want to, you can shoot a beaver even though it is swimming in the water – even though shooting at beavers like this often does not end well. There's a lovely family-holiday memory to take away from sunny Perthshire. *Look at the beaver kids! The one over there being washed out to sea!* as the fatally injured animal struggles, feet in the air.

But what you can't do, under the current legislation, is to translocate a beaver anywhere else in Scotland – even to land owned by someone who would love to have beavers boosting biodiversity in their neighbourhood.

What happens when the farmers – the managers of PALs – and beavers rub up against each other? I wanted to talk to a farmer to hear their side of the story. A farmer agreed to meet me. His farmhouse lies high above the Tay valley, and in the farm kitchen, we drank tea and talked at first about flooding and trees and about sheep. Then we spoke of beavers. There are, or rather had been, beavers in the River Tay at the foot of the farm hill. The farmer thought that beavers were being distributed in vans from one location to another by beaver-advocates.

'How else can you explain how they're spreading themselves so widely?' he asked. 'How can they travel all the way from Crieff to here without help?'

'I'm not a beaver expert,' I said, 'but I'm pretty sure they're just doing what beavers do: they're swimming, making new territories.'

I'm not sure the farmer was convinced. Maybe I should have told him about the beaver dam the size of thirty football fields, but he might have thought that was just silly.

'What about Patagonia?' he asked. 'Have you heard about the beavers in Patagonia? They've wreaked environmental havoc.'

This was indeed true, but it is not true that beavers were re-released; beavers were not native to Patagonia, and the consequential effects of a non-native species on an ecosystem that is not and never was designed to cope are unlikely to end well. If you want to blame someone, don't blame the beavers but do blame the Argentinian military who decided to try their hand at breeding beavers for the fur trade to bring economic regeneration to the region. In 2009, a scientific paper called the impact of beavers in Patagonia 'the largest landscape-level alteration in sub Antarctic forests since the last ice age'.

Beavers in the UK, meanwhile, have only been absent for about 200 of the past 1,100 years. A mere snip of time. The blink of an evolutionary eye. If evolution really exists.

I asked the farmer what he made of remarks made by John Scott, MSP, also a farmer, who, in objecting to the proposed new Scottish beaver-protection laws, said during the Environment, Climate Change and Land Reform Committee: 'As we all know, wild salmon is under significant threat across Scotland … and introducing physical barriers to spawning grounds and a new species of predator to salmon themselves … now is not the time to be affording beavers protection.' As we drank our mugs of tea in his kitchen, the farmer told me: 'I have yet to be convinced that beavers don't eat salmon.'

An obligate herbivore eating salmon? Who should we blame for this lack of understanding? The beavers, for being vegetarian? Why not? They can't fight back. They don't have guns. We could blame C. S. Lewis for planting the imaginative idea of a beaver catching and cooking trout in our minds. But what about the marmalade roll and the table and its cloth and the sewing machine inside the magical, wonderful beaver lodge? In *The Lion, the Witch and the Wardrobe*, when Lewis brings the four children into the world of beavers, he either knew well or instinctively felt that beavers represent the bringing of order to a natural world gone wrong. He knew too that the beavers he imagined into being were the inhabitants of a story. But once we leave our childhood behind, aren't we supposed to be able to distinguish story from fact?

You could picture them like this. It's late and very dark. Tam should have been back hours ago. Isla's anxiety translated into displacement activity. The twins were both fast asleep, so she closed the kitchen drawers quietly, slipping each over-polished item of cutlery back into place, only the slightest chink emanating from the drawer. She heard Robbie turn over in his sleep, always the restless one. She knew without looking that Rosa would be utterly still, flat out on her back, paws above her head. Then the familiar vibrations out in the entrance, and Tam was back. Isla understood straight away the situation was worse. They looked at each other, Isla holding the tea towel printed with the kids' paw prints.

'It's Jim and Helen and the kids,' Tam said, his coat dripping. 'Gone, taken out. Bill found the bodies on the riverbank.'

'Oh God,' Isla said.

'No one's seen the kids,' Tam said. 'They think they've been shot and thrown somewhere out of the way.' A beat passes between them. 'Isla, we have to go. Now. Bill's up on the lane with the van.'

'OK,' Isla said. 'You know what I'm going to say. I'm not leaving the sewing machine this time.'

A friend from the area put me in touch with Duncan Pepper. 'I don't use the word "ghillie",' he'd said, 'that means "manservant" in Gaelic. I'm a fishing guide.' Duncan takes wealthy Americans on salmon fishing expeditions across Scotland. Replying to my email, he'd written, 'I have plenty to say about the beaver,' and I feared that when we eventually spoke, I was in for a jeremiad. But on the telephone, Duncan knocked the wind out of my sails. He'd spent many years looking at how beavers work the landscape and observing how salmon behave in a landscape worked by beavers. How beaver-felled trees create shadowed pools, the kinds of places where you would prefer to rest and recuperate on the journey upstream if you were a salmon. How beaver dams are good because they slow the flow of water and make drought and flooding less likely. How beavers do all this while also cleaning and improving the quality of the water, which, for a salmon, would be one good reason to stick around for a while. And how dams do not, in fact, impede the passage of salmon upriver. Duncan and I talked about all of these beaver benefits and about the hypocrisy of fishing guides who cut down trees so that clients' lines don't snag on branches, yet these were the same people who complained at a recent SNH public meeting about beavers that beavers removed too many trees. Duncan was frustrated and angry that many farmers either didn't get or didn't seem to want to get the many benefits that the presence of beavers in a landscape has.

On a fishing beat of the River Tay Duncan manages between Grandtully and Aberfeldy, he estimates that up to 200 beavers have been shot out in the last two years alone.

'And I don't blame SNH,' he said. 'They've been subjected to some nasty attacks because of the beavers. They're just stuck in the middle of a challenging situation. Many of my clients are already beaver converts; in the US, they're much more enlightened about beavers. These folks don't need any convincing.'

He added that beaver dams do not and have never inhibited the passage of salmon up into the headwaters of rivers and that there are many established links between salmon health and the presence of beavers, proven by the American ecologist Dr Michael Pollock. Before we finished talking, Duncan said: 'Canada is a country built on the blood of beavers.' And in her novel, *Surfacing*, Margaret Attwood wrote that Canada was founded on dead animals, including vast numbers of beavers, and that the beaver is to Canada what the black man was to the United States.

I talked to beaver expert Derek Gow. I'd been riveted by a line he had written about beavers as 'the pilotlight in the boiler of biodiversity; snuff them out and every activity that revolves around their pivotal presence ceases quite simply to function.' I asked Derek about the anti-beaver campaigners – many of whom, in Perthshire at least, are farmers. Derek said, 'They believe what they want to. No matter how hard they carry on wedging their arguments into place, their narratives are utterly flawed.' And to Derek, the Knapdale beaver reintroduction on Scotland's west coast was a travesty because the terrain lacks suitable riverine habitat and so young beavers are taking to the sea to find new territories, but beavers are not habituated to saltwater, and Derek believes that significant numbers of them are dying as a result. He told me about ancient Iran, where beavers were called 'water-dogs' and where a single beaver was considered to have the value of a thousand dogs. To kill a beaver in Iran was an act of such destructive magnitude that the people believed that drought would inevitably follow. A memory surfaced of my conversation with Beau on the waterfront and that idea of how the world's deserts may have been caused by the removal and extinction of beavers.

After breakfast one morning, James, my Perthshire beaver host, made a phone call, and soon we were heading east. We passed out of the Highlands onto lower terrain where serious agricultural land begins. We crossed the A9, the main arterial road linking the Highlands and Inverness to Scotland's southern half, crossing the River Isla and heading into the Angus Glens. James wanted me to meet Paul and Louise Ramsay. We parked at the back of an ancient turreted house. Their home at Bamff has been in the family since the thirteenth century. There's a nice strapline on the website: 'Bamff – Where Wild Things Are.'

'I'm afraid you've missed the pizza,' Paul said, leading us into the kitchen (a poster on a cupboard door: 'Alyth

Floods – The Beavers are Not to Blame'). 'If I give you the
last piece – which rightly belongs to Louise – I fear I may
be shot.' Paul has an MSc in Environmental Conservation,
and as he made us coffee, he told me how beavers are the
last things that should be blamed for the reducing numbers
of salmon in Scottish rivers.

'You can put it down to much more fundamental problems
than that,' he said. 'There's massive issues of overfishing –
especially off Greenland. Then there's the cooling of ocean
currents from melting glaciers. There's industrial pollution
and the construction of weirs and dams for hydropower.
Digging gravels out of rivers. All this *and* reductions in
zooplankton – the salmon's main source of food.'

The Ramseys are self-confessed beaver nerds. They
introduced beavers as a way of improving biodiversity on
the estate. 'Once I knew about the benefits they bring, I
thought – why aren't we reintroducing them across the
whole country?' But the Ramseys became embroiled in a
local scandal when beavers were found to be living wild not
very far from their property.

'In 2012,' Paul said, 'I was asked to go in for questioning
by the local police. They wanted to know if some of the
beavers on our land had escaped. But proving where wild
beavers originate from is rarely a simple business. Afterwards
I thought we'd all say: "Well, thank you indeed for your
time," but when I stood up to go, I was arrested.'

'For what?' I asked.

'For releasing a dangerous animal.'

Not very far away, a wildlife park near Crieff 'fessed up:
some of their beavers had gone missing.

'In 2015 there was a flash flood down in Alyth town
centre – a huge event. People tried to pin the flood on the
beavers up here, but I'm pleased to tell you they were later
exonerated.'

Of course, beavers are the last that should have been
blamed for the flood.

We walked into a field beyond their garden. A small stream ran through it, although its slow waters no longer ran between straight banks but were haphazard, meandering, interspersed with grasslands and damselflies that glided iridescent and turquoise above the wetlands.

'We moved the fence back twice,' Paul said, 'as part of an agri-environment scheme for water margins.'

The ground was spongy and, even though I was wearing wellies, we were forced to navigate our route through the beaver-reimagined wetlands carefully. Dragonflies zinged, and yellow flag iris flaunted their bright-yellow flowers. We walked on, following a path that led through a tangle of beaver engineering: beaver-gnawed mature trees that leaned widdershins towards what had once been a small watercourse and was now a small, shallow lake. Among the wetlands were meadows of grass and tangles of toppled trees. Every so often, we'd come across the beaver-gnawed stump of a tree, from tiny aspens that were, in effect, pollarded by the beavers and from which new growth sprouted – supply and demand: you eat some, you create some. There were the massive stumps of mature trees with beaver teeth marks clearly etched into the wood.

'They keep going back,' Paul said, 'until the tree is about to fall, and if it falls the wrong way, it's bad luck.'

Some of the beaver-felled trees lined the banks, others had toppled into the water, and along their trunks were marks where the beavers had ambled, stripping the bark to cache as food for the winter months. There was a beaver lodge with a birch tree sprouting out at an angle. The watercourse dropped in a series of dams and a chain of small lakes. The branches of willows bowed towards the water, and willow warblers, blackbirds and thrushes called. It was all, I felt, chaotic but vibrant and whole. And beyond the wetlands, beyond the self-limiting margins of beaverly ambitions, the woodland remained entirely intact.

Beavers have self-imposed limits. They seldom travel further than 20 metres from the riverbank. Apart from the river and the riverbank, they don't want anything else. Oh, yes – they want trees. They want trees along the watercourse and some patches of fresh grass to eat, and they want to live undisturbed. Disturb a beaver and what you get is a sudden and powerful slap of that rounded leather spade of a tail that sends an echolocation of danger to any other beavers on that beat of the river or on the pond and to the kits sheltered in the lodge.

When adventurer Rob Mark spent three days trekking through the uninhabited wilds of Northern Canada in search of the biggest beaver dam ever found, he discovered that the wilderness was inhabited by bears and by mosquitoes the size of helicopters with the bite of bears, and finally – although in the last kilometre or so he was forced to wade ever deeper, not knowing where each step would lead as the sludge sucked at his boots – he arrived at the dam and was greeted by the slap of a beaver's tail. *Slap!* I wondered how that might feel, to have lived in splendid isolation for all those years, like a Japanese soldier hiding away in the forest, then someone arrives out of the blue, out of the sludge it had taken forty years to develop. I might want to slap my tail too.

The slap also sent a warning to this beaver-watcher who, on her last evening in Beaverland or Not Beaverland, had arrived with James in another quiet place on the side of a small glen deep in the Perthshire hills. Like the beaver-watcher by the river on my first evening, I endeavoured to walk in such a way that accommodated that idea of non-disturbance, to open that engaged, non-speaking conversation. Over the previous few days, I had become inculcated into the ways of the watcher. I noticed that I moved through the woodland more softly – each step mattered. I was accommodated by the conversational stream and the soft evening wind that bustled through the oaks and birches and the quiet pool into which the stream tumbled. I was accommodated too by the willow warbler whose descending scale of song opened and fell like the light and the stream and the water that, slower now, glided imperceptibly through the beaver-made lochan. We walked on the narrow grassy track that not very long ago, before the beavers came, travelled lower on the side of the hill. The people who own the land here, this out-of-the-way bit of a valley in the convergence of High- and lowlands, when the beavers first arrived and set up home and began redistributing the trees and building that vast architectural pile of branches into the lodge on the opposite bank of the new lochan, as the water levels slowly began to rise, they said that it was going to be a learning curve, of learning to live with chaos.

Among the beavers' anarchic chaos and tangle, we made our way past the sharpened pencil stumps of beaver-coppiced aspen from where new aspen buds were opening. We walked past silver birches whose horizontal trunks were almost submerged, the bark reflecting eerie white light from water that was as black as a folk song. Then, *slap!* I jumped right out of my skin. And what I caught (because the slap happened way too quickly to see) was not the tea-cosy swimmingness of beavers, but the surface of the water as it sloshed from side to side beneath the bridges of birch trunks – it looked as though someone had hefted a huge great cobble into the water. The water rocked this way and that and eventually it resolved. My heart rate resolved too. I grinned and shrugged my shoulders up to my ears, and they wouldn't come down again, and the grin wouldn't go away either. 'A beaver!' I mouthed at James, who, though he has seen it all before, was grinning back at me, and his grin didn't go away either.

We continued, walking between the trees. The beavers, well aware by now of our presence, remained hidden. On the opposite bank of the pool was the massive architectural assemblage of the beavers' lodge: a great flat-topped pyramid, a pile of branches and sticks fashioned together with mud from the bottom of the beaver-made pool. I wondered for a moment if I was disappointed that there was no chimney-pipe protruding from the top. No Mr Beaver guiding us onwards towards supper and warmth with his almost-human hands and his short thumbs. No Mrs Beaver saying: 'Come in, my dears! Come in,' and bustling about her tiny home, not knowing whether to cook the trout or boil the kettle or sweep the floor because beavers are fastidious animals. What the beaver lodge is, is the place where the nature of water becomes an earworm – a liquid sonar system beaming messages downstream, upstream, midstream – about levels, about increased volumes of water after rain, about drought and breaches and holes.

A few minutes later, we came to the dam. At the top of a rocky cleft between oaks and birch and hazel trees, the dam straddled the banks where the stream cleaved the passage of what was once a small waterfall and was now a a beaver-engineered slope of mud and sticks and small branches. Not long after it was built, James and the Scottish Wild Beaver team came and installed a flow device – a beaver deceiver. A little way upstream, a beaver-proof cage had been installed around the mouth of a wide-bore pipe, and the pipe had been pushed through the dam itself, the end of it pouring a steady slow pulse of running water from between the woody debris. The beaver deceiver makes sure that the water level in the pool doesn't rise too far because, even though beavers have limits, their works sometimes flood out on adjacent land. What the beavers make of their subsequent inability to stem the flow is difficult to imagine. The neural pathways of beavers are hardwired into the sound of water – either running or still. And take a look at a beaver's hands; maybe ours were designed after God saw what a good job he or she had made of the beavers, but then he or she decided to give us bigger thumbs. (I wonder what function he or she thought they'd serve – our human thumbs, our hands. Not anything to do with climate change?) With their human-like hands, the beavers fetch woody debris and great sodden bundles of mud to plug the dam. Damming is the beavers' modus operandi, their way of being. Their way of being is flow and stillness and everything in between. But beavers don't just plug the dike; they build the dike. And in doing so, they become the bringers of reason to a skewed world – the bringers of everything that follows in their wake.

And as the light and the swallows drained from the sky and night began to come in – bringing her train of stars and her midge-and-mosquito-hoovering bats that looped the loop above and through the trees and between the light that was reflected in the surface of the pool and the light that was falling and failing in the sky – for an hour, maybe more, we stood with our backs against a couple of big-enough birches because it was way too boggy to sit. At 10.30pm, a song thrush was still singing. The bats flitted over the lochan. And then it came: the furry tea-cosy head of a swimming beaver, eyes scanning at the level of the water and studying the edges of the pond and carrying in its mouth a small leafy branch. We had not seen or heard the beaver coming. It arrived out of the blue. Out of the pond, the evening, bringing in its wake that narrow line of barely disturbed water. Furry teacosy and travelling wake, the beaver travelled upstream. There was a small beaver-made island in the middle of the pond, and the beaver must have swum along or through the channel on the far side of this and reappeared here, like a trick of the light, in front of our eyes. Among the gathering darkness, it was difficult to follow, this beaver, who swam in and out of the shadows and under the toppled trunks of trees, under the midge-hoovering bats and the last swirling swallows. And I lost it. I lost the beaver until, a few minutes later, it reappeared for a second where a muddy intrusion had been made in the far bank – an entrance to the lodge. And that was it. Enjoy it while you can.

Beavers and dams. Beavers and deserts. Beavers and wetlands teeming with dragonflies and damselflies and frogs and toads and invertebrates. Beavers and the return of plants to the margins of watercourses, to the margins of rivers. Beavers and floods. Beavers and dams and beaver deceivers. Beavers as architects. Beavers and the return of reason. Beavers and the making of lakes and – who knows, maybe, if we're lucky – climates that adapt locally and downwardly, as the beavers bring chaos travelling in their wake.

James and I leaned into the two birch trees. We waited, then we waited some more. Tiny moths rose out of the flowering grasses as if they were being blown gently upwards by the earth itself. The quarter moon rose above the trees, the light chalky and diffident through layers of cloud. A fine soft rain began to fall. It was as if I was standing inside a cloud, which, no doubt, I was. I didn't know what the time was, and I found that I was not really interested in knowing. The light continued to fade. The bats swithered among the branches overhead and above the darkling surface of the pond.

Further away from us, the linear intrusion of the beaver-felled birches. The swallows gone. Somewhere over there, a thrush delivered a closing oratorio. We didn't see any more beavers, although, of course, they were here, living in their beavery chaos and listening, as beavers will, to the watery messages being transmitted from their liquid world. It was all fine and, right then, there was nothing else I needed to do.

At the end of August, I returned to Bamff. It wouldn't do just to have seen the beaverlands on the estate without any beavers. An evening was required, an evening with good light and preferably without rain. I was to rendezvous with Paul where the track to the house crosses the two areas of beaver-worked land. Or water. I was in the open, looking upstream, then down. At 8pm, Paul appeared, walking away from the direction of the house and towards me. I waved and turned back to look over the fields. I turned back to the pool, and not a metre and a half away, heading straight towards me, was a beaver. Intense evening light caught the way the water beaded along the animal's back and how the fur divided into fine furrows, the blue-lit water spooling over the nut-brown, gold-brown fur. The beaver was lighter coloured than I'd thought, the animal itself lithe in the water. I don't know if, from that range, the beaver had seen me; beavers have poor eyesight, but their sense of smell is strong. The beaver flipped underwater.

Paul arrived. He had already spotted another beaver, one of this year's kits out on a grassy meadow among the wetlands. And what else was it doing but eating grass? We watched for a while, then moved further along the track. Another beaver, an adult, swam through the water, the light lower, the blueness replaced by amber and lead. Like a broad-notched arrow, the beaver was aiming for the dam. It climbed out of the water and over the top and was gone. We followed, and there it was in the next pool, the furry tea-cosy head and the line of the body and tail behind. The beaver flipped, and I saw how the tail is a rudder for moving the body allowing the beaver to investigate the water as it manoeuvres itself under the surface.

Further on, another kit, eating more grass, its leathery tail laid out behind. Further still, another beaver – the big male. The sun had disappeared below the treeline of the far hill, and the water was pewter and glass. The male swam underneath a fallen tree, where it became lost to us in the tangle of branches. Paul pointed, saying that the main lodge was hidden somewhere underneath. There was a series of beavery grunts as if the beaver were saying: 'I'm home!'

There were dams that were narrow across the top and some that were wider, plugged with sedge grass and branches. There were half-constructed dams, and others where the beavers had judged that the water level in the upper pool had reached the required point and had subsequently dug small side channels through which the water poured softly. There were yet more beaver lawns, and a vast larch tree toppled at the edge of the pool. Across the water was the abandoned house I remembered from my previous visit. As we stopped to survey the water, a barn owl morphed out of the tenebrous pine woods and landed on the exposed lintel of an upper window, its pale moon face angled directly towards us. A second owl flew in silently to join the first, following a trajectory towards a cavity at the top of the crumbling chimney, and I noticed how its white-trousered legs swung forwards, the wings and body rotating so that immediately when it landed, the owl was orientated towards us. Only the head was visible, cantilevered out from the shadows and the chimney stack like a satellite dish.

Both owls appeared to scrutinise us, no doubt assessing the interlopers in their field. Further away, in the night woods above the fields, a tawny owl called. Another answered. The barn owl on the lintel lifted and floated into the darkening shadows beyond the ruin. The owl on the chimney remained, peering towards us. If it was dark enough for the barn owls to stand out from the gloom like this, no doubt it was too dark for us to see any more beavers. We turned to walk away. I took a final glance at the owl on the chimney. It was intent, tracking our human shapes as we began to move further into the woods, and I wondered what sense, if any, it made of our signals.

Dance Halls of Desire

I'm walking along a ride in a Scots Pine woodland. It's barely light. It's so early and so cold that, despite the layers of clothing, my body has not yet acclimatised to being outside the warm van Simon Pawsey drove me here in. Every intake of breath feels less life-sustaining and more as if a blunt-edged knife is being inserted into my lungs. Something has just flown across the airspace above the ride and as it passed over, an enormous body borne along on furious and tattered wings, the bird loomed so large it was as though the sky was temporarily blotted out. No mistake: male capercaillie.

Simon is a wildlife guide and friend, and just ten minutes after setting off to look for one of Britain's most elusive and iconic species, we've struck lucky. It's a win–win. These Strathspey woodlands have morphed into a Scottish theme park; you turns up, you pays your money and the attractions show up – just like that.

We're looking at each other, mouths open and, even though Simon has seen cappers many times, he silently articulates: 'Male capercaillie!' and his arm is still pointing at the sky where the capper passed overhead. I'm shaking and nodding my head simultaneously, and it seems certain that I've been relieved of the power of speech because Simon had told me just nine minutes ago that there was no guarantee we would see one. The best chance to see them is really early in the morning, but loads of times it's a blank, he'd told me, so it'll be a bonus if we find one. He said as well that there could be female cappers up there roosting in the branches now, but you'd never see them against all that russet bark, what with the hen's russet-coloured neck and the barred silver and grey head and wings that are like all the stags' horn lichen dripping in garlands from the branches.

We're in one of the last Strathspey refuges for capercaillie, though it's hardly remote. Back at the roadside, there's a sign on the gate with a capercaillie symbol and a request that walkers and bikers keep strictly to the paths. The ride has been gouged into deep welts by the passage of forestry vehicles.

We're maybe five minutes further in when, with an explosive crack, a second capper bursts out of the heather and blaeberry just a metre or so from my feet. Another male. I'm dazed by the blast but pull myself together to watch how the bird swivels low between the trees and heads towards the edge of the wood, then breaks across open ground. But, as if confronted by something entirely alien, the capper swings back onto a trajectory following the edge of the woods. It becomes lost to sight.

Cappers, huh? Ten a penny these days.

You see them on YouTube – these outlandish, gigantic birds, strutting around the lek site like hedge-fund managers high on profit, acting cocksure of themselves in front of the womenfolk and making that sequence of ridiculous noises that sound like marbles dropping through a marble run followed by a ratchet tightening a rope. But there's little preparedness for the size of the animal in the flesh. We're talking Hercules transport planes here.

The plumage of a male capercaillie is decadently blue-black, the chest a viridian sheen. On each scapular, or shoulder, there's a curious white ellipse and above the confident eye, a bright-red brow. German hunters call the red brows the 'roses'. In among the tangle of the forest, maybe this was what helped the hunters to see the birds. The beak is white and curiously chunky – a tool of a beak that looks as if it could effortlessly wrangle a dead animal. It deals, though, with the more mundane diet of capercaillie: berries, insects, pine needles. Everywhere we look among the blaeberry and heather, the forest floor is awash with the evidence of cappers. Simon picks up a bunch of the stuff and holds out a handful of extruded ellipses, like cords of playdough pushed through a playdough-moulding machine. He rubs a couple between his thumb and fingers, and they reduce back to the mainstay of the capper's winter diet, pine needles – such a bulky bird, sustained by bits of chaff.

Capercaillie are Red Listed under the IUCN (International Union for Conservation of Nature) Globally Threatened index. Because of this, it's illegal to go near a lek site – the clearing in the woods where cocks get it on in front of the hens – without a licence. Watch on a screen, though, and what you see is the male capper pushing out his chest while simultaneously holding his tail feathers like a broad, decorated fan. Like this, the male capper struts. The tail has a curious arc of white markings, like die-cut patterning. Like this, the cock becomes a 'join the dots' bird; join the white dots on the tail, the scapular and the beak and what you get is this: Old Man of the Woods. Horse of the Woods. Europe's largest member of the grouse family, moving in his strangely mechanical dance, uttering that peculiar mechanical-sounding call that is strangely not of the animal world at all.

We're moving forwards through the forest, and I'm looking up because now I think if there are these males around, then just maybe I'll see a female up in the branches. Meanwhile, the ruptured ground demands that I look down and ahead when I'm moving, so I look forwards and then, as we move around a bend in the ride, I see the terminus of the forestry track. Flying hugely, soundlessly across it, is another male. More likely, it's the same male that exploded out of the forest floor a few minutes ago. As the capper crosses that avenue of light at the end of the forest, it morphs into a symbol of what we have left – and simultaneously of what we don't.

I wonder about this cross-pollination between one world and the other, of the bird that sounds like a machine and the noise of the human world where mostly what we do is continue making our machines and our many sounds. I wonder too about connection and separation, especially now in this phase of human tenure on Earth, in the eye of the Anthropocene.

I've warmed up inside my layers. Simon and I move towards the edge of the forest, where we sit and look out at the landscape and think and talk about what we've seen and what the meaning is of what we've seen. In front of us is an area of rough moorland. Away to the south, the low morning sun has turned the Cairngorm mountains into a linear dome of bright white, as if someone has polished the snow until all it can do is reflect itself back at us. The middle ground, though – this area of moorland and, beyond it, another patch of forest – is a landscape under reconstruction.

Cairngorms Connect is the biggest habitat-restoration project in Britain. RSPB Scotland, Wildland Limited, Forestry and Land Scotland, Scotland: The Big Picture and NatureScot – Scotland's Nature Agency, in a mix of state funding and private philanthropy, are working together across 600 square kilometres of contiguous land dedicated to wildlife. From the floodplain of the River Spey through some of the last of Scotland's ancient forests, the project aims to restore a functioning ecosystem around the entire Cairngorms massif. Thinking in terms of centuries – 200 years ahead, rather than the average political regime of five years (five years of this funding, five of that) – the longevity of the Cairngorms vision points to a future that is less about us, now, and is more about an alignment of humans and the natural world. And the kinds of forest repair that Simon and I are looking out at – designed to join one forest relic to the next – represents part of that vision.

Because this is the thing: cappers don't travel in search of a mate. They live in the woods in which they live, and that is that. If you're a cock capper, you're not going to travel to capper discos in woods other than your own. You stay put and you wander those woods and sometimes you fly above the woods at what appears to be the speed of a Hercules aircraft, that strange simultaneity of speed and of slowness. And if you're a female capper, you come down from the safety of the pines to have a look at these few remaining males as they do that male thing around the dancefloor because being pumped and primed for the continuance of their genes is what they know best how to do. And as the female, you wonder which of these males represent the best genetic example because the imperative is to make a choice even though (and I'm anthropomorphising here) you do this *despite* the braggadocio and the fact they all look faintly ridiculous. And when the results of your gene mix come into the world, they too will not travel to discos of other woods, not even to that wood just over there across the open moor.

When that second capper exploded out of the ground, wings smacking together like that to deter me because, fair enough, I might be a predator – when he flew out over the moorland but soon enough swung back towards his familiar stomping grounds, it was because of the cappers' specific inability to cross the divide. Without new pine plantings, what that open ground represents is fragmentation and the consequential loss of species for whom the idea of connection and connectivity is critical. You fly out ... oh shit, you've lost the map ... you fly back. But the moor that Simon and I peruse as we sit with our backs to the pines has been planted up with conifers and other native trees. When this bridge of trees has grown in, and the moor is no longer open and derelict, then the cappers will once again have the wherewithal to wander through the woods to meet other lovely capper hens and cocks in the cold of the early mornings. No longer will they be trapped inside the woodland discos of limited genes and limited opportunities.

A 2017 study by the RSPB revealed that 1,114 capercaillie remain in the last capper stronghold of Strathspey. This might sound like quite a few birds, but the numbers signify that cappers are a hair's breadth away from extinction. We have been here before. In 1785, the *last* last capercaillie was shot in Aberdeenshire. In the first half of the 1800s, capercaillie from Sweden were reintroduced to Perthshire. They thrived, wandering purposefully through the woods that in those days persisted across much of Scotland. Numbers expanded rapidly, to what seems now an astonishing number of 20,000 birds. The capper was doing what it should do and being where it should be.

More recent losses articulate the story of the gradual but systematic erosion of woodland habitat across Scotland. All those isolated woodland discos. Add in the exponential rise of the industrial forest and the protection of those commercial interests. As a forester, what you do is protect your assets from the very healthy numbers of red deer that roam unimpeded through most of Scotland's glens and erect anti-deer perimeter fencing and what you end up with is a very systematic way of wiping out any cappers left patrolling the woods. The capper senses disturbance and bursts out of the blaeberry forest floor: *smack*, that's one less capper to compete at the forest disco.

Too late in this world, we have learned to look at the ways and means our machines of progress impede the stately progress of our most iconic species. Put another way, for far too long, we've been looking at our very human needs rather than also looking at the needs of the wider community of the natural world. But there's a flaw in this human-centric system of looking, and that's the fundamental way that the natural world supports our life systems. *We* cannot do without it. *It* underpins our very existence, and we know this – of course we do – yet on we go, imposing rather than looking at the cappers crashing into fences or the capercaillie trapped in the isolated dancehalls of capper desire.

Much of the work that Cairngorms Connect is under-taking had already been happening inside each organisation.

But by joining together and sharing the guiding principles that underpin the necessary care of the Cairngorms habitats and species, a connected vision of the landscape could be enacted. Capacity and output could both expand. The principal methods of considering the landscape come firmly into alignment.

The project has begun to build relationships in the broader community. I talked to Tors Hamilton, the project's Communications and Engagement Officer, over the phone. She told me that sometimes these community conversations are dynamic, and sometimes they are difficult conversations to have; nevertheless, the conversations are had. People bring many questions to the meetings about the kinds of changes that are happening and the consequential impacts that might arise. About what ways of life and livelihood might be challenged, and then what the gains might look like. You build your community, you build your landscape, and, in the wake of this work and this engagement, those cappers probably won't display anything like gratitude. I think it's us who should be grateful.

Tors told me about the project having commissioned traditional Scottish musician Hamish Napier. They asked him to write a suite of tunes inspired by Napier's explorations of the habitats and species of his home in Strathspey. When he subsequently went for a stroll in Anogach Woods near Grantown on Spey, Napier took along a book about trees. Instead of seeing this collection, this woodland full of trees as a single entity, he began to intuit how each tree species was its own thing, how each species was a character among a landscape of characters. The CD that resulted from the commission, *The Woods*, became a way for local communities to explore the places, the birds, the trees, the flowers and the insects among which they live.

When reading the sleeve notes, what struck me was the discovery that the eighteen letters of the Gaelic alphabet

had traditionally been taught to children using the old
names for native trees and scrub species. I tune in to the
music as I'm writing. It is fluid and solicitous, and by
listening to it, I'm transported to the landscape and forests of
Strathspey. The tunes have their roots in traditional Scottish
folk-dance tune forms, and in the suite Napier has woven
them into contemporary arrangements enhanced
in places with field recordings from the woods. In the notes,
Napier said: 'for me, this is an album of identity, exploring
my native languages, music, folklore and natural environment.'

The Woods is a series of tunes, each of whose titles begins
with one of the Gaelic letters, including all the native tree
species found locally in the wild. There are also tunes for a
suite of other forest flora and fauna. The first tune is for the
letter B – or *Beith* in Gaelic – for the silver birch, the downy
birch and the dwarf birch; *beith-dhubhach, beith-chlumhach,
beith-bheag*. In English, this tune is called 'The Pioneer'
because the birch is the pioneer species that provides
protection and therefore enables other species to become
established in their shelter. The letter *Geanais* is gean, or
wild cherry; *craobh-shirist* or Glocan; bird cherry, hagberry,
hackberry. Letter I is the Tree of Blessings, the juniper. There
are tunes for the Tree of Lightning – the bourtree, or elder,
and tunes to the Tree of Knowledge: the Witch's Tree: the
Trembling Tree and the Tree of Love – the rowan, or Venus
of the Woods. There are tunes for the hawthorn, the
blackthorn, the alder, oak and the aspen.

Next, the Scots pine. Napier tells us that one such
sentinel pine was given a specific name: *Craobh Phillidh*, the
Tree of Return. When local farmers brought their cattle up
the mountain to graze on the summer pastures, they
stopped at the halfway point, at the Tree of Return, where
they would send the cattle on their way to walk
unaccompanied for the last 13 kilometres up the glen while
the farmers returned back to their homes in the valley. In

1927 the Tree of Return was downed in a storm. The bleached trunk remains.

Granny pines are the ancient Scots pines of the Caledonian forest. These are the familiar gnarled forms that can live for up to 600 years and attain a height of 20 metres and a girth of four metres. The Scots pine is Napier's favourite tree; he loves the resinous smell and the nut-brown, weather-reactive cones that litter the forest floor. Most of all, he likes the Scots pine because the bark supports communities of insects that support communities of birds and mammals. The Scots pine, Napier says, is a keystone species upon which many other species rely. These include the pine hoverfly, the red squirrel and the Scottish crossbill. Abernethy is the largest ancient Scots pine forest remnant in Britain, so the lives of those communities of species really matter. Given a voice, I wonder what they would have to say about the future prospect of landscapes. Maybe we should tune in and listen.

The final piece in the suite is less music and more a way of bringing the listener directly back into the heart of the Caledonian forest. It is the peculiar, anti-love song of the cock capercaillie – that weird concoction of marbles and ratchets, accompanied by the tuneless assonance of a slow wind moving steadily through the branches.

We can safely assume that one of the greatest threats to our existence on the planet is our distancing from the natural world. Many of us have a greater knowledge of the inside of our computers than we do of the life-support systems we once lived among more connectedly. Sometimes I can't imagine the future because what I see when I try is the end of the line, which does not make me happy. I find it difficult to see those future landscapes because of the juggernaut of global warming. How do we go about getting out of this mess? How do I? How do you?

I worry about many things.

Once, not very long ago, I wended my way purposefully along Strath Glass to Glen Affric in my car that I should probably not have been going anywhere in at all. From the final car park, I set out to walk to the shores of Loch Affric in blistering August heat, enraptured by the heather and blaeberry that in such a successfully operating ecosystem were the height of a medium-sized child. I reached a viewpoint, and there, on a rocky knoll, among the many Scots pine trees that make this landscape more connected, more sustaining than most of the rest of the more traditionally managed Scottish glens, was a granny pine. And underneath her gnarly branches with my back to the ecosystem that is her continental drift-sequence of bark, I stood and looked out at the glen and the loch that shimmered underneath a seamless blue sky, and I sat down with my back against the granny pine, and I wept.

I'm going to sound a tad 'tree hugger' now, but I think that's OK. I placed my hands on the bark of the granny pine and told her that I was sorry – so very sorry – that, as part of the human race, I am utterly complicit in the unmaking of the natural world. And the tears fell. Other tourists walked past, and I don't know if they noticed this strange weeping woman or not, but no one stopped, and so the conversation between me and the tree continued. I said to the tree that the natural world is so astonishingly beautiful, that this, right now – this landscape that I would never turn my back on – is ravishing, is its own marvellous thing. I said that as a human, I sit at the very edge of the granny pine's world, and when I think about the future landscapes of my sons and of theirs, I really don't want it all to come unstuck because coming unstuck is too awful to comprehend. And I don't know if the granny pine answered or not because you can imagine anything you want to in these kinds of heightened emotional states. You can see the landscape as what it is or as what you want it to be. And maybe what the granny pine said in reply was to remind me of the way that trees ask nothing in return; they are the ultimate gift to the world. And maybe I heard her say that trees ask only that humans allow them to be and that we help create the right conditions for them to get on with living and being rooted and solid to continue giving. Maybe the granny pine also said that if we pay each other respect and show love and care for each other, then maybe we can pull it back from the edge. Maybe.

In its own way, that granny pine *was* the Tree of Return. And I might have said to her that because you, granny pine, have seen such a lot and have passed such a tremendous amount of time being here on this knoll overlooking the loch and despite everything you have not fallen, then maybe everything *will* be OK. Maybe you will be OK, and I will be OK, and maybe my sons will be OK. Then the horse flies began biting, and I knew that the glen's ecosystem was in something like good shape, for now.

In her vibrant, enlightening book, *Braiding Sweetgrass*, the American plant biologist and enrolled member of the Potawatomi Nation, Robin Wall Kimerrer, writes: 'We need acts of restoration, not only for the polluted waters and degraded lands, but also for our relationship to the world. We need to restore honour to the way we live, so that when we walk through the world we don't have to avert our eyes with shame, so that we can hold our heads up high and receive the respectful acknowledgement of the rest of the Earth's beings.'

How might it be possible for us to rebuild our relationship with the natural world? And by 'relationship', I mean to be *in relationship with* rather than to treat nature as a form of commodity – less nature as the salve for troubled minds or nature as something we do on our holidays; more nature as kith and kin.

I think of how we acquire language and how our lives are shaped by the meaning of the language we acquire. I think what it must be like to learn to speak through the naming of trees and animals. Is this what we should begin to do to start coming unstuck? To go back to the foundations of language and learn again? To learn differently from the beginning? A is for Apple, B is for Bat, C is for Capercaillie, S is for Scots pine. The Tree of Return. To see what it is that sustains us above all else. Let's seed the idea of return through the seeding of languages that wander through the world. If we want it, all we need to do is imagine it into being: *3 … 2 … 1 … go*. Hearts and minds. What you don't love, you can't save. Save what you love.

Eighty Fragments on the Pelican

1. Fossils are a kind of stony mirror reflecting the past forwards through time. One of the things fossils reveal is that some 2,000 years ago – in the Bronze Age – Dalmatian pelican paraded their stylish red fish-basket bills through the English wetlands of Cambridgeshire, Somerset, Norfolk and Yorkshire.

2. A wetland is a mirror signalling to the sky. The sky responds by lending the wetlands its many moods and colours and by delivering cargoes of water birds for whom a wetland is a kind of avian magnet. Into this mirror, the birds dabble their many kinds of bill.

3. Dalmatian pelicans work collectively to corral fish into compressed schools, and then in they go, those red pleated pouches scooping up just enough small fishes to keep themselves fed. This is the manner of birds: take no more than you need.

4. The Dalmatian pelican existed in Britain because once-sufficient wetlands existed and because this is the only kind of habitat that a Dalmatian pelican can accommodate.

5. In the case of habitats for pelicans in my country, the impact of humans on drainage and agriculture did away with the gentler impact of pelicans. That Bronze Age farmer over there argues that land for growing food is more important than land for pelicans. I see him now, shading his eyes from the sun as he watches the last pelican escort itself lugubriously into the land of being disappeared.

6. And so we continued, wedging our arguments and the primacy of our human needs firmly into place. The impact of this was that fragmentation really got going.

7. Since the last pelican fished in British waters, 80 per
    cent of the world's wetlands have been lost. A lost
    wetland no longer signals to anything.

8. Writing in 1953, the ornithologist Ralph Whitlock
    gave thought to Britain in the time of the pelican. He
    wanders imaginatively back into the misty landscapes
    of fifteen hundred years ago, a time when the country
    would have been drenched in bird song from shore
    to shore, when wolves, bears and boars inhabited dark
    woodlands, when there were cranes in the marshes,
    bustards on heathland and beavers busy in rivers and
    streams. Into this place, he visualises the great pink
    pelican wafting on outstretched wings over the reedy,
    secretive wetlands of what is now Somerset.

9. I find a webpage on which a curator from the Oxford
    Natural History Museum describes a pelican's humerus
    and ulna bones – a pelican's 'arm' bones – as 'hollow
    tubes; that's all'. The curator says: 'Honestly, pelican
    skeletons hardly even exist.'

10. The expression 'hollowed out' is sometimes used to
    signify places from where species have disappeared.
    When the word 'disappeared' is used like this, it's like
    saying: *this particular animal/bird/insect/habitat just nipped
    out but for some reason didn't come back*. It's like saying: *it
    must be out there somewhere*.

11. When the Dalmatian pelican disappeared from the UK,
    it did not go on its holidays to Northern Greece. It did
    not come back because there was nowhere left for it to
    come back to.

12. On a video on the museum's website, the curator holds
    a single pelican vertebra up to the light to articulate its
    many angles and planes. Held up to the light like this,
    the vertebra resembles a hollow Star Wars TIE fighter.
    Light as air. Fish-powered.

13. In a cross section of bone, the curator shows how the struts at either end of the tube reinforce a pelican's otherwise hollow arm bones.

14. A strut is a structural component in engineering, aeronautics, architecture, anatomy. Struts tie things together. Buildings. Bones. The Eiffel Tower. Arguments. Language.

15. Struts work by resisting longitudinal compression, and they provide tension. In the case of the pelican, the bone struts stop the bone from shattering on impact of diving in water.

16. In flight, pelicans rest their heads on their shoulders and their great pleated bills on their folded necks, alternating between effortless gliding and luxurious, loose, flapping flight.

17. The first time I saw pelicans was from the inside of a bus on the long, see-sawing descent from the mountain pass into the Prespa Lakes region of Northern Greece. Out there in the middle distance, circling in stratospheric thermals high above the nearest of two vast bodies of shining blue water, was what at first glance appeared to be a flotilla of white flying boats.

18. Inside the bus, I craned my neck, eager to catch another glimpse. I had not yet arrived and already I was beguiled by pelicans.

19. In 1575, artist Nicholas Hilliard painted a miniature portrait of Queen Elizabeth I. The gown she wears – or rather that appears to have been constructed about her royal personage – is blood red. The bodice of the gown is encrusted with jewels and geometric patterns fashioned out of tiny white pearls. In the centre of the bodice – centre stage, you might say, because the costume is indeed a kind of stage – a female pelican is embroidered in white silk.

20. This embroidered pelican holds her wings aloft in a gesture of protection for the three fledgling pelicans gathered in their white tininess at their pelican mother's feet. The pelican's neck curves piously towards its own breast, which it pecks to draw blood. The blood is signified by a single, blood red garnet.

21. In wearing this symbol of the 'pelican in her piety' and as a Christian monarch, Elizabeth is saying: 'I am the blood and body of Christ. This is my sacrifice as queen.'

22. In Christian mythology, the story goes that the pelican draws its own blood to feed its young because, in the presumed absence of food, this is how some Christians attempted to make sense of what they saw.

23. Early Christians were present in Prespa. The church in the mountain village of Agios Germanos, lit only by high, narrow and deep-set windows, is decorated by ancient frescoes, including the iconography of a local ecosystem: a badly painted bear, a wolf, a fox, each with a human foot clamped between its teeth.

24. Our small group of abundance-seekers took the boat from the village of Psarades to the immense cave of Panagia Eleousia above the shore of Megáli Prespa. Inside the cave, I climbed up a series of precipitous rock steps and ladders into the vaulted interior. Built long ago into recesses, the monks' individual sleeping platforms were scattered around a tiny hermitage. The chapel's white façade was adorned with geometric patterns, the Jesus child in Mary's arms, prayers and declamations. A doll's house for prayer and meditation.

25. I looked out through the lopsided vertical aperture of the cave's mouth over the lapis-blue waters of the lake and imagined how those sequestered ascetics would have observed pelicans skimming low above the water. I

wondered if, like me, they might also have paid attention to the pelican's alabaster plumage disrupting for moments at a time that boundless icon of blue distance.

26. Like all birds, pelicans pay careful attention to keeping their feathers in prime condition. This habit of long preening sessions is thought to have inspired that religious notion of the pelican tearing its own flesh to provide food for their young. In those faraway days, the luxury of binoculars did not exist, but perhaps those religious seers were not as interested in veracity as they were in story.

27. In the vast wetlands of Lake Mikrí (little) Prespa and Megáli (great) Prespa, pelicans roost and breed on islands of collapsed phragmites reeds. They raise their young and keep themselves pelican-powered by fishing only for what they need.

28. In *Leap*, the American writer Terry Tempest Williams uses Hieronymus Bosch's painting 'The Garden of Earthly Delights' as a vehicle for exploring spirituality, passion and creativity. In Madrid, Williams takes a pair of binoculars to room 57 in the Prado – and goes birdwatching.

29. The conceit of birdwatching in a painting – especially a painting as rich in birdlife as this one (real as well as imagined species) – appeals to me. I like the quirkiness of it. I try to put myself in Williams' shoes and think what that must have been like, a watcher watching and, in turn, being watched by the many visitors because binoculars in galleries would be seen as eccentric or as a form of intrusion that begs the question of how humans choose to look.

30. I also like the idea of birdwatching in this way because Williams and I have both studied that particular painting to make sense of its abundant ecosystem of birds.

31. Williams counts thirty-five species of birds, many of which I could see — or hear — that first morning in Prespa when I woke early and walked over the metal causeway connecting the island of Agios Achillios to the mainland. I climbed a small hill and settled in to watch dawn come in over Mikrí Prespa. In the painting and in Prespa were alpine swifts, great white egrets, little egrets, night herons, squacco herons, magpies, ibis, hoopoes, nightingales, and the glorious golden oriole.

32. Although I have searched and searched in 'The Garden of Earthly Delights', I have not found the white pelican that Williams twitches in room 57 in the Prado.

33. From the little hill, I looked out onto the land bridge dividing Mikrí from Megáli Prespa formed from glacial run-off carried down from the vast range of mountains opposite. If I look down the length of Megáli Prespa, I look into North Macedonia. If I look to the east behind me, what I see are the mountains of Albania.

34. Through my binoculars, I followed the expanse of phragmites abutting the land bridge and found a narrow channel forging its way into the reeds. I followed the channel and quite unexpectedly chanced upon a small body of water — a lake within a lake — where an accumulation of pelicans, white and Dalmatian, a roost of two or three hundred birds were hidden.

35. As the sun emerged incrementally from behind the mountains, the roosting pelicans transposed into a gathering of mystical creatures turned pink and bright by the first slanting rays, as if glowing lights — garnet-coloured lights — were radiating from inside the pelicans' bodies.

36. In the scrub on the hill, bees and insects began instantly to buzz, as if the sunlight had thrown a switch, which, in a way, of course, it had.

37. Watching the pelicans in their roost felt like an act of transgression – as though watching was also a form of intrusion. But the watching was compelling, like coming across yet another among the cavalcade of species and accumulated images in 'The Garden of Earthly Delights'. An unlooked-for moment that takes me both by surprise and by joy.

38. Elsewhere, night herons passed above the reed beds from wherever it is that night herons come from or go to, and pygmy cormorants skimmed the silvered water and reed beds. Dawn's avian commuter belt, all of it unfolding to the background crackle of *chip chip chip, garra garra garra, chip chip chip* – the great reed warbler's constant, clamorous dementing.

39. As I studied the lake within a lake through my binoculars, I came across other little aggregations of pelicans. A half dozen here, a few over there. Some pelicans in pairs with heads high, scrutinising their watery world, or as if taken by surprise. There were circles of pelicans islanded on collapsed reeds and singletons cruising like old steamships. One raised its wings high above its head, the shadowy underwings revealing the markings of a Dalmatian pelican.

40. Unseen behind me in the scrub on the hill, a pair of hoopoes chanted to each other in their customary sonorous call and response, then a nightingale began to sing, and another, and another. I have lived my entire life without nightingales, and there we were – not one, but three.

41. Of the nightingale, Pliny the Elder wrote: 'That little throat contains everything that human skill has devised in the complicated mechanism of the flute.' Over and over, we are compelled into likening ourselves to nature or nature to ourselves. But how often are we able to

contemplate nature as its own valuable thing, its own richly embroidered self, unimpacted by the struts of our human arguments, our impacts, our place in the world?

42. In his book, *Prespa: A Story for Man and Nature*, the Greek ecologist George Catsadorakis said: 'There is very likely no other region in the whole of Europe that has such a great variety of forms of life for its size.'

43. In the 1970s, the Prespa fishing industry began to fail. That it was due to overfishing or the introduction of voracious non-native fish was not then understood. The fishermen looked at the pelicans fishing and noted the volume of those pelican bills, and what happened next is that the pelicans themselves were sacrificed – again – to the greater needs of humans.

44. Catsadorakis paraphrases the response of the local authority like this: 'Pelicans are to be considered vermin. They constitute a threat to the productivity of the fishing industry. They are the enemies of fishermen. Anyone presenting to this department the head or egg of a pelican will receive a reward of 50 drachmas and five drachmas respectively.'

45. When a group of ornithologists visited Prespa the next year, the pelican roosts had been hollowed out. Eggs smashed, nests destroyed or abandoned, the corpses of young pelicans afloat in the lifeless water.

46. News of what was taking place spread rapidly. An international group made up of both Greek and overseas ecologists and ornithologists launched a campaign. Remarkably, in a very short space of time, they persuaded the Greek government to protect the region – and the pelicans.

47. At that time Greece was under the control of a military dictatorship. An alliance between such a regime and

a bunch of nature nerds seems inconceivable to me. Even so, the military leaders were anxious to create a constructive impression of themselves elsewhere in Europe. They took to the task of protection enthusiastically so that the pelicans and all of the other species were once more left in peace – watched over by a resident army in helicopters and armed patrols.

48. Catsadorakis later said the first battle had been won. The campaign to secure the preservation and protection of Prespa, though, was just beginning.

49. Together with ecologist Luc Hoffman and architect and planner turned conservationist Thymios Papayannis, Catsadorakis began to pave the way for a more formal approach to taking the care of Prespa on into the future. In 1991, the Society for the Preservation of Prespa was launched.

50. What is most impressive about the ecologists' reactions and the Greek government's response was the speed with which change and protection took place. Within a single year, the region was declared a nature reserve under which the birds of Prespa were granted full protection.

51. Imagine that – a 'nature junta' patrolling our British farms and countryside at the behest of a bunch of nature nerds! An end to ecocide in our countryside! What's not to like about that?

52. Across the world, governments have yet to be seen to deal with the environmental crisis with the gravitas it clearly demands – five years of this, five years of that. The Paris Agreement signed with much smiling and shaking of hands, then those same governments studiously ignoring the agreements in the document just signed.

53. What's five years, seen through the stone mirror of the fossil record? Seen through the lens of an escalating crisis?

54. As the several nightingales sang and the hoopoes *hoop hooped* and as the day warmed, in ones and twos and in little parties the pelicans began to lift from the water and flapped along the liminal edges of the lake. Eventually, they found what they had gone in search or in sense of: the thermals that rise in the burgeoning warmth of the day and upon whose buoyant, accommodating air the pelicans gathered in spirals, circling higher, soundlessly, to two or three hundred metres, then higher still.

55. And there they were, the pelicans, like atomised particles, getting on in their unassuming way of being, their slow-time swirling together, each a tiny part of a more significant whole, their aeonically unspoken agreement to behave in co-operative ways and thus to make their way environmentally through the limpid, lustrous world of lake and sky.

56. And by now, the world was full of pelicans. Pelicans airborne, flying low over the reeds, occasionally coming in to land, feet thrust forward like the landing gear of a plane, the dark tips of the wings grazing the surface of the water from where immaculate streamers of bubbles washed in their wake.

57. When a chain of pelicans glide one behind another, inches above the water, maintaining lift, surfing through whatever force keeps them like this for fifteen or twenty seconds at a time, I see how improbably large their bodies are. The image that comes to mind is of a Boing 747 leaving the runway – the sheer improbability of it all.

58. Some pelicans crash-land, feet hop-skipping then lifting off again, sometimes wobbling, sometimes certain, rising into the air as the wings flexed and the primary feathers afforded that extra degree of lift at the zenith of each languorous downstroke.

59. An early fishing boat buzzed from Agios Achilios into the western extremity of the lake, unzipping the surface of the water. Unzipping that morning a world until then uninterrupted by human impacts.

60. In Prespa, many species thrive: the pelicans, yes; the bee-eaters buzzing like static and the turtle doves purring in the scrub by the shore of Megáli Prespa; the many pygmy cormorants, the squacco herons, the night herons; the wryneck, the golden oriole and the flute-voiced nightingale whose songs are really too liquid, too resourceful and ingenious, too full of life to be likened to a human-made means of making music; the red-backed and lesser grey shrikes; the ant lion and the common blue, the clouded yellow, the small skipper and black veined white – the too many species of butterfly and insects to count; the tortoise eggs raided by mustelids; the dog-eat-dog nature of it all; the bear, the wolf, the fox.

61. And meanwhile elsewhere – mostly everywhere, in fact – on we go in our badly painted versions of ourselves, our short-termist approaches, our well-practised ways of not looking properly – atomised and separated, mostly with our feet stuck in our mouths.

62. If we know one thing, it is that certainty is a diminishing quality in these troubled times. The abundance that exists in Prespa is a mirror reflecting back to us the way our ecosystems once were and – yes, of course – how they could be again.

63. After four days of this unaccustomed abundance, when
     I awoke in the morning, I knew I was in trouble. I was
     sick, very sick, and I'd begun to slide into what became
     a lucid, corrosive dreamtime. There I was in a room on
     the top floor of the small hotel on an island on a lake in
     the mountains in the remote Balkans, with no concept
     of where or if medical help might be available. I was
     sick, again and again. I couldn't drink. I was unable to do
     anything other than to accept and be pulled back down
     into the strangely comforting world of hallucination.

64. In those uncharted depths, my unmoored mind snagged
     on and returned continually to something I'd seen the
     previous day in the village of Psarades. A man bent over
     and grappling with what at first glance I took to be an
     animal. And there was blood. Whatever it was, whether
     the version held in memory or hijacked by the delirium
     was correct, the creature was being handled in much
     the same way a sheep is grasped by a shearer shearing
     a fleece.

65. When I stopped and looked over the fence in the
     village, there were washes of blood smearing the man's
     hands and arms and the blade of the large knife he
     held over the anticipated sheep or goat, but the animal
     morphed into the body of a great fish – a carp, perhaps
     a metre in length and the circumference around the
     belly equivalent to a border collie.

66. The carp's body was washed in pale watery blood,
     the scales dichromatic pale pink and grey – sizzling,
     you could say, under the heat of the midday sun. The
     man was deep in conversation with a bystander, and I
     noticed the way he wielded the blade but appeared to
     dissect the fish more by feel than by sight as he chatted
     away, inserting the knife into the carp's resistant skin
     and the internal structures of its body, reducing the

mass slice by slice and throwing hefty horseshoe wedges each containing a segment of white severed spine into a white plastic box where, for a greasy moment, each one slid over the slices below.

67. At some point in the afternoon, still deep in my delirium, a couple of folks from our group came and helped me down the stairs and out into the heat and to a small open boat where I lay collapsed against the fibreglass hull, my head on my knees as the outboard zoomed me across the lake to a waiting car.

68. In the doctor's waiting room and behind a desk was a young man wearing shorts and a death-metal T-shirt, twiddling his thumbs as if waiting for sickness to walk in through the door. I took him to be a teenage receptionist. He took my details, this youth, then removed a white doctor's coat from a hook on the wall and shrugged it on over the T-shirt with a skull and thus became a doctor and asked me to follow him through open sliding doors that did not, in fact, slide or, for that matter, provide much in the way of privacy. In the consulting room, the doctor delivered an injection of anti-emetics into a location that shall remain nameless and gave me a prescription for what seemed like a dozen kinds of pills – then he thanked me for coming.

69. Every afternoon dark clouds built into towering presences in the far distances of Megáli Prespa and thunder bellowed, moving closer, tantalising, breaking over the lake and the mountains and forests in fractured pulses. And as the white hyphae of lightning broke the back of the malign sky, the closer waters of the lake became strangely opalescent, becalmed.

70. Just offshore and strangely luminescent against the blue-black sky, pelicans went about their business in

the warm interstices of air above the lake. But in that peculiar luminosity, it was as if the lake was not filled by water, but more by light that radiated upwards from the depths, as if slaking the thirst of water for light.

71. And in these storms and under the monsoon of rain, the fishermen miniaturised by distance turned their backs and continued fishing. In the grip of the sickness, I'd hauled myself from the bed and peered from the window because everything out there had suddenly turned dark. The clouds began to empty themselves like an upturned drum of water, and a single fishing boat turned towards the island, picking up speed suddenly, outboard at full throttle. The prow rose up so that the lone fisherman (who must have been hunkered down against the rain) was obscured entirely, and because I couldn't see him, it seemed to me that the boat was steering itself. And with the throttle reduced to approach the jetty, the prow lowered like a pelican settles into water, and there was the fisherman, encased in voluminous grey waterproofs and sou'wester, hauling buckets of fish from the boat and running towards the village, the storm hard on his heels.

72. Later, I considered briefly whether, in fact, it was the abundance of Prespa that was the source of my illness. That the birds and the insects and the sheer volume of it all had made me enter into delirium, despite the doctor's assurances that I had caught the early-summer virus well known to the Prespan people themselves. Had I become sick with abundance? Had the abundance of Prespa been the catalyst, a way of confronting the deluge of loss that we endure in the UK? And yet, I think this loss we live with has not made enough of us sick. Do more of us need to become besotted with abundance or sick because we have seen exactly what it is we have lost?

73. Prespa, of course, is a garden. A garden in which pelicans in all their piety – in their getting on with not overfishing and with not plucking blood from their collective maternal breast – can be seen as the embodiment of the innocence that existed before the coming of original sin. And make no mistake: the great undemocratic forces that continue to underpin the unravelling nature of life on this planet are collectively a wicked, mighty, unholy, human-made sin. Are we all guilty? I think so. Are some more guilty than others? I think so.

74. When I found the pelican roost in Prespa that morning, it was indeed like birdwatching in 'The Garden of Earthly Delights'. Because Prespa – its hidden pelican colonies and its whole cavalcade of natural life – is a mirror in whose reflection I can not only understand the losses that humans have wrought on my country since those long-ago Dalmatian pelicans made their homes among the reedy waterways of Yorkshire, of Cambridgeshire, and of Norfolk and Somerset, but I can understand that in our not looking, in our distraction in the experiment of progress, what we did was to disappear – or un-home – a species that will forever and everywhere be on the verge of leaving us.

75. The pelican, that weird and perfectly adapted species, offers a way of recalling Hieronymus Bosch's fervent imagination, his intelligence and wit; it is, after all, a bird he could easily have conjured into being. Even so, and despite Williams' assertions, I still have not found it in the painting of 'The Garden of Earthly Delights'.

76. And let us not – I could not ever – forget the great reed warbler's dementing underscore. The rusted hinge of the day-long soundscape. A jangling minimalism that takes over the day shift as soon as those amphibian desperados,

those Steve Reich on a three-note-bender pond frogs
relinquish the dwindling chiaroscuro of night.

77. The great reed warbler I'd observed constructing its
    unobtrusive little nest, a tightly woven basket of stripped
    phragmites, a speculative home among the reeds using
    the struts of the reeds for support and for supporting its
    argument for the need to build a nest. And in it came, this
    little bird, pushing and pulling and tenaciously building
    something from nothing much at all – all innate intention
    and art, discretion and intelligence. A speculative nest
    that may or may not have been considered of satisfactory
    quality or of superior enough location for the female
    great reed warbler to grace it with her presence.

78. And we think we are engineers.

79. The morning of our departure, I awoke to feel weak but
    better. I had passed through an actual and metaphorical
    sickness and was back in the land of abundance. I looked
    out early from my hotel room eyrie on the island and saw
    moving through the water, like an old paddle steamer,
    a single pelican. The pelican paddled into sight beyond
    the open channel in the reed beds where the jetty runs
    into the lake and from where everything needed by
    humans is carried in by boat, and where the great reed
    warbler's nest may or may not have been deemed good
    enough to make a home in.

80. In that early hour and caught in the sun's incipient glow,
    the pelican barely disturbed the surface of the lake. The
    water it moved through shifted from the dull sheen of
    old metal to pearlescent as the pelican languidly unfurled
    its great wings, raising them above its improbable body,
    and there I saw, nested in the underwings, the tenebrous
    shade of diminishing night.

Viewing Stations

Station 1

I'm looking across Ullswater's shining blue surface from the yard at Gowbarrow Hall farm. Ranged around the hinterland of the opposite shore are the hills whose names form part of the distinctive – or hefted – language of place: Breda Fell, Hallin Fell, Loadpot Hill, High Street and the Nab. To borrow a word from the antecedents of landscape interpretation, the view is *sublime*. My own reaction is somewhat more mundane; it gives me that comfortable feeling, like pulling the duvet up around my shoulders.

Across the lake, I can make out small groups of people who've undertaken the short, steep climb to the summit of Hallin Fell, despite the August heat and lack of breeze. No doubt they are doing what we do when we reach the summits of mountains on these clear kinds of days – gazing out at the landscape unspooling beneath their feet.

I'm met by Anne and Richard Lloyd, their daughter Claire and her husband Sam Beaumont and three-year-old daughter Bea. A few months earlier, I'd heard Sam and Claire talk at an uplands conference about how they were regenerating the soils at Gowbarrow. Cue photographs on the conference screen of some of the holes that Sam had been digging to see how the soils are coming along. The first image was taken in sheep-grazed pasture where the earth was compacted through over-grazing. It was dull-looking, the roots making barely any headway into the soil. The second image was of pasture where the sheep had been removed and that was now grazed by cattle. The grasses were significantly longer, with roots that penetrated deep into the soil. The soil itself was crumbly and rich, chocolate-brown. I know nothing about soils, but the difference was palpable.

'I've developed something of an obsession with digging holes,' Sam said at the conference.

When Beatrix Potter fell in love with the Lakes and came to live there full time, she became deeply enmeshed in farming and with the local farming community. She recognised the contribution that sheep farming made to the local landscape and economy. In addition to functioning as this more prosaic working landscape, the Lakes is also known as the birthplace of Romanticism; the heartland of Wordsworth and Coleridge, their friends and families. Between the Neolithic landscapes of stone axe factories and stone circles to the later industry of slate mines and the modernity of Cumbria's nuclear west coast, when we look at the landscape, whether by walking or by driving, it gives back what my colleague Charlie Gere calls in his book *I Hate the Lake District* (he doesn't), 'a cinematic experience'; a series of sweeping vistas of mountains, lakes, farms and grand houses that were built in specific locations to provide their owners and visitors with the most sublime views possible. From all this, how do we begin to disentangle a time when the land here was not instrumentalised by somebody and for something? In 2017, under the cultural landscapes category, the Lake District was granted World Heritage status. A significant element of the inscription was the idea that a 'cultural' landscape had been fashioned over centuries by the farming of mostly Herdwick and Swaledale sheep. Under areas of common grazings – the commons – sheep roam the fells in over 600 parcels known as 'hefts' that exist entirely separately to ownership of the land. More than 60 per cent of the uplands here are designated common grazings. The sheep become hefted to particular places in the hills, and this genetic memory is transferred down through the generations.

To be hefted, therefore, means to know your place in the landscape. To be hefted means understanding the lie of the land, knowing where to retreat in hard weather and where to find the best plants to eat. Of course, people are also hefted to the land and to ways of working and making a living from it.

In this way, the lives of the farmers and their sheep are entwined, one with another. Some of the less helpful ways we look at and consider the Lake District landscape create an elision of time. As if in the way we want to see it, not very much has changed since siblings William and Dorothy Wordsworth and friends took to walking and looking and thinking and writing in response to it. But the landscape itself can also be thought of as a mirror that reflects ourselves back to us. If we look more deeply, if we listen to what the land itself tells us, we find there is more than one way to look. When we look through the lens of the Anthropocene, how is it that we should see?

Station 2

Anne's father bought Gowbarrow Hall in the late 1970s, and from then until the death of her mother in 2017, most of its 250 hectares had been almost exclusively sheep-grazed.

Anne and Claire lead me through the yard, and we enter the upper storey of a big barn, swept clean. Daylight from the lower storey seeps through the cracks between the boards. There's a laptop set up ready on a table.

'We've tried showing people around the farm without the context,' Anne says, 'but gradually we realised it's better to give some of that first. That way, people get it; it helps them see more easily when we're out on the land.'

Anne projects images of the land onto a limewashed wall and begins to describe the changes they'd been making over the past year or so. The root of their methods, excusing the pun, is about looking at and thinking about what the ground beneath their feet is telling them. To begin the process, most of Gowbarrow's sheep were sold, replaced by shorthorn cattle, and the use of chemical fertilisers was stopped. In

Anne's parents' time, she explains, the land would be dosed
with fertiliser three times: once in the spring, then after the
first cut of grass, and again in September to give the grass a
boost to help keep the sheep in condition over the winter.

'But we know that all fertiliser does is compromise the
soils. Good, healthy soils have trillions of microbes available to
feed the plants. Keep fertilising,' Anne says, moving her hands
apart to illustrate the vacuum, 'and all of that is destroyed.'

We venture outside and set off walking uphill through a
field of long grass towards the higher ground of open fell
and shelter belts of woodland.

Claire and Sam are engineers by trade, and Claire still
works part-time.

'We were so happy when they said they wanted to move
back from London,' Anne says. 'It meant we could really get
stuck in to making the changes happen.'

As we climb higher, the lake comes increasingly into
view. Small sailing boats are white nymphs balanced on the
water. The lake steamer ploughs towards Pooley Bridge, and
behind it, a couple of orange kayaks roll through the wake.

'We're turning things on their head, doing Lakeland
farming in reverse,' Claire says, pointing at the higher
ground. 'In the Lakes, it's traditional to put the animals on
higher ground in the summer and bring them down to the
in-bye land in the winter. We're putting the cattle and a
gang of native fell ponies up there to overwinter. They graze
in the open or shelter in the woods where they browse
vegetation from the trees. The test comes when we see how
they've fared come spring. What we're seeing is, they're not
losing condition. When the cattle are ready in the summer,
they go to the local abattoir. The butcher says the meat is
fantastic quality – all on 100 per cent grass. Now we have a
waiting list for the beef.'

We contour along the hillside through meadows of
flowering grasses and thistles. For the first time in this topsy-
turvy year of weather, I count a dozen or more peacock

butterflies painting the thistle flowers and seed heads in a drift
of red and black. When a peacock lands close by, the outer
wings are dark and subtle, illuminated with tiny segments of
buff like the buff of thistle seed. The women occasionally stop
to identify plants that have returned in the time since they
began to reimagine the farm. There are sneezewort, bog
asphodel, betony, broad-leaved dock and shoots of lilac
heathers, and small bees making sorties from plant to plant.
Through the decades that the land was sheep-grazed, these
tenacious plants held their nerve. Lying dormant in the dark,
they sensed when the time was right to emerge into the remit
of the sun and the light, the weather and the seasons.

In Half Moon Field, we approach a herd of shorthorn
cattle lying down and ruminating in the shade of a streamside
bank of sycamore, oak and alder. The calves are standing,
scrutinising us as we wander closer. If ever there was an
English idyll, this is it – Albion in all its summer glory. A
painting by Gainsborough, albeit with added electric fence.

'It's called mob grazing,' Claire says. 'Once they've eaten
the grass in one section, we move them to the next bit – and
they're dead keen to get at that next lot of fresh grass! When
they're grazing, the birds come in – swallows, martins – lots
of other "little brown jobs". That's the ecosystem working.
When the soil rests, the grasses and wildflowers recover and
set seed and that provides the right kinds of habitats for
insects, voles and birds.' She points into the middle of the
herd. 'There's Lionel the bull – the one with the curly hair.
He's very happy just now. Sometimes, if the bullocks get
uppity, he's on the case.'

The grass is strewn around the cattle like new-mown hay.

'When we first put the cows out into the fields,' Anne
says, 'three days later we looked at the ground and gasped
and we wondered what on earth we'd done. It looked like a
mown hay field. Our farm worker shook his head. "It's no
good," he said. But we held our nerve. Four days later, the
new growth began to come through.'

I wonder what their farmer neighbours thought of this idiosyncratic approach to farming.

'When we chat with other farmers, they say things like, "That grass has gone over." But they're looking from too far away; they're not seeing what we see.' To illustrate the point, Claire pushes and pulls the grasses apart, revealing the close structure at the base of the plants.

'You remember Sam's holes from the conference? When we started, he'd dig a hole, pour water in. The water just sat there; it couldn't do anything else because the ground was clay. Now when we do the "slake test" the water runs straight into the ground, like when you pour water into the moat of a sandcastle.'

'We've begun to see how different kinds of worms inhabit different levels in the earth,' says Anne. 'It's really very exciting. And we've had surveys done. Our ecologist says he can tell what's in the soil just by looking at it. We're building the microbial bridge, which means these organisms act as a bridge between the health of the plant and the soil.'

'Now we've got worms and roots aerating the soil,' Claire adds, 'and if the soil is aerated, then the water is absorbed and held.'

There is a pause, and I wonder if, at that moment, all of our synapses connect back to the way the rain slid off the fells in vast grey sheets during Storm Desmond. If you live in Cumbria or in North Lancashire, any conversation about the weather – especially about rain – contains an add-on narrative, one that hovers darkly overhead, somewhere on the periphery of vision. If you experienced Desmond, the way that water behaves becomes pivotal.

Over five and a half years have passed since that particular storm did its terrible work across the north of England. The weight and rate of the floodwaters being forced out of Ullswater into the River Eamont sundered the bridge supports at Pooley Bridge, leaving the fractured carriageway and ramparts lying in the river like the remnants of a previous civilisation. Which, in a way, it was. Late in 2020, the new bridge was opened. When you have to wait more than five years for the rebuilding of a bridge, the way the land is managed and therefore the way rivers can behave becomes an issue of connection or separation.

We are living in a time of unfettered species loneliness. We have cast ourselves far adrift from the natural world and what we are seeing all around us is the manifestation of that loneliness.

The American environmental philosopher and writer Aldo Leopold wrote that much of the damage that has been inflicted upon the land remains unseen by laypeople. He notes that an ecologist needs to either harden his or her shell and pretend that the consequences of their learning have, after all, nothing to do with them, or else become the medic upon whom the responsibility lies for confronting a community with the damage imposed under their watch.

Under the Lake District World Heritage designation, if you want to plant more than a handful of trees, the World Heritage folks need to assess the nature of the proposal. If the plans are likely to impinge too significantly on how the designation is framed (remember that 'cultural' landscape of the sheep-cropped sward), projects can be refused. But if the planting of trees and scrub is something to be so studiously excised – if the idea of restoring habitat for pollinators is to be so vigorously resisted in this time of drastic and dangerous loss of pollinators – then what exactly is the nature of the fear? Let us not forget that sheep farming – and any farming where the attendant destruction of surrounding ecosystems are lost as a direct result – is an extractive industry. It cannot, by its own nature, be otherwise.

The grasses at Gowbarrow were becoming increasingly entangled, and if this was so on the surface, then in the ground below, the roots and the soils and invertebrates were entangled with each other too. I learned a lot at Gowbarrow Hall. I learned enough to allow me to begin to see the land differently. I remembered something Claire had said to me before I left the farm that August afternoon: at the Knepp rewilding project in Sussex, it had taken twenty years to bring the soil back to fully functioning health; at Gowbarrow, it had taken just over a year.

There was something else I learned too, and this was the idea of reciprocity. When the cattle at Gowbarrow graze, they eat a third, trample a third, and leave a third behind. This practice, this husbandry by animals that are genetically encoded to act positively on the health of the ground, is the mechanism of creating plenty. The topsoil is developed, and the grass is duly provided with the nutrients of success. Not only this, but the thirst of the land is slaked.

If we build the microbial bridge and slake the thirst of the land, what we are doing helps ameliorate the cause and effect of our increasingly heavy rains, allowing them to be slowed sufficiently to help stop our communities from becoming divided – again. If we engage with slowing the flow, what we are also doing is reflecting a more useful version of ourselves back at us.

Station 3

When travelling cleric Thomas West published the first comprehensive guide to the Lake District in 1778, he provided readers with a set of instructions about how they should look at the landscape. He established dozens of 'Viewing Stations' at various locations around the Lakes, from Claife Heights above Windermere, from the top of Castle Crag in Borrowdale, to the view along Bassenthwaite from Armathwaite. And West had other 'visitor experience' tricks up his frockcoat sleeve. Along with the telescope (better to collapse distance and engage more closely with that sequence of lofty vistas), he also introduced the 'landscape' or Claude mirror – a folding mirror small enough to be carried in the pocket of the walking tourist. Once the visitor was in position at the chosen station, the guide instructed them to turn their backs on the landscape and view it instead through the mirror's lens. When you look like this, West said, your perception of the landscape is heightened. Follow me, he said, and I guarantee you the ultimate way to see the Lakes; you will be greatly stirred. The capacity of your soul will be increased. West, then, was an eighteenth-century travel agent directing the flow of tourism into specific locations – a kind of early Tripadvisor – and, with him, the commodification of the Lake District began.

Sometimes I daydream about what those pioneering conservationists William Wordsworth and Beatrix Potter might have to say if they could see things from this point in the evolution of the world. In this imagining, I have them take part in a panel discussion at a Lake District literary festival and, to make sure there's a balanced set of views and because I see him as the eighteenth-century manifestation of the World Heritage way of looking at things, I also invite Thomas West. Once they, and we, have got used to the idea of sitting beside people who should not, of course, be there, I also imagine someone (it could possibly be me) putting their hand in the air, and what this person says goes something like this.

'I'd like to know how you feel about the idea of preserving this landscape as "cultural" in this time of climate breakdown and failing biodiversity?' (We'll assume for the purposes of the exercise that our illustrious guests are familiar with these twenty-first-century terms.) 'Do you think we should preserve the landscape as it is – that this should be the precedent, the guiding principle of how we see the land – or do you think there's a moral obligation to look more closely at what the land is telling us?'

I'm beginning to think this person is one of those literary festival types who come across as a little bit too self-important. This person who might or might not be me looks William directly in the eye and says: 'I remember the bit in your poem about the leech gatherer and the questions you ask him in the poem: "How is it that you live, and what is it you do?" Do you think we should be asking ourselves those same questions?'

Imagine them like this: William has his hands clasped together on the table in front of him. He nods his head slowly back and forth. From his demeanour, I assume that he understands what this person is getting at and thinks their questions are useful and valid. I'm concerned about Thomas West. I think he's going to toe the World Heritage party line: 'But think of all the tourists!' and perhaps, like in a cartoon, dollar signs begin ringing up in his eyes. Beatrix Potter, meanwhile, shuffles her sensible sheep farmer's best shoes underneath the table. Perhaps she feels conflicted about the relationships between sheep and the loss of biodiversity. Maybe she doesn't think she can say what might be coming more and more to the front of her mind. But then let's remind ourselves that, as well as being an illustrator and storyteller, Potter was an astute scientist. She was the first to identify the reproduction systems of lichens. She grew fungal spores on glass plates and tracked their development under the microscope. Beatrix Potter fundamentally understood the nature of cause and effect.

There's an uncomfortable pause, then William speaks.

'I don't know what to say. I was poet laureate but here I am, rudely posited back into a landscape that I simultaneously recognise and don't recognise, and I'm lost for words.' He gestures towards the landscape outside our imaginary festival. 'I'm lost also for knowing how it is that I should feel when I'm confronted by the nature – or by the lack of nature – in the Lake District in *your* century.' And William looks at us as we begin to shift uncomfortably in our seats and asks: 'What on earth have you done?'

As Wordsworth's words trail away, Beatrix picks up the thread. And what she says is that the consequences of our collective actions upon the planet, and particularly on the Lake District, are unimaginable from her time in tenure on the land. She tells us, in her no-nonsense way: 'Without biodiversity, we can stop worrying, because there'll be nothing left for us to worry about.' She says: 'Where have all the wildflower meadows gone? Hilltop was surrounded by meadows until well after my time.'

I can vouch for this. I can vouch for this because in the late 1970s, as a seventeen-year-old in need of finance for my newly acquired hobbies of cigarettes, alcohol and parties, one of my ways of earning was to help the farmer across the road to bring in the hay. And I can vouch for the sweet smell of the hay as we piled it up onto the trailer, as well as the thistles and the flowering plants that were compressed along with the grasses into the bales – the entangled stems and fading flowers of ragged robin, knapweed, Yorkshire fog, dog daisies.

As recently as the late 1980s, farmers in the Lakes were bringing in hay from traditional meadows. A few years later, as young adults in search of the wild and finding it – or something we then understood was the wild – my friends and I made expeditions to one of the more remote western valleys where on our way out to walk the fells in the early morning, the farmers would be working together to bring in the hay. In the evenings when we wandered the narrow road to the pub, they were piling the hay onto the bale lifter that carried the bales to the upper floor of the barn at the side of the road, and when we meandered back to the tent in the not-quite-dark, there they would still be, illuminated by soft electric light emanating from the barn doors and windows. It was as if we had walked into a painting by Joseph Wright of Derby.

This was all within my living memory rather than in some lost era hovering between fixed and faded, like my old 1970s colour photographs where the colour inevitably migrates towards oblivion.

I can also vouch for the way farmers have been paid through EU subsidies to behave in certain kinds of ways and, therefore, to look at the land in certain kinds of ways. That engine of destruction, silaging, which, in a very short time, has reduced the countryside to a palimpsest of its former self, is a manifestation of how farming mostly lost its way and industry took over. It is under the mantle of industrial farming that pollinators and invertebrates haemorrhaged from the land. This, we know, rang the death knell for pollinators, invertebrates and for ground-nesting farmland birds across most of the rural British landscape. Not for nothing did the curlews and lapwings disappear from our fields. Where there are no invertebrates in the soil, there is no health in the soil – and of course, if you are a curlew chick, neither is there any food.

I should pause here for a moment. I want to say that if I had been a farmer at the advent of this industrialisation, had I been incentivised to act in a certain way – to silage instead of making hay or to heft my sheep to the uplands rather than thinking about the greater commons (that of the wider public good) – then no doubt I'd have done the same too. The pressing issue for us all, of course, is one of repair and restoration across as much of the land as is humanly possible.

Back at the imaginary literary festival, Beatrice points an astute, no-nonsense farmer's finger at the World Heritage folks and says: 'Your way of looking at the Lake District is not mine. Cultural landscape? Not in my name.'

Thomas West looks at his pocket watch. He's wondering how soon he can get away and mutters: 'I didn't think it would end up like this.'

Station 4

In the spring of 2020, I rode my bike into remote Swindale. Here, in the Haweswater catchment area, the RSPB, Natural England, United Utilities and the Environment Agency have undertaken a joint project to restore Swindale Beck and bring scrub habitat and trees back to the land.

I stopped my bike and paid attention to the cuckoo calling on repeat from the blackthorns on the fellside beyond the river. Over there, the bluebells were now just a fading smudge of phthalo blue. Bluebells are a clear genetic marker of what was once woodland. I traced that fading colour into the head of the valley as it ambled into and out of the woodland and scrub and open spaces all the way to the glacial moraine under Hobgrumble Ghyll.

Previously canalised to make way for more grazing land for sheep, Swindale Beck now carries itself in a series of naturalised graceful curves that meander through restored flood meadows. Lee Schofield, the RSPB's farm manager for the Haweswater and Swindale valleys, says that the beck has been given back its sinuosity. And with this sinuosity and the meanders come deep pools and shallow gravels, and because of this, the Atlantic salmon has returned. Cause and effect. Those flood meadows are not only awash with spring flowers and attendant biodiversity, but they are also repositories for storing vast amounts of CO_2. The loss of soils from the mountains and fellsides is slowed, fixed into place through the restoration of wood pasture – the mix of open ground and woods and their attendant understorey that previously existed across much of our landscapes. And with these new habitats comes the building of biodiversity and the return of abundance. When I look from inside the Anthropocene, I see the return of pollinators and their habitats and the fixing of our shallow soils on the fells as more purposeful ways to consider the landscape.

Another day I took a walk with Simon Stainer, one of Natural England's ecologists in Cumbria. We headed into Rydal and Scandale in the heart of Wordsworth country. Simon talked about how, in exchange for agri-environment payments, two local farming families had removed their sheep from extensive parts of the valleys. Where the sheep once were, a forest of scrub and native tree species now cascaded up the flanks of both valleys. There was a herd of shaggy-coated longhorn cattle too, and as we wandered among them, Simon told me how their heavy feet poach open the ground, allowing seeds to germinate, and that by browsing the trees, they create open spaces in natural woodland. A rich variety of wildlife follows in their wake.

'What we see in the Lakes,' Simon said, indicating the bare fellsides across the valley, 'is the result of decade upon decade of unameliorated losses of flowering plants and grasses, of rowan, hawthorn, birch, cherry, bird cherry, crab apple, blackthorn, aspen and willow species – all of which support countless thousands of invertebrates.'

Hawthorn are commonly encountered in the landscape of the Lakes as isolated specimens. The species can live for 400 years, so an individual tree represents loss of habitat and biodiversity on an immense scale. Sculptural, they indeed are. Hardy, unquestionably. But each one is also adrift and unconnected. Were we to reimagine this hawthorn as an individual – a person, for example – we would immediately get the nature of their isolation. Trees are sociable beings that communicate with and feed one another through a range of subtle interventions – a bit like humans, then. Who, we might usefully ask, are these lone individuals able to communicate with? Does the lone hawthorn suffer from loneliness?

Simon and I walked on over the brow of the fell. A peregrine dropped like a stone from the sky, plummeting into the upper reaches of Rydal. A minute later, Simon became ecstatic. He'd found a bramble looping its spiny tendrils out of a crevice in a rocky extrusion. Above this, a birch had taken root in a fracture in the rock. The humble bramble, he said, is a vital plant for insects because of its long flowering season and abundant autumn fruit.

The going got steeper and, as we crossed the rounded ridgeline of the fell, my boots began to sink into boggy ground. Simon calls this a 'wet flush'. I am learning the language of ecologists. Simon studied the ground. Soon, he found what he was looking for: a constellation of low-growing, unassuming flowers that I had to get my eye in to see – one here, one over there, another right here, and here a little congregation. Bird's-eye primrose.

'These species are all very patient,' Simon told me. 'They lie dormant and, when the conditions are right, they do it all for themselves.'

Balanced upon minutely wavering stems, these pink acolytes, these little clusters of dish-faced flowers are miniature Jodrell Banks or tiny Earth-bound satellites circumnavigating the sky in thrall to the sun. They are also tenacious packages of emergent life and sensors of the planet's hum in a way that we, in this time of anthrophony, can barely imagine.

A couple of months later, in late August I spent a morning with Jim Bliss, the quietly enthusiastic young conservation manager of Lowther Estates. From the tiny hamlet of Whale, we strode off across an open field with Jim's German Pointer, Sully. Work had just been completed on creating a new wetland scrape designed to attract wading birds and to allow ancient – or what Jim referred to as 'Paleo' watercourses – to reconfigure the land. The estate had begun to sell on their flocks of sheep. A whole suite of regenerative farming methods was being deployed, including the creation of new wood pasture. Much of the restoration work was being funded through environmental grants of the kind used elsewhere in Cumbria that are implemented to support environmental changes in soil health, slowing the flow, bringing back pollinators and more.

We headed from Whale to the River Lowther and stopped on the wooden bridge so that Jim could show me where redundant stone from field clearance had been dumped into the channel of the river. This had the effect of raising the water table behind the new low rapids, allowing the river to widen and slow, and for more ancient Paleo channels to work out the most natural way to carry water back into the main channel of the river. Somewhere beyond the bridge in a woodland enclosure, the first beaver to be reintroduced into Cumbria had recently taken up residence, and, although he didn't know it, he would imminently be joined by a female.

'What's the idea with the beavers?' the sceptic in me asked. I feared a bank of remote cameras relaying images to the Lowther Castle's visitor centre or pre-booked visits to the site for a fee. I couldn't have been more wrong.

'We want them to impact on the landscape – to bring more wetland habitat back and all the other species that come on the back of that. Part of the thinking is that sometimes what nature needs is to get on with being itself, without constantly being disturbed by people.' This was music to my ears.

Framing the horizon beyond the beaver enclosure were the slopes of gently rising land where other wood pasture habitats were being created. Beyond that was the line of hills that rise up towards the mountains of Haweswater. When you look at the landscape in the way the folk at Lowther are doing, you automatically begin to consider the potential expansion of these ideas into that wider landscape. After all, nature doesn't begin and end with fences or hedgerows. If nature could communicate her thoughts on the potential for regenerating that wider landscape, I'm sure she would tell us it was a no-brainer, though no doubt she'd employ more elegant language than that.

A series of surveys are being commissioned to reveal the habitats and species that used to exist at Lowther. Looking at the land in this way – as a crucible of prior abundance – is also a way of opening up new ideas about what kinds of species could potentially be restored. Looking into the past is a way of informing the present, of leading towards abundance rather than shrinking from it. There was talk of the corncrake, a migratory bird whose vastly shrunken breeding range in the UK is ample illustration of the

war-zone impact of silaging. To return the corncrake would
be turning modern farming on its head; it would mean
putting the lights back on instead of allowing us to continue
turning them off.

The last stop on our walk was at the restored wildflower
meadows adjacent to the river. I'd noticed the meadows
from the road as I'd driven the narrow lane, but until you're
right in among it all, the full-colour picture remains unseen.
That walk through the meadows remains locked in my
memory. Seed had been taken from meadows a stone's throw
further along the valley – of red clover, red campion,
constellations of bright-yellow corn marigolds, yarrow,
mayweed, the bright red of smooth-headed poppy, geranium,
ox-eye daisy and leaning blue towers of vipers bugloss – but
there were also species from further afield: wild carrot,
marigolds, cornflowers.

Later, when I showed the photographs to my friend Peter
(my go-to person for anything flora), he put a slightly
different spin on that array of species. He called it a
'tumbledown' mix resulting from agricultural land that has
been left or abandoned, and so into the genetic mix arrives
other species that add complexity and diversity. Forget those
1970s colour photos; this was the full digital colourscape.
This was nature dialling up the filter on Instagram, a field
shouting the entire colour spectrum.

This is what we have forgotten we should see in fields.
This is how we have forgotten to see the land.

Those wildflower meadows are to the sheep-farmed
backdrop of the fells what Gauguin and Van Gogh were to
Courbet's muted tones or the restrained palette of Constable.
They tip the percentage up from the 3 per cent of traditional
wildflower meadows remaining in Britain towards 3.333
recurring, signifying that change is coming – but oh! What
a long road there is yet to travel.

When the first surveys were carried out in the meadows
at Lowther, they counted one wild bee species. This season,

there are five. What began as a hobby for Jim Lowther – a
couple of hives of honeybees – has developed, and there are
now more than 300 hives on the estate. As we walked
through the flowers, the honeybees busied themselves
around our calves and our feet.

The return of bees to our meadows and dragonflies to
wetlands and the kingfishers that arrive with the wetland
creation of beavers – and not forgetting the invertebrates
(how exactly did we manage to forget the invertebrates?) –
make manifest the whole glorious, riotous, entangled
assembly of life on Earth and in our fields. And all of it is
possible. Abundance has the potential to arise from the
ways we choose to look at, consider and act upon the land
around us.

Station 5

A couple of years ago, on a blustery day in December, I
went to meet another farming family in a remote valley of
Cumbria. As I chatted in the yard with the farmer and his
farming-partner daughter, contract tree-planters were
zipping over the nearby fellsides in all-terrain vehicles. As
part of their agreement with Natural England, the headage
of sheep on the farm had been reduced from 1,000 to 800
animals. The farmer told me he'd only gone in for the
scheme because of the financial uncertainties around Brexit.
I'm not party to what kinds of sums we're talking here, but
later, Simon Stainer told me that the benefits were 'generous
for doing ambitious conservation'.

Those contractors on the fellside were putting in
thousands of birch, holly, hawthorn, rowan, oak, alder and
aspen. They were returning to the fells an ecology that
had been an intrinsic part of this landscape in the past –
too long ago, of course, for human memory to recall. The
tree plantings will create new habitats (or, as Simon calls
them, niches) into which associated species can insert
themselves. The previously canalised beck that runs

through the valley and that had in earlier times already been picked up and moved – or re-engineered, if you like – to accommodate increasing numbers of sheep was again being re-meandered. Eventually, together with the plantings, this would help slow the flow of our increasingly heavy rainfall. It's a win–win. The farming family benefits through financial security. The land and nature benefit through being revitalised, and, crucially, communities downstream (in this case, my town of Kendal) benefit from the effects of flood amelioration.

In Kendal, we know too well about the nature of flooding. In Kendal, as elsewhere, and as we have already seen, those predictions of once-in-200-years events are unhelpful and largely inaccurate because of climate breakdown. By now, though, we understand that this calculation is unrealistic at most, unhelpful at least. If we think back to that idea of the commons – which in this county refers to the right to graze animals in delineated parcels of land – then I'm also interested in the idea of reinterpreting those commons, to repurpose or reimagine them for a whole suite of benefits. Benefits that extend far beyond the farmers and World Heritage officials who continue to be hefted to the idea of sheep as the predominant cultural narrative of our time. What I am calling for, therefore, is the long-overdue and radical re-evaluation of what exactly is meant by 'the commons'. If the commons can be so reimagined, restructured, redesignated, the pay-off would be an amelioration that is also a far greater, more altruistic way to think about landscape – one that will help to alleviate the suffering in our communities downstream, as well as the common good that would arise in the wake of the reinstating of biodiversity.

High above the tree contractors and the new fences that ascend and contour along the top of the fellside, a buzzard hovered against the headwind, its underwings stained like the vestiges of snow on winter bracken.

As we talked in the yard, and as this more fully functioning habitat was being put into place, the farmer and his daughter told me they were not happy about the changes. I wondered why. They worried that the tree plantings would spoil the look of the valley. I didn't understand what's not to like about reducing soil run-off and increasing biodiversity, but thinking about it later, I saw the matter differently. If you've lived in a place all your life, if you're *hefted* to it, if you're used to looking at and thinking about the land around you – land you know intimately and whose moods you know well in any kinds of weather and of which you have the kind of intimate knowledge that tells you instinctively where that missing sheep and her lamb might be stuck in the bog or that snowdrift – then you too might feel conflicted about change.

A couple of years later, I heard from the farmers again. They had, they felt, become adapted. The valley was still home – even with the burgeoning abundance of new trees gracing the fellsides; it was, they said, just a different way of looking at what home meant.

If I'm honest, I'm really not good at sudden adaptation. What I like is certainty. I like to know where I'm headed, and I like to know this in advance. Where we're all headed at the moment, I don't much want to look. I avoid looking at that place between the eyes; I'll keep my eyes on the ground, thanks.

That buzzard up there, hovering in the indifferent onslaught of the wind in the way buzzards do, is all aerodynamic bluster as he drops through the air and slides across the valley. His whole life is an arc between certainty and uncertainty. Every day he knows where he's going but never knows exactly what he'll find when he gets there (if there even is a getting there when you're a buzzard). What he needs is to find food. He needs food and a mate, and he needs to deploy that neat buzzard dodge and swipe to avoid that pair of crows who really don't like the fact that he's a buzzard hanging around in what they see as their airspace and theirs alone. The buzzard does not know about the Anthropocene. The buzzard has no idea what's around the corner or over the horizon of the fell. I envy the buzzard all that sliding around on the sky, but I find I am more drawn to knowing about the ground under my feet because without knowing about this, there is no buzzard anyway, and one day, maybe there'll be no us, unless, of course, we all begin to look.

Station 6

I've become interested in looking at what's happening in the ground under my feet because of the Anthropocene and because of my sons, and also because of Sam and Claire. I remember the roots of the grasses at Gowbarrow Hall entwined with all the other living organisms that live inside the soil, which is how they would like to be if only we custodians of the earth would let them. I want us to return to the idea of entanglement. I want to think of humans becoming much more closely entangled with the ground that we often look at from just too far away. What would it take for more of us to become entangled, to bring life back to the ground under our feet? How closely can we look?

In its current iteration, the Lake District World Heritage designation seems to me, and to many of the conservationists and NGOs and individuals I speak with, to be nothing so much as an eyeball floating around the world and failing to see the evidence of climate breakdown and biodiversity loss that's staring the rest of us in the face. I wonder precisely what they are afraid of, these guardians of the countryside who ask us to view the landscape in a single and particularly constrained way. Perhaps they consider the nature of life on Earth as something entirely other, something that exists separately to humans, something that ought fundamentally to be kept at bay.

If the humble, vital worm and the microbial bridge are the ancestors of and the precursors to and future engineers of regeneration, then we need to spend more time looking at what is happening in the earth under our feet. In his agrarian essays, Wendell Berry writes that soil is Christ-like in its passivity and beneficence, that its nature is exemplary; that there is a peaceable quality that emanates from its penetrative energies. Seasons pass over it. Growth rises from it. It is enriched by all that die or enter into it; its fertile nature builds from death into promise.

If we look through the lens of World Heritage and of landscape preservation, is the humble, vital worm transformed into an eco-warrior, a nuisance glueing its life to the doors of the train?

Claire and Sam are engineers both in the hard world of construction and in the much softer, more porous world of the engineering of microbial soils. At Gowbarrow Hall and at Rydal and Scandale, and in the west at Ennerdale and on the Lowther Estate and in Haweswater and many other elsewheres, a quiet, startling emergence has begun. These land managers, these farmers of resurgence and regeneration have all held their nerve. So too the plants themselves – the bird's-eye primrose and the bog asphodel and the humble bramble and the birch – coming out into the light when the time was right. Or rather, when the time is way past being right.

Hill-farming subsidies have maintained and driven the narrative of farming in the uplands and ensured its financial viability. In the UK, as across Europe, we know too well how the CAP (Common Agricultural Payments) system has been responsible for the wholesale sweeping away of nature. In the UK, in 2027, they come to an end. What kinds of landscape do we have in mind for the next phase in the life of this cultural landscape? There exists between now and then a hiatus, a lacuna in which it becomes possible for us to reimagine this landscape that, in actuality, is all of ours.

Scientists say that without dynamic and imminent restructuring, there are only sufficient soils on Earth for sixty harvests. In sixty years, my sons will be elderly men. If they have children, those future generations will be middle-aged, and if they have children, that generation will be roughly the age of my sons now. I want the future lives of those sons and those daughters – my future family – to be as secure as possible from hunger and want. The methods are within our grasp. The changes underway at Gowbarrow are being replicated across increasing numbers of farmed landscapes.

In the United States, the film *Kiss the Ground* shows the incredible potential that rebuilding soils through 'no-till' regenerative methods of farming can and does sequester carbon. They have shown how the Loess plateau, the cradle of Chinese civilisation and agriculture has, in a few short years, been restored from desert to green where wildlife and people once more coexist and where the land once again yields crops and wider sustenance. They show too, how if enough of the world's farming systems convert to regenerative methods, then this would be a significant contributory factor in reversing global warming.

The American landscape photographer Ansel Adams once remained fixed in place in the landscape for an entire day. He was there in the morning when a party of visitors passed by, and he was there in the evening when they returned. He was waiting for the light to fall in the particular way he wanted it to fall for the shot he planned to take. This is a way of noticing and a way of looking. If we choose to preserve a landscape in the Anthropocene without regard for the greater good, then we have pressed the shutter and kept it depressed. Too much light gets in and washes away the image. To preserve a deteriorated landscape is to render it obligately dull, a palimpsest of what it once was. If we look like this, then that act becomes a long, immovable moment that pays no heed to the subtle qualities of shifting light or of the weather or the life that could and should be there, whether we can see it or not. I prefer my landscapes to be animate. To be full of fleeting moments and life and immediacy. I want just enough light to get in.

When we are further along the restorative road, when more of the land has been reimagined and re-engineered into something more alive with possibilities and with pollinators, we will be able to look at the world around us, having recalibrated the material nature of what a cultural landscape is. I think this would be something worth celebrating. I think we would all feel more hefted and that yes, indeed, we would experience more deeply the how and the why of our belonging. We could look at the view and pull the duvet comfortably around our shoulders, knowing that we and our children can sleep a bit more safely in our beds. Knowing that the next storm raging outside is being helped, a bit at least, by all the entangled roots and the creatures in the world around us, some of which are just too small to see, and by the holes that Sam has or hasn't dug to show us how the land holds more water.

I think that William and Beatrice and even Thomas would be with us. And yes, I think they would be smiling.

Ecdysis

It's called ecdysis, the shedding of skin. A young meadow adder sheds its skin many times as the adder outgrows itself again and again. Like this, the adders move on while simultaneously inhabiting the place they need to be. How many times have I wished I could shed my skin, begin again?

In a clearing in a small wood in the Hungarian steppe, Tamàz Pèchy pulls on a pair of thick red gauntlets, leans over the rim of a circular concrete enclosure and, from the tangle of grasses and plants inside, lifts and extends towards me a meadow adder. I have never before looked into the eyes of an adder. For a second or two, I regard the nature of those bronze, vertically elliptical pupils. Look how vital the adder is. Vital and intently focused, as if being lifted out from the shade has flicked a switch, and instantly the adder constructs all that it can or cannot see, all that it can or cannot scent. In Tamàz's practised grip, the adder swims through the air like an eel through water.

Tamàz tells me that a bite from a meadow adder is like a sting by a bee. Still, I have no problem not handling the adder, and anyway, Tamàz doesn't offer. Each adder's head is marked with a unique sequence of sinuous lines or irregular spots – dark inky purples for a male, paler purples for a female. A meadow adder focuses by articulating the lens of its amber eye outwardly or inwardly, like the focus button of a camera. The lens Tamàz looked at meadow adders through showed how, in an unusually short time, the species had passed through a metaphorical door marked 'Edge of Extinction'. Tamàz believes no more than 950 individual adders remain in Hungary.

A meadow adder has no say over those vast incoming corporations from Austria or the Netherlands that prefer their fields devoid of anything but the crop. What adders like is grasses and wildflowers, places to bask in the sun having made a woven basket of their bodies, or to articulate that amber lens backwards and forwards to locate that grasshopper or that small amphibian for the next meal.

In the clearing in the forest are avenues of large netted boxes in which meadow adders are housed and can breed. One day, when they are of sufficient size, they will be released into the surrounding steppe agricultural landscapes of Kiskunság. In the spring, male meadow adders twine themselves around other competing males in a sinuous, competitive dance. And then the victor repeats the dance – with a female adder.

The viper safely deposited back inside the enclosure, Tamàz invites us into the cool of his red-roofed, white-painted house. His daughter Zita makes lemon tea. On the wall adjacent to the table are paintings of Second World War fighter planes – dogfights against orange skies. On the opposite wall, a watercolour of a dipper. Over in the corner, an electric guitar and amp.

Tamàz apologises for his lack of English.

'I don't have …' he says and shakes his head.

'I don't have …' I say in return. We smile warmly.

As we drink tea, Tamàz tells me more about meadow adders. Zita translates. Zita studies at university in the UK; her English is perfect. Tamàz tells me how the traditional habitat of hay meadows have mostly been swept away under the rise of industrial agriculture, that the winters are sometimes not cold enough now, so the adders are unable to enter the state of brumation. (Brumation is the lowering of the reptilian thermostat – the beginning of saving energy by entering the hibernaculum.) Tamàz has configured his own adder hibernaculum by manufacturing clay pipes, each one a metre and a half high, augmented along the length with circular chambers. Once buried deep in the earth, the adders can place their bodies into brumation inside the chambers and slumber the winter away. When Tamàz holds up one of the pipes to show me, as he stands there dressed in a checked shirt and denim jeans and hat, the image that comes to mind is a weird fusion of cowboy and Alice in Wonderland.

Perhaps Hungary's general public is not so keen on the idea of meadow adders. People worry about their children playing outdoors being bitten. But Tamàz and the team take films of adders into schools and communities and host press conferences to build trust and break down the antipathy to adders.

The adders that are sufficiently grown are released. When the adders are released, Tamàz and the team have no idea whether the adders will survive. By now, though, the team has created a panopticon of suitable habitats in the fields that radiate from the adder centre. In these fields, they have restored ditches and field margins and, in so doing, have provided shelter and habitats that support quantities of crickets because this is what meadow adders most like to eat.

It's not rocket science. And it's all achievable because nature is benevolent like that. Give nature a bit of support, and it pays you back tenfold. Put back the field margins and the ditches for water, and the return on investment is the return of an adder that would otherwise no longer be seen either as a threat or an integral part of the dynamic whole. Occasionally a meadow adder will be fitted with a satellite tag that, even allowing for ecdysis, remains in place implanted beneath the abundant layers of the adder's skin. The tags allow Tamàz and the team to work out how long the adders might survive and how far they might travel. Mostly, though, the adders are spared the tags because these veterinary procedures cost money. And anyway, who wants to keep putting all these young adders through that?

In the winter, the adder centre facilitates brumation. In the spring and summer, it offers a safe place for adders to eat and sleep. And on top of this, the centre even provides meadow adder dating opportunities – all that sensuous snaking around. The team keep going because not to keep going is to abandon hope. They look through a lens that moves backwards and forwards in time, and that clarifies the achievements that become possible on the back of challenging the imperative of loss. They are determined to keep moving forward in their own small way and in their own back yard. And by looking through this particular lens, the world of the margins of fields are populated with hope. They do this because they understand that, in the face of the alternative, this – for now – is enough. The team keep going, releasing adders into the world even among all the not knowing of whether they survive or not.

You shed your skin because the old one is holding you back. You create a renewed version of yourself. You keep going. You never stop.

The Bear, the Taxi Driver and the Custard Cream

The pawprint indicated that the bear had been moving uphill ahead of us.

'A female,' Liviu said, then he and Daniel crouched, and Liviu extended his hand, fingers wide, though the bear's footprint was larger still. 'It's very fresh,' he said, then the two rangers stood and looked along the track between the trees as if by doing so they might conjure the bear back out of the forest. 'Maybe she passed only minutes ago.'

My son Callum and I hunkered down to inspect the print. Tiny electron signals began zapping over the back of my neck and scalp. I had entered the forest knowing that inside it was the possibility of animals that could, should we encroach in the wrong way and if they so chose, effortlessly rip us apart.

The indent of the toes made an arc of rough moons of increasing size. Extending from these moons were five elliptical incisions where her claws had sliced through the red earth as she ambled uphill along the logging track. The impress from the inside of the pad was shinier and deeper where the foot carried the greatest weight. The bear's trajectory mirrored that of a logging vehicle that had also recently passed through and, where the two coincided, the animal's weight had obliterated the tyres' chevron tread. Writ large in this muddy section of the path were two very different ways of inhabiting the forest: that of an indigenous animal going about its business in the way that it had since it evolved into being, and the more complicated way of the human. What, I wondered, do chainsaws sound like to a bear or a lynx or a wolf? How did that sound make them behave? The whereabouts of the loggers was manifest to us by the industrial racket of chainsaws somewhere not very far ahead; the whereabouts of bears – who knew?

'She has two cubs,' Liviu said, indicating the less obvious prints of the youngsters, one travelling either side of the female.

We stood and scanned the depths between the trees. I really wanted to see bears, but then the reality of bears came crashing in. Say a bear came close – what then? Would I mess up entirely and set off, running? After all, wasn't that what our instincts told us to do? And what about Callum? In his early twenties, my son was agile enough. But then, what if? He was here because of me. And could bears really climb trees, or would we have time (or would I even have the ability) to climb a tree? What if there weren't any low branches for me to clamber onto? What then? Say I did manage to scale the tree and a bear climbed up after me, would I be capable of kicking it away to protect myself and my son? Like in a cartoon?

I'd noticed a can of bear repellent in the pocket of Liviu's rucksack, and initially, this had been reassuring. Now, though, I began to wonder where the tipping point would be and how close a bear would have to approach before, well, before Liviu might decide to act. And how many seconds would it take him to remove his rucksack, grab the can and take aim? The question I'd sworn all along not to ask came spilling out.

'What happens if we see a bear, and it sees us?'

Liviu looked directly into my eyes.

'We carry on talking quietly and calmly, and they go on their way. The only problem – if you come between a mother and its cubs, you can do nothing,' and Liviu gesticulated, sweeping his arms up towards the branches. 'They run faster than us – and they climb trees.' Cal and I exchanged glances. I was trying hard not to show the whites of my eyes.

Under Ceausescu, Romania's forests were designated as the playgrounds and preserve of the political elite. In the early 2000s and after the gruesome dénouement of the Communist regime, the state restituted areas of forest back to their original owners. But what happened next was that significant numbers of those duly reimbursed landowners entered into the types of opportunities the newly capitalist economy presented: they began to sell. The Romanian government safeguarded the forests through legal protection, though this meant little to the international logging companies who had already crossed the threshold. In the vast and remote Carpathian mountains, legislation was of little consequence. The real predators had not only moved in; they had taken up residence.

In the mid-2000s, animal scientists Barbara and Christoph Promberger visited Romania to monitor Transylvania's wolf populations. Deep inside Piatra Craiului National Park, when crossing from one side of a mountain to the next, they chanced upon a scene of carnage. The mountainside had been reduced to vast acreages of tree stumps strewn with a chaotic mess of brash – the uneconomical wands of small branches and branchlets – everything else hacked out and shipped away by illegal loggers. With the trees gone, there was nothing to ameliorate the flow of rainfall and consequently, the ground had been gouged into ugly channels riven by the weight and speed of rainwater run-off. Nothing animated the scene; with no trees left to nest or perch in, the birds and animals had vanished. The National Park was about to lose control of almost half of its 15,000-hectare estate to timber companies. The belly of the forest was being ripped apart.

The Prombergers decided to fight from the inside. They moved to Romania, bought a farm, ran a guest house, raised a family and set about building conversations to underpin the beginnings of protection. To protect forests in Romania, it is necessary to own the land. To protect the habitats of

bears, wolves and lynx, the acquisition of hunting rights to
the land in question is critical. The protection of the forests,
though, was utterly contingent upon finance, but what were
the chances of raising appropriate funds? In a stroke of
timely good fortune, a Swiss environmental journalist called
Hedwig 'Hedi' Wyss came to stay at the guest house. Hedi
had already founded her own conservation organisation.
She offered the Prombergers financial support to fund the
tagging of wolves and lynx so that accurate numbers of
animals could be determined. Lynx hunting had already
been banned, but evidence was needed to determine
whether the ban had been successful. And crucially, Hedi
knew exactly who else the Prombergers needed to talk to.

Hansjörg Wyss is a Swiss biotechnics multi-billionaire –
and, importantly for the Prombergers, he is Hedi's brother.
Wyss travelled to Romania, chartered a helicopter and flew
with the Prombergers over Piatra Craiului National Park.
For Wyss, the idea of continuance and the measure of success
is found in what he refers to as 'cathedral thinking' – the
fundamental understanding that we, the current generation,
should hand down the environments under our care in the
best possible state of repair. Wyss offered to help – on two
conditions: first, that the area of work should be significantly
increased; secondly, that more investors were brought in.
Phone calls were made. Before long, a succession of wealthy
benefactors who all had the pressing needs of the
environment on their mind were queuing up to invest. In
2009, Foundation Conservation Carpathia was launched.

That first day with the rangers, we'd set out from the
Transylvanian town of Zarnesti, driving in a convoy of
FCC's mucky white Dacia Dusters up into the foothills of
the Fagaras mountains. In the Barsa valley, we parked up at
the side of a small and sparkling river, and the team of six
guys organised themselves into pairs. Cal and I were to walk
with Liviu and Daniel. Checking watches and agreeing on
the rendezvous time, we set off, each pair heading in a

different direction. There was that particular scent of autumn in the air and, as we entered the forest, brambles thick with berries spiralled over the edge of the narrow path.

Liviu had short dark hair, a trim moustache and beard and wore his baseball cap back to front. His English was flawless. Daniel, meanwhile, appeared to understand us when we spoke but talked to us most often through Liviu, and I wondered if he was bemused by this British team of mother and son. We were the first outsiders to spend time in the mountains with the rangers.

After an hour's increasingly steep climb, we emerged from the path's confines into an upland meadow. It was an unexpected place, framed by the shadowy green of fir, hornbeam, oak and beech. The path continued, meandering uphill. There was a newly planted orchard with fruit trees encircled by wooden pickets. The meadow had recently been scythed, though little edges of tenuous grasses had been left behind in which wildflowers grew. Liviu brushed his hand over the white flowers of yarrow as we walked.

'Achillea,' he said, 'for making tea – and for curing infections and illness.'

This was the first evidence of Liviu's generosity in sharing his knowledge. Over the coming days, our ways of seeing the forest were greatly enhanced through his facility in interpreting the places we passed through, along with the things we saw.

To one side of the meadow, someone had built a hayrick, heaping the grass up to two or three metres tall. A couple of thin branches of birch, still in leaf, had been pushed in at either side, making the hayrick strangely human, like a woman in voluminous skirts. Further uphill was a tiny wooden cabin under construction. It had a Dutch barn roof of overlapping clay tiles, a single PVC window frame and a narrow second floor built into the roof space.

At the meadow's highest point, sheltered in the forest's lee, was a small timber dwelling, black with creosote. The back wall was partly sunk into the ground as if it had begun to grow into the earth. The roof was black corrugated metal, its pitch precipitous, and from a wonky red-brick chimney stack, a rusted stovepipe projected at a jaunty angle. Liviu and I peered through the small window but a lace curtain obscured our view. Someone had locked a metal superstructure over the door.

'To keep intruders out?' I asked.

'No,' Liviu said, 'to keep the bears out.'

Cal and Daniel came over, and Cal said: 'What a place,' and I said: 'Like something from a fairy tale.' And indeed it was, although the place also told the more prosaic story of whoever had hefted all the paraphernalia up the mountain – timber, ceramic tiles, food, cooking gear, even the plastic window frame.

As we set off back into the forest, Liviu told us how as a young boy he'd spent most of his holidays in his grandfather's cabin in the mountains.

'One time,' he said, 'in the middle of the night, we heard something outside. I remember looking out through the window and there were bears in the garden, raiding the apple trees. My grandfather said: "You stay here OK? Your mother will kill me if you don't," and he took the only oil lamp outside to scare the bears away. That was all that it took! The bears don't want to be near humans, but they definitely want some of our food!'

It wasn't very much further when we came upon those first bear paw prints in the mud of the logging track. At that point in my journey, the bear prints manifested not only as the possibility of real danger but also as the certainty of that danger's origin. The logging vehicle tracks, meanwhile, I took for granted.

The bear prints made the forest come alive in a way that was entirely new to me. For much of the subsequent days, I carried an almost overwhelming sense not only of coming to terms with the epic scale of the terrain but also an unshakeable sense of having crossed a line in my experience and of there being no going back. The potential for possible encounters with an animal at the apex of the food chain was also the first time I'd ever been faced with the possibility of being prey. Being in the forest, then, was to vacillate between a sense of awe at the nature of the Transylvanian landscape and of feeling extremely small and entirely vulnerable. Nothing in the forest, I began to understand, was wholly straightforward.

The previous morning in FCC's offices in Brasov, I had a meeting with Technical Director Mihai Zotta. Mihai heads a team of sixty, many of whom are rangers like Liviu and Daniel, but there are scientists, a communications team, fundraisers and administrators. The offices had the ambience of a quiet, fully functioning and smoothly operating machine. Mihai set up his laptop and began to project images onto a big screen, the first of densely forested mountains receding into translucence under milky blue light, then an exposed ridge of glittering, castellated pinnacles.

'This is Piatra Craiului,' Mihai said, 'the mountain at the centre of our area of work. The forests here are one of the last great refuges in Europe for brown bears, wolves, lynx and wild boar – large enough to allow natural processes to take place. We know that less than 2 per cent of Europe's surface remains in its original forested state, so these places really matter.'

Next, he showed us aerial photographs of forests marked with red lines indicating the boundaries of Piatra Craiului National Park, then images of white tracks and hairpin bends that scored the landscape like the drawings of burrowing beetles.

'After Communism, these old-growth forests were given conservation status; in reality, this meant little to people in desperately poor rural areas. When you have been poor for so long, when food has been scarce for so long and everything is in short supply, when part of the act of recovery is to hand back the forests to their rightful owners and you have this one chance to obtain a significant amount of cash, no questions asked, of course you want to sell. Most of the repatriated forests were parcels of 50 hectares or less. These are what the illegal logging companies targeted. To the people selling the logging rights, it didn't matter who these companies were or where they were from; their criteria was to sell to the highest bidder.'

And directly in the face of protection, the timber companies began to offer bonuses to remove greater quantities of lumber. For the forests and the animals that live in them, the rate of change and the damage done became catastrophic in a very short time.

Mihai was forthright, sombre:

'None of the logging companies were Romanian; they came in from Western Europe, from Austria. They log out an area and sell the timber to China. In China the timber is processed then shipped back to the West. No one asks where the timber comes from. For the local communities, there are no long-term benefits; when your cash is gone, it's gone. You build a nice house. Then what? The financial gains remain external. As a country, from all of this, Romania gained exactly nothing.'

Mihai was telling me this but in my mind, what I saw were fleets of container ships ferrying tat and furniture and timber across the world. I was caught in an existential loop inside the existential loop of the consequences of illegal logging.

The image on the screen changed – more photos of white roads mining the forests. The white roads give access to places that are too far away from small villages for anyone to notice. Once the roads have been cut in, the hardwood forests of beech and hornbeam are cut out. The blanks left behind are dead zones, though few knew they existed until the FCC came into being. You can find them on Google Earth, resembling tiny white imperfections at first glance.

But zoom in, and they morph into arterial networks plugging the world outside the forest – of modernity and the gaze of speculative extractive industries – into what was previously intact. Not for nothing is the term 'virgin' forest used in such circumstances. And if, like undetected cancer, you don't know something exists, how can you do anything about it? Between 1990 and 2011, 366,000 hectares of Romanian forest were illegally logged. Some of those places were Natura 2000 sites protected under EU law.

'When you cut the forest like this, the large mammals that live there are placed under enormous pressure. They can no longer move freely. This is not what we – or they – want.' Mihai continued in that measured, matter-of-fact way, talking now about the critical role that major forests play in ameliorating climate change. 'You remove the forest – we know what happens. This is nothing new.'

More than 20 per cent of Romania's forests were destroyed in only a handful of years. During the 1990s, many of those logged-out areas were immediately replanted – with spruce. And spruce is a known harbourer of the invasive bark beetle. An image on the screen showed red lines that highlighted areas of spruce sewn into logged-out areas, like poorly done darning. Little, other than bark beetles, lives in industrial forests. Of course, the animals retreated.

'Since we began, we have monitored to make sure that only these industrial areas are logged. Then we go in and replant with indigenous species. It will take some years,' Mihai shrugged, 'but we work steadily. We move forwards. The forest will not recover overnight.'

The scale of the work is staggering; the scale of the vision that underpins it is monumental. Over 200,000 hectares in the Fagaras Mountains are fully protected, undergoing piece-by-piece restoration. Some 700 hectares of forest are now repaired, with more than two million native trees planted.

Recently FCC created an app. If a lorry is suspected of transporting illegally logged hardwoods, an observer enters the registration number into the app, and the technology alerts the police. Surveillance by citizens – yet another way of inhabiting the forest.

'In the longer-term,' Mihai said, 'our aim is to create the largest National Park in the European Union. Once the objectives have been ratified, FCC will hand the park back into the hands of the state – but at a time when the state is better equipped to protect it. We know that in terms of international tourism, Romania has achieved nothing like its potential, and we know there are huge possibilities for ecotourism. Hungary has six and a half times more tourists than we do – even Albania has 70 per cent more. But nowhere else outside Russia has this scale of forest or this amount of endemic wildlife. If we go about managing it correctly, ecotourism can provide economic regeneration. And bring that regeneration to the communities where it really matters.'

When we came across dumps of treacly black bear scat, they were plump-full of berries or sweetcorn or pieces of apple.

'If you're a bear,' Liviu said, 'it's not easy to hide what you've been eating!'

Such massive animals – sustained by something or nothing.

If the scat was fresh, the guys set to. Either Liviu or Daniel identified the exact location with GPS while the other dug into it with a wooden spatula, sealing a small sample inside a plastic bag labelled with the date, time and location.

'This is what we do 365 days a year. Well, OK, not Christmas Day,' Liviu shrugged, 'but apart from that, this is where we work. You can say the forest is our office.'

I liked this idea of the forest as your office. You drive out of town and into the mountains, and you begin. Stuff the computer and air con. But then Liviu continued: 'When we finish in the mountains, it's more work back in the office. We have to enter the day's data onto the system.'

'You don't escape that,' Cal said. 'Too bad.'

Liviu shook his head. 'Every day we co-ordinate our movements, mapping one area at a time. When we complete one area,' he nodded, 'we move on.'

Though it may be tempting to attach romantic ideas to this way of being in the forest, there were also all the prerequisites of any other job. There were targets to meet, government inspections to undergo and a reducing living wage because the country's economy was beginning to tank in the face of the end of EU financial support as the country transitioned into the wider free-market economy. All this, along with the stamina and endurance required and that background hum of risk.

Sometimes Daniel went on ahead. Once, as we caught up, he held out a hand, indicating for us to stop, and turned towards us, finger on lips. We'd all heard it: an indistinct, gruff moan coming from the bottom of a steep escarpment beneath the path. Daniel moved silently through the trees and disappeared over the edge. Cal and I glanced at each other, wondering if this was it; I wasn't sure I was ready to come face to face with a bear. By the time I'd talked myself down, Daniel reappeared, and he was grinning: 'It was only a deer.'

Another time, after Cal and I had walked blithely underneath it, Liviu called us back and indicated a wound high up in the bark of a tree. He reached his arm as high as he could; the bite mark was higher still.

'A big male,' he said. 'I'm glad we weren't around when he passed through.' From a platelet of bark, he extricated a few strands of hair caught as the bear had been scratching an itch. I caught Cal's eye, the forest around us electrically charged. For Liviu and Daniel, collecting the sample was just another part of the job.

Not only was I building a picture of the tensions between destruction and repair, I was also building a picture of Liviu and his own particular way of inhabiting the forest. Knowledge of the forest and the richness found there must have flowed into him under the guidance and familial tuition of his forester grandfather. Once, he stopped to pick a birch bolete – 'Have you seen this?' – and when he broke the fungus apart, a transfiguring, woad-like blue leached from the outer gills through the colourless flesh of the fungus. Translated by Liviu, the forest was beginning to get under my skin; his knowledge and ability to interpret were the oxygen that transformed my understanding, my ability to see.

Overhead, the muffled battering of a black woodpecker. Further in, the neurotic call of a three-toed woodpecker looping across the track ahead of us. Out in the grasslands of an alpine meadow, something black and undoubtedly dead – the tail of a black squirrel.

'And the rest?' Cal asked.

'Eagle,' Liviu replied.

Somewhere, not very far away, a chainsaw revved into life.

Always, just as we drew closer to the roar of chainsaws, the sound retreated into the trees. The loggers were never, it seemed, around the next bend in the path. For all their racket, they were proving more elusive than the bears whose evidence we came across regularly. It was as though the loggers slipped continually into an alternative layer of the forest's consciousness, or as if they were already manifesting as a myth, a symbol of the days before the forest was released back into its own deep silences.

At some point in the hot afternoon, on an exposed slope, there was an area of clear fell – cut some time since judging by the scrub and the young birches already populating the hill. We picked and ate wild raspberries from towering banks of briars, and as we did, Liviu said: 'The foresters have done a good job.' Daniel nodded in agreement. 'They leave the brash like this across the hillside so that the soil is not washed away in the rains. It's OK. All good.' Higher still, a section of logging path had been littered with torn-off branches, everything confettied with pine needles. Liviu scuffed at the debris with his boot.

'There's no need for this,' he said as if the damage to the trees was a personal affront. 'They can drive without harming the forest if they want to. But no, this is what they choose.'

We repair the forest. We take out the industrial conifers, and still we forget that the forest is more than its monetary worth.

By now, the heat was intense. Nothing moved. At the top of another long steep section, we stopped to catch our breath, and for the first time, there were panoramic views of the Carpathians rolling northwards, the more distant peaks masked by haze. Midway, a sequence of summits rubbed out by soft grey clouds. The Carpathians twist like a weather system up from the coast of Bulgaria and the Black Sea, then spiral northwards in an unruly S into Serbia and Romania. And here they were, surging blue and translucent into the distance, like the images we'd seen in Mihai's office. Somewhere beneath us was the road through the Barsa valley and the way back to Zarnesti. In a distant valley, grazing land dropped from the treeline, the fields scattered with the traditional red roofs and white-painted walls of farm buildings. To the north, perhaps a kilometre or so away, the long sparkling ridge of Piatra Craiului broke through the forest, its limestone crest rising and falling into vertical gullies of scree. In the middle distance were the forested flanks of a spur of our mountain, the ridge interrupted by a pale green meadow. Above this, tall old-growth forest. The nearside, meanwhile, was like the image of destruction I imagine had affronted the Prombergers on their seminal walk. But Liviu pointed, and through the binoculars, I made out the scrubby growth of recently planted indigenous trees. The forest broken. The forest repaired.

We navigated on through glades of beech and poplar or indigenous fir. That familiar frisson of autumn occasionally infiltrated the senses. At some point in the afternoon, it became apparent that Daniel was no longer with us. That sense of anxiety began to surface again. Was it, I wondered from my singularly British perspective, safe to go into the forest alone? What if there were bears? Liviu, of course, missed nothing.

'Sometimes, one of us goes ahead, the other moves more slowly. That way, we miss nothing.'

'What happens in the winter?' Cal asked. 'Do you still work in the mountains?'

'No matter the weather,' Liviu said, 'snow, rain, fog, whatever – we work. When we take a sample, we're building our knowledge about individual bears or wolves and lynx, about how far they travel and whether one particular individual might be causing problems around houses – bin raiding, orchard raiding. We can identify the exact animal. Having a picture of all these individual animals, we can intervene with potential problems. Every time we do this,' Liviu indicated a pile of black spoor dumped in the long grass, 'we can say categorically: "No, this particular animal in this particular area is not a problem," or: "Yes, this one seems to be," and if we have to, we relocate it. Mostly, though, the bears just go about their business. Mostly, no one sees them.'

'And how many bears are there?' I asked.

'If you ask the authorities or the hunting organisations, they will tell you there are 6,500 bears in Romania. That the numbers are sustainable, but this justifies their intention to hunt bears. Now, we think only 5,500 or even, it's possible, fewer than 5,000.'

On a narrow path where fir trees pressed increasingly close, Liviu stopped: 'The path is here, but you can't see it.'

He checked our position by GPS. Another way of being in the forest – the satellite offering lines of sight that, on the ground, are just too tricky to see. The entrance to the path was like any of the other millions of gaps between the trees but – with the certainty of space–Earth co-ordinates – Liviu set off with us following, winding our way down the slope through a slalom of firs before the path became evident, continuing between the trunks, the damp ground imprinted with the hoof marks of cattle.

'At different times of year the shepherds drive the cattle through the mountains to different pastures. Some of these tracks go back hundreds of years. We don't really know how old they are.'

The path as genetic memory. The path as cathedral thinking passed down from generation to generation.

As we contoured along the side of the mountain, in an unremarkable patch of churned mud were animal prints. Liviu hunkered down and placed a pencil across the print; the pencil defined a straight line between the outlying digits.

'Wolves,' he said. 'I've come upon them only a few times, even in all these years. They travel incredibly fast and without sound; they can be here, and we would never know.' He nodded towards the forest above us. 'They behave as wolves, right? They could be just on the other side of that bank. Maybe they are watching us now!'

A spool of wildlife documentaries began running through my head: images of wolves loping through dense forest, a wolf scrutinising the side of a valley. I willed a real wolf to appear, to nonchalantly observe us as we looked back at it.

We came out of the forest onto a high meadow, a broad and complicated place where the grasses underfoot had yellowed in the summer heat. The meadow was bounded by isthmuses of indigenous pines, and there, some 800 metres distant, was Daniel, following the wavering green line of the path.

We were walking deeper into Romania, deeper into the limestone heart of the Carpathians. I was beginning to understand how the nature of the forest changed continually as if we were walking through a series of dreaming rooms, each interconnected but separate, their borders fluid, one melting into the next. There were mature beech woods and mixed forests of poplar, beech and hornbeam. There were groves underscored by hawthorn and scrub and areas that were constituted entirely of native fir. There were banks of wild strawberries, the seed heads of wildflowers, and always, distantly, those receding blue mountains.

We took a break on the trunk of a fallen pine. Liviu extracted a brown paper bag from his rucksack and handed each of us a couple of huge purple plums, entirely unsquashed.

'From my grandmother's garden.'

We bit into the fruit, juice dripping into our hands.

'I can tell you a story. I was in the mountains with another colleague. It had snowed and he'd gone far ahead. After some time he sits down to wait for me – like this,' and Liviu indicated our seat on the trunk of the tree. 'He was writing his notes and eating lunch, and then, he sensed something.' Liviu paused. 'When he looked up, he was surrounded by a pack of wolves. Young wolves, in a complete circle around him. This is what young wolves do. They are stupid, right? And they have not yet the experience to stay away, and I think they were interested in his food!'

'What happened?' Cal said.

'So, my colleague thinks: "Shit, what the hell do I do now?" and he looked at the wolves and the wolves looked at him, and when they had looked enough and thought about him enough, they went away. And do you know what he said? He said: "It's true, they didn't make a sound."'

'And what about lynx?' I asked. 'What are the chances?'

Liviu shrugged. 'They can be within sight, and you will never see them.' He pointed into a nearby tree. 'Maybe there is a lynx up there now; we would never know. My grandfather spent his whole life in the forest. Twice only he saw lynx.'

Liviu told another story, one that engaged with a very different way of looking at and thinking about the forest. How one of the rangers once surprised a bunch of loggers illegally cutting down trees at night, and the loggers came at him because, of course, if you are illegally logging, the last thing you want is to be exposed. So the ranger fired a single warning shot into the sky. The ranger was well aware that other rangers attempting to prevent illegal logging in Romania had been beaten, left for dead; the less lucky had been shot and killed. This ranger was fortunate – the loggers scarpered. When he reported the incident to the authorities, the police confiscated his rifle for one and a half years.

'This is how the police respond: they leave a guy vulnerable, unable to defend himself against the real enemy. He knows how to handle the bears well enough. They leave him with bear spray as his only line of defence – and what use is that against a logger packing a rifle?'

After a long and knee-bracing descent, we came out of the forest onto the mountain's lower slopes. It was late afternoon. On the forested hillside opposite, viridian shadows lay deep aslant the trees. Parked on the grass below were the FCC Dusters, with the rest of the team leaning against the cars. One of them shouted: 'What took you so long?'

I turned to look back at the forest. Its dark green seam had already closed around the path as if it had never existed. The border between the forest and us, for now at least, closed.

That night in Mimi's guest house, I tried but failed to sleep, my knees throbbing from the long and difficult descent. Intermittent thumps and rumbles broke in as salvoes of ripened pears dropped from the enormous tree outside my window, each one thundering down the corrugated metal lean-to roof before falling soundlessly to earth. And when the pears were not dropping, the town dogs gave voice to the chill, starry night. On and on they went, in crazy Mexican waves of baying that reverberated around the small town nestled against the mountains. On the edge of sleep and far away, I thought I heard a wolf howl.

Early the next morning, Bogdan Sulică collected Cal and me from Zarnesti. Bogdan is FCC's head ranger for wildlife. We drove south-west, passing through small villages with fruit trees whose branches plunged low under burdensome cargoes of fruit and where the occasional tethered cow grazed next to the driveway and the car. In the bustling tourist town of Bran, tourists climbed the steep path to the house once imagined as Dracula's castle. The Duster climbed higher, passing even deeper into the heart of the Fagaras mountains. At the summit of a dramatic pass, we stopped to check out the view. An elderly woman dressed entirely in black waved at us from the back seat of a car. I thought she was being friendly, then Bogdan pointed out the home-made brandy for sale in recycled Fanta bottles packed into the open boot. Twice we passed the bodies of dead dogs at the side of the road.

We turned off onto narrow gravel roads that mined their way through rounded hillsides, passing small villages of traditional Transylvanian houses, foursquare and turreted, the walls decorated with patterned shingles of flaking, painted wood. But the houses were mostly unoccupied, and everything about them was elegantly rotting away. In a long-abandoned, once-handsome house in a field, the large wood-framed bay window bulged as if the house had taken a huge intake of breath, everything on the point of bursting. Frequently, the most recent evidence of human activity was the hand-painted signs on wooden boards: 'De Vansare' – for sale.

At the entrance to the Dambovitsa valley, we negotiated a narrow ravine where vaulted tracts of rock pressed close on either side and where even Bogdan had to reduce speed. Beyond the ravine, the valley opened out again like a hidden land where high forested mountains piled around alluvial grasslands and meadows.

Further on, among billowing inflorescences of dog daisies, achillea, knapweed, buttercups and common daisies, we stopped to see the work taking place in one of FCC's tree nurseries.

The day was sunny, and there was a warm breeze. A small group of Roma men and women were weeding the ground. The women wore bright headscarves and using small mattocks, they deftly excavated weeds from among countless tiny saplings, bent double and throwing the scoured weeds into plastic buckets. As they worked, the ground was transformed into orderly rows of baby trees and crumbly tilled earth. Beyond were rows of bushy sycamore and beech in full summer leaf, like so many small and boisterous hedges. Bogdan talked with the supervisor, and Cal and I – encumbered by our inability to speak either Romanian or Roma – smiled at the workers, who smiled back at us warmly. The Roma were some of the local communities employed by the project to nurture saplings ready for planting in those damaged or logged-out industrial areas of the forest. Cathedral thinking requires that there are benefits for the communities who live in those places, and here in the valley was the manifestation of that investment in action.

In places, the saplings were so small and lost among the weeds and grass that I'd begun to walk through them – until Bogdan pointed at my feet. Failing to notice the next generation of indigenous trees like that, I felt I had transgressed. Despite this lapse in attention, when it was time to move on, the Roma waved and smiled at us enthusiastically, and we all said our goodbyes in whatever language we had.

Miles further, at the vast Dambovitsa dam, Bogdan stopped the car: 'I heard one of the roads is closed; I'll check.' We got out, and as Bogdan talked with the engineers, Cal and I leaned over the railings to look down at the massive sloping wall of the dam. Thirty metres below, the Dambovitsa river shone distantly as it threaded itself through the valley bottom in a thin and sparkling stream. Bogdan said: 'We can go this way,' pointing at the left-hand dirt track. 'The other road is closed – there's been a rockfall.'

For another hour, we bounced and skidded and rattled on a logging road that deteriorated increasingly by the mile. It was less of a road, more of an endurance test for vehicle and humans. The Duster jolted and jounced around rock-strewn excavations. I braced my knees against the car's interior in an attempt to retain a degree of self-control. In the back seat, Cal held on. The welts of logging lorry tyres gave a false sense of a safer route. Bogdan gripped the wheel and countered continually as the Duster slewed around like a boat on a rough sea. On a sharp bend, the mud gave way to an ambiguous edge with a drop – of how far exactly? – down to the sheet of water.

Where the reservoir finally petered out, we got out of the car and let the bone-shaking journey subside as the infant Dambovitsa River chinked down from the mountains through open glades of pine.

We set out to walk a redundant logging road contouring above the reservoir, the water's surface shining with refracted light. I'd not seen any bear spray in Bogdan's rucksack, and a wave of anxiety surfaced. Like a persistent fly, I swatted it away. Over the water, a migratory gathering of martins swooped and chittered and fed.

'There has been no activity here for a long time – you can see how the path is becoming overgrown.' Frequently, our sightlines were obstructed by invading birch and scrub where the forest had begun to reclaim the track. Here, on fertile ground and in the shelter of an industrial forest, the withdrawal of human interventions had enabled the forest to get on with the job of repairing itself.

'This section is due to be logged soon,' Bogdan said, indicating the plantation's steeply rising ground above the track. 'But look in there – you can see nothing grows. It's a dead place.' He stayed a while, looking at the darkness between the trees, shaking his head. Further in, on high rocky outcrops, we saw tree trunks that had been tossed down the slope but lay snagged and balanced precariously on lips of rock.

'How on earth do they manage to work on such ridiculously steep ground?' I asked. 'It's almost vertical.'

'Well, it's their job,' Bogdan shrugged.

On the opposite shore, a lorry stacked with spruce rumbled slowly back along the mud road. The engine gunned for an eternity. We were 35 kilometres from the nearest house and 55 from the nearest main road. The place should have been a haven of peace. With all this repair and restoration, how long would it be before humans withdrew and the forest was able to get on with the business of being itself unencumbered by industry?

'We should be thankful, I guess,' Bogdan said as the lorry appeared and disappeared between the trees. When we first began to monitor Dambovitsa, there were a hundred logging lorries a day.'

'Do the logging companies pay for the road to be remade?' Cal asked.

'No,' Bogdan laughed, 'they prefer to spend their money on heavier logging machines and bigger lorries.'

A yellow butterfly landed on the pale rock of the path up ahead. I tried to sneak up to take close-up photographs, but the butterfly swithered into the air again and skittered low along the track ahead, flying and resting intermittently on sunlit rocks where only the dark borders of its wings distinguished it from its surroundings. A Camberwell Beauty, the wing edges a band of red so dark they were almost black, and each border embellished with pinpricks of white.

By now we were used to the routine. 'I think this one is from just a few hours ago,' Bogdan said, and we watched as he took samples of bear scat and logged the GPS co-ordinates. 'When people ask me what I do, I tell them it's a shit job.'

We clambered underneath a fallen tree where the young birch and scrub made an almost impermeable barrier. Then we all heard it: the hollow, rustling slap of something making contact with something else. In all that scrub, our sightline was reduced to nothing. Cal and I froze. Here I was – a mother with her son – not knowing what I might do to protect him or myself because we'd never have known if we'd come between a mother and her cubs. After all, the forest was the bear's habitat – and who were we to intrude? Bogdan moved towards the edge, then turned and smiled. 'It was just a wave hitting the shore!' and we carried on, the adrenaline rising and ebbing inside me in transitory tides.

Rounding a bend in the track, a long view opened over the reservoir. The water and the forest that encircled it continued on and on. High up on the mountain's side, nestled behind a craggy outcrop and alone in all that wilderness, was a small house. I took up my binoculars. Of wooden construction, the upper floor cantilevered slightly over the lower. The two sides in our line of sight were almost entirely glazed, the curtains inside drawn. There was a smart red chimney and, on the ground floor, a wooden door.

'This is the new hide,' Bogdan said. 'This is the beginnings of ecotourism for FCC. You want to see bears and wolves; you book the lodge – then you wait for a few days! Hopefully you get lucky.'

A couple of kilometres in, laced with shadows from overhanging branches and a welcome respite from the heat, a stream bed interrupted the sandy track; in the soil at the stream's edges and under the meniscus of water were the perfect prints of a female bear and bear cubs.

'Two cubs, I think,' Bogdan said.

We took off our rucksacks, drank water from our bottles and hunkered down to inspect the prints. But there was more; running lengthwise along the line of the path were the tracks of a pack of wolves, travelling. Then Bogdan handed over a pellet, a matted roll of grey felt, compressed and crammed with mice hair and bones.

'Lynx,' he said, then showed us how the prints of the paws indicated the animal wandering in the soil around the stream bed. In my mind, I picture the lynx on the late summer edge of night, her body barely decipherable from the forest backdrop, dropping her head to sense the scents of others then lapping at the water. I imagine her pausing and lifting her head as if something has snagged her attention, her ears and ear tufts receiving incoming signals. She leaps the stream and disappears between the trees.

On our final evening in Transylvania, we drove south along the main road from Brasov, passing hotels, motels, roadside restaurants, train stations and billboards. At a nondescript pull-in at the side of the road, Cal and I joined a small group of tourists on a trip arranged by the regional forestry service. The head guide instructed us on how to behave in the forest.

'As soon as we are inside, keep your voices right down. Stay close together.'

Towering fir and beech and an impenetrable understorey of fallen trunks, young beech, hazel, grasses and brambles receded on either side of the track. Within minutes, the sound of the road disappeared. I overheard an American woman ask one of the guides that question: *What do we do if a bear comes too close?* And the answer: *You can do nothing.* Slung over his shoulder were a canvas bag, and inside this, a rifle.

We turned on to a narrow path to climb the hillside and crossed a dry stream bed spanned by a wooden footbridge. A few minutes later, perched on the lip of a low escarpment, I saw a wooden hide, but it wasn't the hide that drew my attention. In a clearing on the far side of the building and at the bottom of a long slope were a dozen or more bears. The guides ushered us inside the hide. We pulled chairs close to the open windows taking it all in, counting bears (initially, there were eighteen) and beginning to accommodate ourselves to the nature of the bears.

The feeding station was, of course, the result of human intervention, a place that provided tourists with the authentic Romanian forest experience. And here we were, and there the bears were, and after all our time in the forest not seeing bears, the fact of so many in one place was, well, like being suddenly transported into the land of fairy story; that mix of wonder – and clear and present danger.

In the centre of the clearing was a big male, the guide told us, its back marked with a splash of pale fur. I focused the binoculars on the bear's immense and tubular snout, then on those great bear claws, and remembered the scored marks of the claws in the red earth on that first walk with Liviu. Another bear was sprawled over a horizontal section of tree and was pushing his snout into the trough chiselled into the trunk as a container for the food. Whenever another bear came close, this particular bear was agitated, antsy. Four juveniles emerged from the trees. One of them clambered onto another trunk, the second followed, another reached up with his paws on either side of the trough, and the fourth remained on the ground, hoovering up all the corn the others spilled.

When the bears first emerge from hibernation, the guide said, they're wary of the world outside. Throughout spring and summer, their confidence increases. By September, the bears have become finely attuned to the forestry Land Rover's burr as the rangers bring food into the clearing. I wondered what it must be like to go on ahead – as the female guide had that evening – and to move about the clearing, pouring corn into the troughs chiselled into the trunks of those specially toppled trees, watching for bears from the eyes in the back of your head.

Another male ambled into the clearing, a granddaddy of a bear, the weighty claws swinging inwardly as he shambled forwards, the coat striated with browns and golds and greys. Next, toddling down the bear-worn path into the clearing came three little bears, each marked by a distinctive white furry collar. The cubs set about hoovering up crumbs of corn from the ground. A moment later, the mother bear paced along the path into the clearing and continued walking nervously up and down, swinging her great head from side to side, her massive snout quivering, testing the air, and I couldn't take in how enormous, how *bear-like* she was. Through the binoculars, I saw how she panted as if being in the clearing was the most testing, most vulnerable place for her and her offspring to be, her anxiety a tangible, physical presence. Something resonated about the vulnerability I had experienced regarding my own and my son's safety in the forest, but I had not considered that bears were also a danger to bears. Another bear waded into a deep puddle at the side of the clearing then plonked himself down in the water like a person in a bath, sliding until he was half-lying, half-sitting, most of his bulk submerged. The bear was searching for something. 'This bear loves being in water,' the guide said, and then the bear retrieved the stick he'd deposited last time and proceeded to chew one end before dexterously turning it around and chewing the other. Then the three cubs were roly-polying on their sides down the sandy bank and biting each other's paws and ears. By now, the mother bear appeared to be apoplectic with anxiety and, as she paced up and down, it triggered a memory of teenagers still not home, an hour after they should have been, mobile phones unanswered.

A juvenile bear headed towards the hide, passing only a metre or two below the window so that I was able to look directly into its eyes and, for a small moment only, the bear looked into mine. It was clear the bear knew we were there;

from the bears' point of view, I suppose we were something to be endured if they were to take advantage of that effortless and regular supply of food.

Into the quietest corner of the clearing, a small mother bear entered and at her side a cub, not very old at all. This, the guide said, was a very young, very inexperienced, first-time mother. To give birth to a single cub is a genetic way of allowing young bear mothers to learn the craft of bear motherhood. Each time she twitched or gave out some hidden signal, the cub scarpered up the nearest tree and waited, apprehensively, peering anxiously down at the ground beneath. Moments later, down it came, its unease evident, and scrambled the short distance back to the mother. And so it went, this dance between mother and cub and tree and ground. After a few minutes, the cub shot back up the tree as a much larger female bear ambled over and, with her snout and head, barged the new mother out of the way to pirate a cob of sweetcorn. Of course, the new mother understood her place in the bear scheme of things. She had had enough. With a short, high-pitched whine, the new mother called to her cub. When finally it had clawed its uncertain way down the trunk, stopping and pausing and scrutinising the space beneath, they scarpered away into the trees as if a huge brown male bear was on their tail. And if you're a small inexperienced mother with a tiny cub and that male wants to get rid of the competition and establish his own gene pool, your cub could be collateral damage.

It was a bear-eat-bear world out there, a functioning flow chart between long-established hierarchies and dangerous unpredictability. Nothing was straightforward about the bears' way of being in the forest. And the clearing in the forest was pure bear theatre. The dramatis personae came and went, the lead characters, the bit players and the light relief, all entering and exiting by the tree's proscenium arch as the audience in the hide wondered at this proximity to bears, at the drama and joy of it all.

Walking back to the road, the forest seemed weightier, a less certain place. Later, I read somewhere that some of these bear-feeding stations may also be used by hunters. The drama had its *raison d'être*: ecotourism as one income stream among possible others. I hoped it wasn't true.

There's a story about Ceausescu and the bear. From one of his luxurious, infrequently visited hunting lodges, Ceausescu set out with a bevy of politicians and, if he had them, possibly even a few friends. They hadn't walked far when they saw a bear, and when the bear caught sight of the humans, it didn't run. The party drew closer, then closer still. A huntsman handed the president a rifle. Still the bear did not run. The president stood in front of the bear and took aim. The rest of the party retired behind a wooden blind. Just as Ceausescu was about to fire, the bear reared onto its hind legs. For the president, this was an unexpected feature of bear behaviour and the shot he fired volleyed up into the tree, and the president lost his balance, toppling over backwards into the mud. The huntsmen, however, were well accommodated to the possibilities of hunting with the president. Simultaneously with his, they had fired three shots into the bear, and that was that. Of course, the bear had been caught and drugged and chained to a tree in readiness for the dictator's bullet. The president's party being late to set out, the bear had been kept waiting too long, and the drug had begun to wear off. For Ceausescu, to kill a bear was the ultimate form of masculine achievement; for him, though, danger had never been part of the equation.

We admit ourselves into the forest. We *intrude* into the forest. The forest in the area immediately adjacent to Brasov is busy being gobbled up. The demesne outgrows its old foundations. There are so many blocks of flats; they are the new fortress walls of the twenty-first century. New petrol stations serve the residents of the new blocks of flats. New hotels cater for Transylvania's nascent tourist industry. New schools for all the new children of the families who have

abandoned the old family home in the village in Dambovitsa
for a better life in the city. And who's to say they shouldn't?
To earn good money through the tourist dollar. For the
burgeoning tech industries and the banks and all the other
global businesses that are now building their steel and glass
towers and citadels through the middle of and around the
uncertain edges of Brasov and other cities, including the
capital, Bucharest, the only certainty is expansion.

The bears don't understand expansion. They cannot
because it is not in their genetic memory to understand that
the back gardens and the dustbins inside the new wooden
fences or left outside the gardens and yards and all the other
new perimeters do not now belong to them. The forest is
shrinking. One day here, the next not. But the bears continue,
testing the genetic memory of where the forest should be.
And sometimes, they leave behind evidence in the shape of
those colossal bear paw prints with their rims of small moons
after foraging in those bins over there. Forget apples and
berries; rubbish isn't going out of fashion anytime soon.

Only expansion is inevitable. The old Romania falls away.
The places we saw miles away from main roads. The old
women in colourful dresses and headscarves knitting and
chatting on the steps of brightly painted houses. The spindly-
legged, dainty-hooved donkeys conveying hefty milk churns.
The abandoned homes that even inside their skins of flaking
paint are beautiful still, the lacy curtains engulfed in grime
as the outside begins to get in. The many *De Vansare* signs,
the villages abandoned. The brand-new primary school that
never opened its doors because no young families and no
children remained in the village by the time it was built. The
water-treatment plants guarded by a chained and maniacal
dog inside intruder-proof fencing – and, having seen those
images, I couldn't shake off the idea of the dogs living out
their small, angry lives compared to the expansive if
complicated lives of the wolves and the lynx and the bears
and the wildness and the hugeness of the forests.

On the walk out from the bear hide, I get chatting to one of the rangers. He tells me a story. A taxi driver has a great idea. Tourists call his number, and he collects them from the railway station in Brasov and drives them to the edge of town. From the boot, he retrieves a heavy-duty rubbish sack inside of which is something dreadfully heavy. The taxi driver hefts the bag to the bonnet and, upending the bag, out crashes the carcass of half a sheep. In the car's back seat, the tourists are watching, wondering what exactly is going to happen. The taxi driver ties the carcass onto the bonnet, and inside the car, they all wait. And from the edge of the forest, a bear does come, it comes right up to the car, and that young tourist couple in the back have never seen anything like it in their life. And, of course, the bear clambers onto the bonnet of the taxi to get a good hold of the carcass, and it wrenches it to the ground then retreats back into the shadows between the trees.

Generally, this new method of being an *Ursari*, or bear trainer, is useful because the income comes in. One evening, though, an overly large bear arrives and, in its enthusiasm to get at the meat, it rips the bonnet off the car. This is less good. New tricks are called for.

The taxi driver refines his twenty-first-century bear-baiting-for-tourist skills. Most evenings, a young bear has been visiting the bins in the parking area at the back of the taxi driver's home. The driver begins to offer the bear food. The young bear learns that it's OK to take food from a couple of metres away from a human and, later, from the man's hands. And so it goes, this refining of skills as the bear becomes adapted to this new way of obtaining food. The bear is there in what used to be forest and is now the parking area at the back of the house. Inside the taxi are the driver and a couple of tourists who've been patiently waiting. The taxi driver gets out of the car. He takes a custard cream from his pocket and gestures with the biscuit towards the bear. The bear has been uncertainly entering and exiting the parking area on the edge of the forest and now it approaches the driver. He leans towards the bear – and I don't know what that might be like, being in such mind-boggling proximity to the bear, its forest smell, its bulk and height as it joggles onto its hind legs, the terrible claws that hang by its sides as it steps forward and inclines its head towards the driver – and the driver places the biscuit between his teeth. The young bear peels its lips apart to reveal those black gums and dreadful bear teeth and delicately takes hold of the other end of the custard cream.

The divide between the wild and the human has never been so complicated.

It's easy to imagine how, if the trick goes wrong, there will be only one victim, and it's unlikely that this will be the bear. Neither should we assume that we understand the taxi driver's way of being in the forest, that he does not love bears, that he is nothing but utterly fascinated by their proximity. Or that, if the bears did stop coming because there is insufficient forest remaining for the bears to live at all, he would not mourn the end of the line of a species that once existed in his own back yard. But while the biscuit trick is just another form of theatre, we should not forget that the bears' presence – the *bearness* of bears – will always be a source of possible threat to humans. It is merely in the beasts' nature.

In the uncertain ideological space or lacuna that exists in the aftermath of a dictatorship or strict ideological regime, two things occur. First, there is the imperative to forget, to remove from the communal consciousness the repression and dogma that have, without any sense of choice, had to be endured for however long. Part of what the human psyche needs is to obliterate the trauma. But to fully process what has taken place, we also need to remember, so that mistakes of the past are not repeated. Somewhere in all this need to simultaneously leave behind and move forwards is the acknowledgement of truth. The Greek word for truth,

Alethia, signifies memory, justice and light. *Lethe*, meanwhile, is aligned with oblivion, with hiddenness, silence, darkness, blame. Somewhere among all the uncertainty, the damaged landscapes, the threatened species, the beginnings of a free market, the vacillating economy, the *Ursari* tricks of taxi drivers, the inevitability of expansion, there has to be room for the forest.

In ancient Rome, a clearing in a forest was called a *lucus* – an opening, an eye, space through which light can enter. I think of the images Mihai showed me, of the *lucus* of the broken forest as a particular eye for seeing. The restoration of the forests that follows is a way of paying close attention because the continuance of the other kind of looking is inconceivable. Environmental philosopher, Holmes Rolston III described forests as 'a kind of archetype of the foundations of the world.' that carry upon their dynamic and vulnerable ecosystems the autograph of continuance. When the forest is under threat – whether it be the burning of the Amazon rainforest for beef and soya, the systematic replacement of Indonesia's tropical forests for palm oil, or the small but irreplaceable ancient British woodlands that are collateral damage in the wake of HS2, we invariably also lose the culture that exists within them. Destroy the forest, and there can be no more writing about forests, no more art made about forests. Remove the forest, and we render ourselves smaller and increasingly unexceptional.

How many ways are there to be in the forest? There are the juvenile wolves fascinated by the ranger and his sandwiches, the three little cubs and the bear in the bear bath, and the lynx who right now might be watching that unsuspecting shepherd drive his cattle from one side of the valley to the other. There is also the way of me as a tourist, passing through, gaining an impression. Or Liviu's way of being in the forest – the forest as the office and the front line between protection and exploitation, where life and job and experience and knowledge merge in a continuous act of

looking and listening and needing to make sense and to
understand – the way of seeing the forest as a prerequisite
for the animals for whom the forest is everything. The way
of protecting the forest because the forest breathes with us
and for us. Forests; the lungs of the world. Or the way of the
illegal loggers, though we should not presume that the
Romanian loggers are the ultimate problem; it isn't as simple
as Romania creating the need or feeding the demand, after
all. Think container ships. Think tat. Think of shopping as
the not-so-new religion.

Repairing the forest, then, is a form of mediation between
one way of being and the other and between one set of
possibilities and another. Illegal logging began as a
manifestation of getting lost in the enchantment of
exploitation, a place where it is not possible to understand
the consequences because the wrong kind of light entered
the forest. You fire up the chainsaw, you turn around – and
you are lost.

Thoreau said: 'not till we are completely lost, or turned
round, – for a man needs only to be turned round once
with his eyes shut in this world to be lost, – do we appreciate
the vastness and strangeness of Nature. Not till we are lost,
in other words, not till we have lost the world, do we begin
to find ourselves, and realise where we are and the infinite
extent of our relations.'

In 1990, the poor woodcutter sold his portion of the
forest to put food on the table, or buy medicines, or keep his
family clothed and fed after the long absence of food and
medicines and clothing and warmth. He sells to the highest
bidder. Of course he does; wouldn't we all, if we were in the
same situation? And the loggers cut down the long-grown,
old-growth forests, regardless of the animals that may or may
not want our food but definitely want to be left in the
profound peace of the forest. And the multinationals, for
whom the idea of continuance and the notion of deep
peace in the forest is neither here nor there, pocket the gold

and, in so doing, forget, if they ever really understood, that
the nature – of forests and of human consciousness –
therefore becomes fragmented, that the connection between
the two is severed. The multinationals enter the forest
disinterested in *Alethia*. They do not have climate or the
drying out of the soil or the challenge of replanting into
desiccated earth on their minds. What they see are gold and
silver spun out of beech and pedunculate oak and sessile oak
and downy oak and fir. The West comes pouring in, filling
these new niches, dragging behind it the terrible attendant
machinery of dislocation. In Romania's virgin forests, the
West is a parasite that has fed so persistently it threatened to
destroy the host organism.

On the long, arduous journey out from the Dambovitsa
forests, for the first time, I saw rather than heard a logging
team at work. I shouldn't have asked the question – of
course, I shouldn't.

'Is it OK to get a photo?'

'No,' Bogdan said. 'We work hard to keep the peace. If
you take a photo, they won't appreciate that.'

Since 2014, six forest rangers have been killed in Romania,
and there have been 184 cases of violence against rangers.
Most of these take place outside of the protected zones
established by FCC. In October 2019, another Liviu, Liviu
Pop, was shot and killed with a high-calibre hunting rifle –
for doing his job. He was the second Romanian forest
ranger to be killed in just over a month. Under the idea of
restoration and repair, and with the imperative of defending
the forest, it has become harder to log illegally. (Remember
the illegal logging app?) And while profits from unlawful
logging prove harder to come by, the job of being a
Romanian ranger becomes increasingly perilous. You go to
work in your forest office and bears are not the first thing
on your mind.

When I read of the rangers' deaths in the UK press, and
when I read that one of them is called Liviu, the hairs on the

back of my neck stand on end. I email FCC. Thank god, the team are all fine.

There are, of course, many ways of being in Romania, but wherever you live, if you care to imagine it, cathedral thinking is about creating a world for the ones who come after; who *succeed*. But what does succession mean – whether you live in an ex-Communist block in Bucharest or a new build outside Brasov or a little wooden house adorned by a *De Vansare* sign and flaking paint in a village where you are one of the few left – if your son or your daughter goes to work in the forest one day – and doesn't come back? And the lives of another mother and father disintegrate under the irreparable grief of loss, over which the veil of forgetting simply *cannot* be drawn.

I'm searching on Google Earth for the places that Cal and I travelled with Liviu and Daniel and Bogdan: the tarmac road from Brasov to Zarnesti; the looming stone walls of the Dambovitsa gorge and the dirt road into the valley; the forest where the ground beneath our boots was a sea of wild strawberries, wildflowers and thyme; the path that disappeared only to be found again by GPS where ancient and modern collided among the trees. But the past has closed around me; I can no longer find my way back into the forest.

When I first entered the forest in Romania, I did so with the certainty of how, if it did happen, danger might present itself. For a time at least, I was concerned with our personal safety; after all, where would Cal and I have been without Liviu, Daniel or Bogdan? But that certainty, I later understood, was born entirely out of assumptions, misunderstanding and a lack of experience. I came to understand that to be in the forest is to exist in a continuum of the shaping of thought. One that is about mapping those thoughts onto cultural and economic identity. But the continuum is also about what happens when a space arises in the forest, and what subsequently pours into it are external – I might say *alien* – forces.

Just as in nineteenth-century Germany when the Brothers Grimm saw their task partly at least as the collecting of stories as a way of restoring lost unity to the country, so it is possible to think of the restoration of democracy and the partial unravelling that took place, and that takes place still among that restoration, along with advocacy for the forests and all that inhabit them, as an act of reunification. To restore the forest is to lose the piece of apple from the princess's mouth or to bring the long-dead Beauty back to life. After all, the bear carries with it the heft of a far greater story.

When I recall my time with the rangers, I see how implicitly my ability to understand the forest had been mediated by them. My son and I were only passing through; our experiences were transitory, ephemeral, like the moment at the stream bed where our human prints intersected with the animals' prints. To have more deeply experienced the forest, I would have needed the luxury of time.

A memory of the cabin in the little meadow surfaces. How would it be, I wonder, to be alone in the cabin in the forest? And how would it feel as the tenebrous forest delivered a cargo of bears into the meadow – perhaps a mother and her three little cubs? And if I was alone and had a single oil lamp, would I have gone outside into the darkness to chase the bears away – with light?

Cathedral Thinking

Interference

In the early pre-Covid spring of 2020, I'm making lunch in the kitchen. I look out of the window where a small bunch of starlings are strutting around the ground feeder, stabbing into the food mob-handed as if the Ramones have just dropped in for tea. The starlings are hungry birds, and there are many of them. My concern is mostly for the smaller garden birds, the sparrows, the dunnock, then the blackbirds and thrushes, but still, I recognise the starlings' place in the scheme of things, so the feeder must be refilled to feed the hungry spangled ones along with everyone else.

Our son Callum is visiting for the day. We carry the salad and bread and cheese to the table in the dining room and sit and begin to talk. There are many things on my mind.

On the news this morning, I heard a scientist talking about rising sea levels. The scientist tells me that sea levels could rise by as much as a metre by the end of the century. That's perfectly reasonable, I hear myself say in response. Then he says that for every centimetre of sea-level rise, six million people will be displaced. The water will rise up their beaches and coastlines and spill into their cities, and six million people will begin to travel to higher ground. At the lunch table, I recount the information and, to illustrate the point, I hold my thumb and forefinger apart by one centimetre. What I see in the gap between my finger and thumb is the edge of the blue and yellow ceramic bowl and the topmost layer of carrot and apple salad, along with the edge of my son's glass.

My husband is an optimist. He says there's time left yet. But, I say, what about the lag in the system? I didn't want to get into all this. What I'd planned to do was to pay attention to my son because these days, I have to grab any opportunity to spend time with him and his brother. My husband reminds me that we live at the top of a big hill. I take some comfort from this.

I ask Callum what on earth he makes of the state of the world. The answer he gives – and gives instantly – is not the pessimism and despair I'd anticipated because of how I fear for my children's future on the planet. He says that of course the world is in trouble, that we are all in some way in trouble – some of us much more so than others – but that, nevertheless, it is a fascinating time to be alive. I am in awe of my son's words, and I am deeply humbled. He tells me that part of his fascination lies in how everything is connected: the way news travels; the way corruption is outed – if not always solved; the way the seeding of ideas about change arises out of the very connectedness that some forms of globalisation provide. Without a doubt, the Arab Spring would not have become the Arab Spring without the digital world.

What I take from our conversation is that deeply entangled with that idea of fascination is the possibility of change. To be fascinated, it is necessary to have curiosity and a sense of enquiry. Without my son's fascination with world politics (he is a student of international relations), I would not, for example, understand what I now know about regime change in Brazil (oh god) or how in Chile, Pinochet's constitution was only recently restructured. And we know too well that what occurs in the sphere of politics impacts hugely on what happens in the natural world. Everything is connected.

When we were children, my brother and I sometimes tuned in to the world outside through the radiogram in our sitting room. When I turned the dial, I tuned in to a Babel of languages other than mine: languages spoken in Helsinki, Stockholm, Riga, Budapest, Helvetia, Munich and Marseille.

On the radiogram, each burst of language was divided from the next by white noise. My father called this white noise interference.

When our first TV set arrived, the signals were sometimes unreliable, so my father would climb up into the attic where the TV aerial was and swivel it this way and that to find the most constant source of the broadcast signal and thus bring the picture into focus. Sometimes it was my job to stand in the sitting-room doorway and shout up through the hall and the open hatch of the loft if and when the TV's picture became clearer. Sometimes the picture didn't want to be clarified, and then, even though my dad was never one for giving up, we would revert to the radiogram.

This backwards and forwardsing of signals, this tuning in and out. This not knowing whether looking or listening is best.

Anthrophony is the term given to sounds created by the human-made world. The word itself is derived from the Greek prefix *anthropo*, meaning human, and the suffix *phon*, meaning sound. Anthrophony is me attempting to sing. It's our hand-push lawnmower and Mozart, the jet engine, the container ship and the cruise ship. In this first lockdown, machine-made anthrophony took a break. I think it had become tired of itself – there was too much noise, too much continuous everywhere noise. Because of too many cruise ships cruising the coast of Alaska, entire generations of humpback whales have never experienced a day without the enervating, far-carrying thrum of ships' diesel engines across their entire feeding grounds. Sometimes the whales don't call to each other because too much underwater anthrophony inhibits their ability to communicate. Why bother to talk if you can't hear yourself think? All those cruise ship travellers, travelling to engage with the fascinating nature of the north. I wonder if they understand the nature of the noise that travels in their wake.

Because of the quieting of most of the world's mechanical noise, we humans began to tune in to ways of listening to the world we'd forgotten it was possible to do. For the first time in a long time, we tuned in to what modernity has allowed us to lose. We tuned in to birdsong, to the quiet thrum of birds' wings in flight, to the thrum of the insect world, the thrum of conversations in the back gardens of houses unhindered by the noise of cars on the road outside. The spring lockdown was an interlude, a fracture in the human-made world in which the lack of our mechanical selves gave us back ourselves in an almost unrecognisable form. All those humpback whales calling to each other through the ocean. If I tune in carefully, I think I can hear them. They're singing in that otherworldly, far-reaching way that whales sing because now they can hear themselves think, and they're saying to one another: *Listen – only us again! Only us and those herrings over there! Dinner time!* All that consuming of how the oceans should sound.

Lockdown was a new form of orientation. It orientated us to a state of uncertainty that previously we'd not had to encounter. Under lockdown, we learned that the food supply chain was never under serious, long-term threat – at least, that's what the supermarkets told us. In the face of uncertainty, some of us became hoarders of tinned goods and pasta, of flour and toilet roll, and you couldn't buy a freezer under lockdown because all the freezers had been hoarded by hoarders.

I dug three new beds on our allotment and edged them with planks of oak sawn from fallen timber. (I was not present to hear the machine cut the timber into planks.) The allotment turned into a bathysphere in which I can travel deeper into the sounds and the absences of sounds I'd forgotten existed. In this augmented reality, I plumb the depths, tuning in to children playing in back gardens a few hundred metres away and to the sing-song thrum of conversations. These natural cadences merge with the

cadences of the closer-at-hand: the thrushes, chaffinches and
great tits that are right now belting out their territorial
spring songs from the trees, hedges and bushes of the
allotments. I wonder if the birds have noticed the lack of
machine anthrophony. I wonder if, because of how we have
taken ourselves away, the birds no longer need to belt out
their songs quite so forcefully. I wonder if nature has begun
to relax. To be more at home.

I dig the soil. I straighten my back. If I wanted to, I could
walk down the middle of the road, carrying my spade and
my fork and my seedlings. If I wanted to, I could lie down in
the middle of the road. I could lie down in the middle of
the road and listen to the birds. Had the birds also forgotten
how easy it is to tune in to each other when machine
anthrophony is taken away?

I have a photograph of my brother and I standing on a
bridge over the M6, one of the first sections of this
transportation marvel to open. (This is how exciting our
lives were back then – a day out to see the M6!) My brother
and I lean on the railings and smile at the camera. The
three-lane carriageways stretch into the monochrome
distance and are, of course, mostly devoid of the very thing
they were constructed for: the motor car. But then the
motorway was a cause of fascination – the idea that we
could all travel further and faster and easier (though we all
know how that particular story advanced). Under lockdown,
the anthrophony of motorways is reduced. I talk to a friend
who walks across a bridge over the M6 during her daily
hour of exercise. She sends an image. Here, one photograph
overlaid across the other, hers over mine, fifty years of
exponential traffic growth are more or less instantly
eradicated. My friend said that looking at the motorway like
this was like being in a zombie movie. When I drove across
the country to collect my younger son from university and
experienced this phenomenon firsthand, the volume of
traffic was like those dim and distant days when 'motoring'

was something one did as a form of engagement with the 'countryside'.

Under lockdown, all I can think about is getting away. I'm not constrained by any underlying condition. I don't live in an inner-city high-rise without air con or in an emergency bed and breakfast with three children and another on the way. Still, I'm not satisfied. I relish the absence of mechanical noise, and at the same time, I want nothing more than to get in my car and drive away. If I get in my car and drive, I'm bringing back the noise I'm learning to listen to the absence of, that I'm revelling in the lack of, that vast numbers of us were revelling in. I sneak away. I go to the woods. Over my allotted hour of exercise I may be, but it is spring, and I need to get out there to hear those incoming birds arrive in my favourite woods. I cycle. Sometimes, I admit, I get in my car and drive. I walk in the woods and beside the trees in whose branches the inflorescence of spring is so fulsomely, shockingly green but that, at the same time, prevents me from tuning in visually to the incoming birds. I linger underneath the trees and tune in to the audiosphere of the territories of the chiffchaff (*chiff-chaff, chiff-chaff, chiff-chaff!*) and those of the plaintive descending scale of the willow warbler – a diva dying in a pool of light at the edge of the stage – over and over again. To miss this, for me, is unconscionable; my fascination with the arrival of spring and her train of marvels must be let loose in the woods and along the lanes of my immediate world.

The grip of lockdown begins to reduce. The world of the machines returns. The motorways fill, and I return to the world of the machine. I get in my car and drive. If I walked down the middle of the road now, someone would call the police.

Pan is alive and well and living on the golf course
After lockdown, we get in our car and head north to Scotland. Being with our sons again after months is a form of

abundance. Going away on holiday with them aged twenty-seven and twenty is another. For two days, it rains. Rain is a form of abundance. Is too much rain still abundance?

We get up in the morning, sit down again on the sofas and read for hours, which is mostly not like us when on holiday. Sometimes the rain loosens its drenching grip, and from our various positions we comment on the filamentous clouds evolving and dispersing above the woods beyond the river's alluvial flood-plain. But there's only so much sitting a frustrated walker can do. In the afternoon, I pull on my waterproofs and walk the waterfalls where Rabbie Burns once walked and sat and wrote about waterfalls. I doubt he did so on a day like this because now the rain has resumed its torrential force, and the pages of his notebook would have been pulped in seconds. Despite the Gore-Tex, when I reach the halfway point in the climb beside the falls, I'm as wet as if I'd swum here.

On the second day, we seek shelter in the town's bookshop cafe. On the third day, the sun returns.

From the German for 'environment' or 'surroundings', an *Umwelt* is the biological foundation underpinning the study of communication and signification in the human and non-human world. An *Umgebung*, meanwhile, is an *Umwelt* seen by another and the word *Innenwelt* signifies the mapping of the self onto a world of objects.

When I set out on an evening stroll on our third day, I need to cross the local golf course. You can think of a golf course as a basic organism, and the broad river that divides the golf course and the abandoned golf course on the far side as another more complex organism. As I cross the golf course, I map myself onto the fairway and feel that I don't belong. I'm passing through on my way towards the kind of landscape and objects I'm more familiar with mapping. (As for the golfers, the golf course is an *Umwelt* made up of the tees, fairway, greens, bunkers and what signifies for them as the 'rough'.)

As it interacts with the world around it, an organism creates and reshapes its own *Umwelt*. Because of climate change and the increased incidence of flooding, the land on the far side of the river has assumed a very different kind of *Umwelt* over the past few years. The footbridge from one side to the other is an *Umwelt* that signifies the passage from modernity and control into abandonment. I dare say not all of the golfers are happy about this. To the golfer on the bridge's fairway side, the flood meadows on the far side have become *Umgebung* – a place beyond their ken. I walk the bridge.

What was once fairway has been reimagined by the forces and fuses of nature. The high-summer meadow grasses and wildflowers are intersected by desire lines that have been fashioned by human or non-human animals walking through this reconfigured *Umwelt*. I follow one particular desire line and notice the sinuous stitching of grasses with red campion, sneezewort, with betony, marsh valerian, knotweed, wild angelica and, yes, with Himalayan balsam. Himalayan balsam, the purists say, has no place in Britain. Some golfers might say that none of these has a place. I move on.

This new way of being a fairway makes me smile, like watching the golf course reinterpret itself for the Anthropocene or like encountering Pan on the golf course. Not Pan as devised by religion – that goat-legged, wall-eyed satyr – but Pan as a force of nature that is terribly alive to the world.

On the far side of the river, among the grasses, wildflowers and scrub that is developing in the absence of golf, the landscape has risen above itself. A couple of years into this rising, a pair of beavers arrived. The beavers are busy mapping their own *Umwelt* onto a world of natural objects. That tree, the one by the little footbridge over the narrow beaver-dammed stream that feeds into the big river, has been worked and reworked over months by those made-for-the-job incisors and will, at some point in the not-too-distant future, be felled into the stream. And behind this barrier, the water will slowly rise, and the wetland will expand, and in the wake of the absence of golf, more species will arrive to feed the new ecosystem. Included among these will be pollinators who in turn feed us; they are, after all, our natural life-support services. All this generous, unpaid support for the human world is the result of the beavers' ability to map the effects of damming. The beaver-felled tree is part of the beavers' grand plan to bring back Pan (not, of course, that the beavers understand this to be the case).

When I arrive at the edge of the new wetland and lean forwards, attempting not to map myself too visibly onto the surface of the water, there's a speedy movement to the right of my field of vision. A streak of blue flashes above the water and disappears into the entangled banks of willow around the wetland's watery margins. Kingfisher, a lapis chimera. A daydream of a bird that maps itself onto a world where once there was golf, and now there are fish. The fisher would not be here without beavers and wetlands and food.

The light dims. I move back to the slow-flowing stream. From the narrow wooden footbridge, I peer down and there, swimming like shadows, are the backs of one beaver followed by another. I'd noticed a jumble of branches and sticks where the channel and the big river meet, and I'd taken the pile for debris swept downstream, trapped in a gyre of woody flotsam. The beavers slip underneath the water just ahead of the pile, and I now understand that this is the lodge and, because it is August, no doubt this year's kits are at this moment being woken and washed and provisioned with willow from the wetlands' borders.

I wonder what Pan would think about all this. I believe Pan would settle back in the river with her or his arms behind her or his head or lie among the grasses and wildflowers, luxuriating in this uppity landscape that has shaken off its former manicured self. Pan is here in the beaver dam and in the fisher bird fishing the wetland and in the lines of desire through which animals and humans walk and that allow us to pass along the continuum of bringing reason to a troubled world.

D. H. Lawrence wrote: 'In the days before man got too much separated off from the universe, he was Pan, along with all the rest.'

Honey as reciprocity; honey as capitalism

One evening during the first UK lockdown, I watch a film called *Honeyland*. Set in a remote corner of Macedonia, the narrative explores the life of Hatidze Muratova, a sixty-year-old woman living without electricity, running water or phone in an otherwise unoccupied village, four hours' walk from the nearest road. The opening sequence shows Hatidze manoeuvring along an airy ledge a hundred metres or so above the valley to approach a colony of wild bees. She removes a wedged stone to expose the nest, places her bare hand inside and removes a slab of honeycomb. The honeycomb is encrusted with golden honey – and also with its attendant corpus of bees. The bees do not sting.

Shot using only available light, the scenes filmed inside Hatidze's house are like watching a Velázquez interior come to life – *An Old Woman Cooking Eggs*. When I watch these sequences, I see that the house is also a hive in its own way. Hatidze cares for her octogenarian mother, Nazife, like a worker bee attends the queen. Hatidze is loyal to the role she was ascribed by an accident of birth, but she is also clear this is not the life she would have chosen for herself. As I'm watching, I question what I see as her acquiescence, though who am I to judge the happiness or culture or ways of living of others I have no understanding of?

Frequently, though I'm sure this is incidental, the women dress in the colour of bees: yellow shirts or jumpers over dark skirts or trousers. In one of the tender and poetic exchanges that pass between mother and daughter, Nazife says: 'The spring will come again,' then: 'I have become like a tree.'

A nomadic Muslim family returns to the village each spring to graze their cattle and for the cows to birth their young. Hatidze teaches the father and a son the art of beekeeping. She does so generously, the sharing of skills transcending any thoughts of what might be lost – she thinks only of what might be gained. Hatidze takes a particular interest in one of the family's many boisterous children, a boy of about twelve. The boy and Hatidze sit together as Hatidze extracts honeycomb.

'You take half,' she says to the boy, 'and you let the bees keep half.'

In this way, both humans and bees are provided with food; survival is implicit in the acts of reciprocity, respect and co-operation. You feed the bees, and the bees survive the freezing mountain winters and, when the swarms follow the new queens out into the golden light of spring, more hives are the result. As the bees swarm, Hatidze sings the song her family has sung to the bees for centuries. Had the bee song become imprinted into the bees' genetic code? Had it fostered understanding through successive generations, imprinting upon the bees' collective consciousness that their keepers do not pose a threat, that they are concerned with beekeeping as an act of respect and reciprocity?

In the stone bee enclosure in the village, Hatidze scoops paper-conefuls of bees and pours each boiling scoop out again into a new hive. As they work, neither Hatidze nor the boy is stung.

Hatidze's teaching signifies honey as a form of compassion and respect between both humans and bees. Teaching the boy in this way, his deep sense of engagement is intensely apparent. As for Hatidze, it seems to me that she gazes at the boy as if he is the son she was denied through the accident of her birth.

What the boy's father sees in the bees is a new business opportunity. The market economy invites him to take more, far more, than half of the honey. A visiting tradesman sees the potential and pushes the father to sell the too-much honey for cash. When the father insists that the same son helps with the extraction of honey from his hives, both are stung repeatedly. When I watch the scene unfold on the screen, I feel the hot electric stings in my own hands and arms, my face, my back and my head. The market way of thinking is the Babel that, through the film, allows us to see that the real impact of the free market moves us increasingly away from the idea of plenty. And we know that things will only get worse.

Without food, Hussein's bees attack and kill all of Hatidze's bees. And in this way, honey is signified as capitalism and commodity – all for me and none for you.

In the spring, Hatidze begins again. She visits the wild hive on the mountain, scooping up wild bees and pouring them like treacle inside a wicker bee skep. She wraps the skep in a cloth and secures it to her back. Then she carries the bees along the escarpment and down the side of the mountain.

Out in the world, the film is greeted warmly. The film-makers take Hatidze to film festivals in Switzerland and the United States, where the film, the crew and Hatidze are all celebrated, and this is its own kind of abundance. Emerging from her seventeenth-century life, Hatidze takes to the stage in a flowing golden gown, her long black hair arranged over her shoulders. She takes hold of the microphone and, through an interpreter, answers questions from the audience: *How did the film crew find you?* 'I always knew my story would find its way out into the world.' *Do you still teach beekeeping?* 'Yes, all the time, and the family have learned a great deal and are now beekeeping in the right way.' She takes to the stage at an after-party where she performs Macedonian folk songs. In this way, unquestionably, Hatidze steps into the role of queen bee.

We cannot know what it was like for Hatidze to return to the village and the bees. I follow trails online. I find an interview where she says she can never be lonely because she has the bees for company. I find another in which her nephew has found her a house in his village and where Hatidze calls for a mosque to be built: 'There are forty of us now, but the children don't know the prayers.' These days, when she takes her honey to Skopje to sell, she has to allow extra time for all the conversations and the selfies.

The natural world works hard for us. It asks nothing in return other than to be treated with respect. When I look to the natural world, what I see is a place that is both salve and saviour but suffers because we have not shared with it sufficiently well, and we have not practised the idea of reciprocity. Above all, we have not treated it with respect. When I think of Hatidze and her bees, what I understand is that hope and regeneration, after all, are only facts of life, wherever they are allowed to be. Visiting a school as a guest speaker in Macedonia, Hatidze urges the children: 'Love bees, they keep the world alive. Split everything you have evenly.'

Watching the film, I understood that Hatidze's philosophy is not only applicable to bees and honey but to all natural resources, and how respect and reciprocity are themselves scarce resources at risk of extinction because of our problematic ways of being entangled with the world. I want Hatidze to become a special envoy for the United Nations and the G20 and for her to talk to politicians and business leaders about fascination and about reciprocity. I want her to teach them to sing so that they can tune in to the sounds of singing and bees swarming. So that politicians and lobbyists and climate deniers learn to quieten down. So that the bees in our hives can look after their queens and make honey, and the whales in Alaska can more frequently dine unimpeded by the heavy drone of our engines. So that the bees can tune out the Babel and tune in to the singing. So that the herring can be consumed in the moderate way that whales consume: half for me, half for you.

Restitution

'The great River flows from the mountains to the sea. I am the River, the River is me.' When Sky Father let loose a tear, and the tear fell at the foot of Ruapehu mountain, the river was born. So say the Maori tribes of Whanganui, New Zealand. That statement of being possessed or *inhabited* by the river is an expression of the inseverable connection tribe members feel – have always felt – in relation to their ancestral river. The Whanganui rises among the snowfields of three volcanoes in the centre of the North Island. For more than 700 years, the Whanganui tribes exercised a duty of care for the river and, in return, were provided with clean water, food and spiritual cleansing. The Whanganui is the people's *awa tupua*, the 'river of sacred power'.

When European settlers arrived in the mid-1800s (that word 'settler' – now we know things are not going to go well), the tribes' traditional rights of care for the river were initially weakened and eventually extinguished altogether by the white man's government. Of course, then the waters became polluted and commodified: touted as 'the Rhine of New Zealand', its rapids dynamited to facilitate passage by tourist paddle steamers; its gravels extracted for railway ballast and road metal, harming both the river's bed and its fisheries; the river's mouth repurposed as a drain for a city's effluent.

A feature in *National Geographic* showed how the river's headwaters had been diverted into a different catchment as part of a new and vast hydroelectric scheme, the result of which was to deprive the river's upper stretches of their natural flow. And this act of 'aquatic decapitation' was 'a deep affront to indigenous cultures'.

On 20 March 2017, something remarkable occurred. Accompanied by music and by the spilling of more than a few tears, the New Zealand parliament decreed that the Whanganui River was now recognised in law as a living being. The river was bestowed with 'the rights, powers, duties, and liabilities' of a person, encompassing the physical and the metaphysical. Now, if someone were to abuse or harm the river, the act carries the same legal weight as a physical assault on an individual or tribe. Following the legislative precedent, 2,124 square kilometres of forests, lakes and rivers of Te Urewera, a former national park, were also granted legal personhood. In a third piece of legislation, a mountain called Taranaki was also granted the same rights as a human being.

On the one hand, that these far-seeing acts had to be fought for is a sign of our arrogance, that we cannot be trusted with the care of the world we are part of. On the other hand, these exceptional examples of advocacy are sourced from a philosophy of giving rather than taking away. They underscore the notion of positive change and facilitate a return to a way of seeing that is humble and generous, and affirmatory.

My son tells me that, even with the dominance of exceptionally right-wing governments and however hopeless the situation may appear to be, history tells us that the status quo is never permanent, that with hope (for how else is it possible to live?) before too much longer the situation will change. And Trump has gone, so now I know that my son was right all along.

In New Zealand, Jacinda Ardern's premiership is an example of this. The granting of legal rights of protection to rivers, mountains and forests is another. Closer to home, in Deeping Fen in Lincolnshire, farmer Nicholas Watts puts back the ditches and field margins around the edges of fields that were silent before he took over the farm. From historical records, he noted the once-common farmland bird species that had vanished with the industrialisation of farming. Watts leaves uncultivated strips of land – over 30 kilometres at the last count – to provide corridors of connectivity that teem with teasel and poppies, with vetch and clover, dog daisies, knapweed and bugloss. And the barn owls return because now there are voles in the field margins and amphibians and insects in the ditches. And the farmland birds return – the corn buntings and tree sparrows and skylarks – because now there is food for all of us on the farm.

At the International Union for the Conservation of Nature and Natural Resources (IUCN) in 1968, the Senegalese forester and conservationist Baba Dioum said: 'In the end we will conserve only what we love, we will love only what we understand, and we will understand only what we are taught.' Political systems and formal education are failing our children's futures. They have failed spectacularly to understand that becoming entangled with joy and awe in the natural world is the simple transformation in seeing that will carry a quiet revolution rustling in its wake. Being entangled is the means of protection for the future of the planet, for our children and for theirs. We need the ability to be deeply humbled by a life-support system that gives and continues to give, that does not stop and asks nothing whatsoever in return other than to be treated with respect. Hearts and minds – we cannot save what we don't love.

We humans have made a rubbish job of being custodians of the planet. Stock has been taken on our tenure, and we have been found badly wanting. If this custodianship were a place of employment, we'd all be out on our ears, P45s stuffed in back pockets. Therefore, I want us to dig deeply into that idea of reciprocity. I want pollinators – the birds and bees and animals too – to be made citizens because we have proven that we are incapable of looking after them just as they are. I want all our towns to be Curridabat, the city that gave pollinators, birds and animals equal legal status to citizens. I want to green the fellsides with scrub and with trees, and I want us to love bees and understand that sharing is a prerogative rather than something for birthdays and holidays. I want what philosopher Bruno Latour calls a 'Parliament of Things' in which people are the advocates speaking on behalf of the pollinators and animals that are unable to speak for themselves. I want us to want to see more.

C. S. Lewis wrote that joy is a signpost to those lost in the woods, pointing the way towards the future. He was writing here about faith, but spiritual faith is not for me other than the innately numinous faith and deep sense of joy I find in the fields and forests and wetlands. What else, I ask myself, can I believe in but a natural world that is my fundamental life-support system?

Zugunruhe

The word *Zugunruhe* – from the German *Zug* for move or migration and *Unruhe* for anxiety and restlessness – is a behaviour seen in migratory animals, especially in birds, during the lead-up to and through the migratory season. Scientists have observed this behaviour under lab conditions where caged wild birds displayed anxiety and restlessness and were continually observed to orientate themselves to the direction they would migrate towards if only they could. We humans also experience a kind of *Zugunruhe*. I'm sure it was at least partly *Zugunruhe* that was behind my longing to get away during the first lockdown. After all, what on earth was there to get away from, what with the quieting of the machines and the succession of lengthening sunny days and the opportunity to tune in to that ethereal season of birdsong?

Again in lockdown, I watch the film *I Am Greta* about Greta Thunberg, and I feel nauseous not merely because of the journey she made across the Atlantic on a yacht that one correspondent described as a steel drum attached to a

gigantic sail. I think of her on those wretched days, the hull
thumping onto each successive wave – because Thunberg was
not prepared to fly and because she had the guts to take that
long, drawn-out alternative (unlike the world leaders and the
NGOs and the abundant teams of attending staff) and because
she had the courage to endure it. At the United Nations conference, Thunberg tells the world's leaders – again –. that they
are failing us. Thunberg says that 71 per cent of global CO_2
emissions are generated by just one hundred companies. She
says that G20 nations produce 80 per cent of all CO_2 emissions
and that the world's poorest countries produce 0.05 per cent.
Thunberg says that 'people are suffering. People are dying, yet
all you can talk about are fairy tales about eternal economic
growth.' She says: 'The eyes of all future generations are
upon you. The world is waking up and change is coming –
whether you like it or not.'

Fairy tales of eternal economic growth. More than half
for me, not much left for you. The world is fascinated by
Greta Thunberg. Where did she come from? Another planet?
But there is no Planet B. In *I am Greta*, when I hear those
Australian extremist right-wing politicians describe her
during broadcasts in words that are jammed with bile and
with anger and hate, I understand that these are the voices
of interference, the white noise of a capitalist machine
hardwired to evade reciprocity and respect. My son tells me
that at least the digital age has allowed us to tune in to and
take note of the anger and hate and understand how it feeds
the extremes of a particular mode of living. I am fascinated
to know if these people have children.

Wendell Berry wrote that there is no need to plan a
world for the future if we take care of it in the present. That
should we choose to do this, the future will have received
full justice from us. The same pressing needs exist that have
always existed – to take care of and teach our children to
also take care of the world around us; that this is our only
legitimate hope. I understand how Berry's thoughts here

align with Hansjörg Wyss's notion of cathedral thinking, of
taking care of our planet sufficiently well that we pass it
down in better condition than the condition the current
generation inhabits. I wonder if we can learn to love the
natural world sufficiently well to allow this to occur.

It is a fascinating time to be alive. I know this because
my son said so, and he, after all, is the inheritor of the
future. He is part of the generation for whom *our* cathedral
thinking is everything. Without this, I just don't know
what his future will be. But my son reminds me again that
things change, that not everything stays the same, and from
this thought, I take a deep breath and push further into the
back of my mind the possibility of not changing, the life
raft horribly out of reach. He tells me that the path towards
a more sustainable future is (albeit not quickly enough)
being taken by an increasing number of companies,
governments and farmers, and this is some comfort to me;
from this, I take some hope. I allow myself to tune out the
interference because to live in hope is really the only way
I know how to live.

Can we hold on to the idea of fascination as a way to
rebuild our relationship with the world? Can we think of
fascination as a means of tuning out the interference, of
tuning out too many distractions? So that Hatidze can get
on with singing to the bees, and the bees can get on with
whatever it is that bees get on with. So that the too many
starlings in my garden can carry on being the punk rockers
of the avian world. So that the whales in Alaska can sing
unimpeded and the world my sons inherit is a place in
which to live fully; to be continually fascinated by.

At a press conference, a journalist asks the directors of
Honeyland whether Hatidze still keeps bees. The directors
answer: 'The bees are her children; she will not abandon
them.' Indeed, how could any of us abandon our children?

There is, I believe, a growing feeling of *Zugunruhe* in the
world today. Of more and more of us coming home to our

home in the natural world. The more of us that do this – the more of us standing at the living-room door, shouting up into the attic that the picture just became clearer – the more effect we have in the world. We need to tune out the white noise. We need to exchange it for hope and for actions. We need to feel hope, to be humbled, to feel awe and joy. We need for love and fascination to be the portals for getting away from ourselves more often. To be fascinated by what happens when we quieten down. To swivel the television aerial of change. To tune in and to tune out. To listen to the conversational babble outside all the houses in Marseille and Manchester, on the allotments and in the gardens and parks of Edinburgh and Budapest, in the streets and offices in Helvetia, Helsinki and Hilversum. In the hills and along the rivers and on the mountains who are anyway, all persons, in New Zealand and in Costa Rica. In Riga and Vienna and in the forests of Transylvania. And not forgetting in the Shetland Islands, where in her poem 'Flightpaths' the poet Roseanne Watt writes:

> these are the waiting days
> at the seam of springtime
> an ache growing in the hollows of our bones
> which only sky can ease
> the day is nearly here when the balance of light shall tip
> and the wind will bring that northward call
> these paths of air and light shall take us home

Incoming

There's a big sky going on, what with all those various clouds building themselves into prodigious swags and the way showers are blowing in across the surface of the bay. When I look down into what remains of the previous tide, the sky is restless underneath my feet, hurrying somewhere.

We're a couple of hundred metres out on the sands. From here, the Moray coast is reduced to a thin wedge of pine forest beyond the dunes with here and there a house, an occasional farm building, a church spire. Beyond this, the long slopes of distant hills. Back where we parked the cars, Findhorn village lies hugger-mugger, the shellfish business mostly gone, the fishermen's cottages repurposed for blow-ins from the south. I'm a blow-in myself – here to meet birding pals for a few days 'vis-mig' (birders' slang for 'visible migration') but, what with that bitter wind coming in off the sea and the way the scope shakes dementedly, this isn't exactly how I'd pictured it.

Findhorn Bay is frequently the first landfall of geese incoming from their autumn migration south from Svalbard, Greenland or Iceland, given the plentiful feedstuffs on the marshes and surrounding fields. Up to 50,000 geese have been counted here, resting and gaining strength before setting out to their wintering grounds further south. What is it that makes a skein of geese in the sky so much more exhilarating than a whole bunch of geese in a field? In the interstices between their feathers, they carry motes of the Arctic with them – this and the romance of land, sea and sky of the north. I think that, somewhere deep in our psyches, their arrival calls to us. It's a way of finding something positive, exhilarating even, in winter's approach.

We'd been tipped off that somewhere at the head of the bay, thousands of geese had already gathered. I look through the scope, but all I can make out is a line of thirty or forty pinkfoots on the far side of the River Findhorn. There is also the white head of a herring gull, the rest of its body hidden below a channel in the sands – a sore thumb among so many grey-brown bodies. Through the scope, I spot black-tailed and bar-tailed godwits, lapwings, ringed plovers and curlews whose calls cut through the latest squall. The wind's way too strong; the scope shakes, and I tell myself – again: *For heaven's sake, why don't you invest in a decent tripod!* There's a constant dance: gloves on to keep my hands from freezing, gloves off so that I can wipe the wind-tears from my eyes or alter the focus wheel snug under the scope's protective jacket. The jacket itself is a survivor.

'You can have this,' the man in the shop said of the jacket when I bought the scope. 'It's one of the few bits I managed to salvage after Storm Desmond.' Most of his stock of optics was ruined when floodwater spilling out of the River Lune in Lancaster reached even his highest shelves. All those water-logged, contaminated binoculars and scopes, all that wasted potential for the paying of close attention. I wasn't sure if the story the jacket carried with it was a good thing or not, but here we were, still together through days of good and bad birding, sun, rain, wind, whatever.

A mighty shower hurls itself upon us; it is like having buckets of water chucked from close range. I've all the right gear, so keeping dry isn't the problem. It's this enervating cold. I pull the hood of my jacket tighter. I take up the bins, hoping I'll see more clearly, but the lenses fog instantly. So it goes: all these different ways of looking – or of being hindered in the ability to look.

Somewhere amid a flock of several hundred golden plovers, there's another blow-in: a Pacific golden plover. The

Pacific plover has no business being here in the north of Scotland. We train the glasses and the scopes, searching for a bird from Siberia or Alaska blown off course on its migration south to China or New Zealand. And here it was, testing our abilities to distinguish. This is what happens when you're blown off course: you seek out others of your kind – or as near as. But what are the chances among so many almost identical birds?

Gloves on ... gloves off ... wipe the lens ... look through the lens ... fiddle with the focus wheel. I try to pick out the Pacific plover. My friend has a picture on his phone of this very Pacific plover in the flock of golden plovers. Telling them apart is nigh-on impossible; the incomer is slighter, a more diminutive version of the same bird, the plumage almost identical but paler by a degree: that same pert bill, the dark, glassy eye.

If the plovers are calling their sad, anticipatory calls, their voices are lost to us as the wind funnels in over the sand spit at the entrance to the bay. We watch the birds needling the sands, exploiting the topmost layers of interstitial life – so many lengths and different kinds of bill, so much adaptation from deep ecological time. A godwit plunges its bill into the silt and walks in a circle around it – a road mender with a pneumatic drill. From time to time, the plovers lift, agitated by the frayed edge of the tide, incoming. Sometimes, when the plovers lift into the air but are yet to become orientated together, some individuals shift into what seems an alternative layer of consciousness as here and there they turn against the majority, and their bright-white breasts catch low sunlight, neurons firing among all that grey weather. When the birds eventually coalesce, they shift downwind of the tide and settle down to the sands just a matter of metres upwind.

A couple of big guys join us, all dressed up in camo fatigues, and God knows how many layers underneath – the Michelin men of the birding world, complete with giant scopes (I take note of the weighty tripods) and cameras sporting massive lenses hefted on shoulders.

'Is it still here?' one asks as if we should comprehend their meaning immediately.

'As far as we know,' my friend answers. 'Not that we've got it yet.'

I like this 'got it' – the idea that by seeing we come into possession.

'Bloody cold,' one of the newcomers says. My friend orientates them to the flock of plovers.

When I look through the scope again, there's a movement among the plovers, each of them dropping and lifting slightly in sequence like a Mexican wave at a football match or as if they are attempting to make themselves smaller. We wonder if a marsh harrier or a peregrine has entered their visual field. If it has, we don't see it. Suddenly, the sun exploits a fissure in all that grey cloud, flooding the wet sands with light. In this abrupt illumination, the backs of the plovers swirl iridescent gold, the glint and gleam flickering across the distance between us, demonstrating their name *Pluvialis apricaria* from the Latin words *pluvia* ('to rain') and *apricaria* ('to bask in the sun'). In the grey and rain and cold of a Scottish autumn, the plovers bask in the golden glow of their own plumage.

I didn't get those big skeins of geese coming in overhead. So it goes; you can't demand nature does what you want. I give in. I'm soft like that. I give in to the freezing wind and walk back over the sands, piped along by a lone curlew. Another birder is heading out from the car park, and as we draw close to each other, he says: 'Has it gone?'

'Not as far as I know,' I say. 'Not that I've seen it.'

I reach the car and begin to peel off layers and untie my boot laces. From overhead, a faint call catches on the wind. That particular querulous call of geese, travelling. I look up to a skein travelling very fast and very high: pinkfoots.

I watch them, perhaps a couple of hundred birds moving on the wind as if late for a party.

A few days later I'm back home and taking out the rubbish. It's dark, and as I go through the side gate, there's that same high call catching on the wind like a fissure in the seam between this world and another. Pinkfoots. I look up, and of course, I can't see them, but I hear them and recognise their flight path is south towards Morecambe Bay. Then the sun-reflecting body of a satellite cuts across their trajectory.

I think about this, about how as a species, we have shown ourselves capable of the most astonishing ways of being in the world. You build a satellite and project it into space and there we are – living in the certainty that, for the rest of its working life, the satellite will continue to pass over the surface of the Earth on a trajectory mapped out in advance and that exists in nothing other than certainty. This, against the wavering nature of geese – the imperative to travel and to migrate because, in their genetic memory, that is how they are conditioned to behave. Even so, among all this, you carry a deluge of uncertainty in your wake.

A day or so later, I'm heading back down the fell towards home, and there it is again. A skein of pinkfoots flying south, but then they veer towards the east, and I wonder where on earth they might be going. I lose them as the path dives into a tunnel of low-growing trees. They're there again when I emerge, and I watch them begin to shift direction, first the lead bird and the rest in that characteristic trailing, ragged V. Now I get it. The geese have reorientated themselves, and this new direction will take them south to the bay or further to the salt marshes of the Lancashire coast, which is exactly the kind of place to be for a pinkfoot goose.

So there we are – you realise you're headed in the wrong direction, you recalibrate the trajectory. Blown off course you may be, but like the lone plover, you seek out the nearest thing you can find to your tribe because to stick together is better than acting alone. You understand that to continue in the wrong direction is to take yourself somewhere you really don't want to go. And you change your bearings. Of course you do. Wouldn't we all, given the knowledge, the choice and the ability to act?

Acknowledgements

A great many people assisted in the process of the writing of this book. First and foremost, I am indebted to the Faculty of Arts and Social Sciences at Lancaster University, whose 'Literature, Landscape and Environment' scholarship enabled me to undertake the journey. Secondly, to Professors Paul Farley and Jenn Ashworth in the Department of English and Creative Writing, without whom I would no doubt still be lost in the forest. The idea for the book followed a conversation with my good friend Astrid Hardwick. Through family connections to the forestry industry in Germany, Astrid had early knowledge of wolves travelling back into countries across Europe from where they had long been absent through changes to legislation. To Astrid and those pioneer wolves, I owe a great deal. To my sister-in-law Cathy Proudlove for introducing me to the work of artist Mary Newcomb. I owe a debt of gratitude to Mark Cocker for introducing me to Extremadura and the Prespa region of Northern Greece and to the many firm friends found in those fields.

In Extremadura, I'm grateful to Martin and Claudia Kelsey of Birding Extremadura (RIP lovely dog Moro) and to Christina Gtz. To Karen Izod for inspired company and conversation on our travels. I am deeply indebted to my friend Szabolcs (Szabi) Kókay for setting up research visits and for putting time aside to share the journeys in Hungary with me. (Szabi's wonderful paintings of wildlife can be seen at https://kokay.hu/en/paintings/) I'm grateful to Lóránt Miklós of Kiskunság National Park's great bustard project, to Imre Fatér of the Pannon Eagle project, to Tamàs and Zita Pèchy of the Hungarian Meadow Viper Centre, Tibor Juhász of the Eagle Centre, Jászberény, the Bird Hospital Foundation, Hortobágy and our genial hosts Judit and

Albert at Hajdu Lovasudvar. In Romania, I am deeply
indebted to the team at Foundation Conservation Carpathia,
to Angela Boghiu and Georgiana Andreea Andrei for
arranging our schedule and accommodation. To Mihai Zotta
and rangers Bogdan Sulică, Daniel Bîrloiu and in particular
to Liviu Ungureanu for making the forest come so alive to
Callum and me, and to Mimi and Gheorghiu Surdu, for
such a warm Transylvanian welcome. In the Netherlands I
am grateful to Yvonne Kemp of Kennemerland National
Park Bison Reintroduction project, Ellen Van Norren
and Glenn Lelieveld of the Dutch Mammal Society
(Zoogdiervereniging) and wolf volunteers Carolien Koldyk
and Jaap van Leeuwen. To all the other wolf volunteers for
making me so welcome; oh, how I long to be a wolf
volunteer! To Peter Venema of the Province of Drenthe. In
Perthshire to Polly Pullar, Linda Cracknell, Duncan Pepper,
Paul and Louise Ramsay, Martin Kennedy and special thanks
to James Nairne for introducing me to the tribulations of
beavers in Scotland and for providing such excellent
hospitality. In the Cairngorms, to Tors Hamilton of RSPB
and Cairngorms Connect for such illuminating and
thoughtful conversations on changing land use and landscape
restoration. Thanks to Hamish Napier for permission to
quote from his album notes from *The Woods* suite. Hamish's
music can be found at www.hamishnapier.com. To wildlife
guide Simon Pawsey and the team at the Grant Arms Hotel,
Grantown on Spey. In the Lake District to Anne and Richard
Lloyd and Claire and Sam Beaumont at Gowbarrow Hall
Farm and to Jim Bliss at Lowther Estates. To Gill Mason for
conversations on language acquisition through nature. To
Carry Akroyd for permission to quote from her work on
John Clare. To Julian Hoffman for details on Prespa. To
Ysbrand Brouwers of Artists for Nature Foundation and
Manuela Seifert. To Mike Toms at BTO and Kit Jewitt for
the excellent fundraising publication *Red Sixty Seven*, which
commission set me off on the quest to find capercaillie. To

Nicholas Watts at Vine House Farm. To Peter Corkhill for help with plant ID. To my dear friends Katherine and Nick Gray for conversations about hope in dark times and again to Katherine for accompanying me on my first visit to the Netherlands. I'm indebted to my colleague at Lancaster University, Professor Charlie Gere, for permission to quote from his book *I Hate the Lake District*, and for our ongoing conversations, together with Professor Ian Convery at the University of Cumbria, and Simon Stainer and Karen Slater of Natural England, on the precedents for urgent landscape change and biodiversity restoration in the Lake District. To Roseanne Watt for permission to reproduce her poem 'flightpaths.' To my agent Jenny Brown and Julie Bailey, my editor at Bloomsbury, and the rest of the team; your combined faith in the book is sincerely appreciated. No doubt there are omissions to these acknowledgements – for my lack of attention, apologies. Last but not least, to Steve Leach for his unstinting support and for the reading of terrible first drafts. Finally, to our sons, Callum and Fergus, may your way in the world be ever-fascinating, ever-fulfilled.

Permissions

Bloomsbury Publishing would like to thank the following for providing permission to reproduce copyright material:

The epigraph from *You Can't Be Neutral on a Moving Train* by Howard Zinn on page 9 is reprinted by kind permission of Beacon Press, Boston.

The quotation from Caspar Henderson on page 17 is reproduced by kind permission of the Society of Authors.

The extract on page 19 from *John Clare by Himself*, eds. Eric Robinson and David Powell (Carcanet Press, Manchester, 2002) is reproduced by kind permission of Roger Rowe and Curtis Brown.

The extract from *Forests: The Shadow of Civilization* by Robert Pogue Harrison (new edition, 1993) on page 28 is reproduced by kind permission of the University of Chicago Press.

I am grateful to Bruno Latour for permission to reproduce the quote on page 28.

The quotation by Derek Gow on pages 148–149 is reproduced by kind permission of the author from *I Must Tell You Something of the Beaver* published on Mark Avery's blog.

The quotation from *Braiding Sweetgrass* by Robin Wall Kimmerer on page 169 is reproduced by kind permission of Milkweed Editions.

The quotations on pages 177 and 178 are from Georgios Catsadorakis' book *Prespa: A Story for Man and Nature* and are reproduced by kind permission of publishers The Society for the Preservation of Prespa.

While every effort has been made to trace and acknowledge all copyright holders, we would like to apologise for any errors or omissions and invite readers to inform us so that corrections can be made in any future editions of this book.

Select Bibliography

Akroyd, Carry, *'natures powers & spells': Landscape Change, John Clare and Me*, Langford Press, Exeter, 2009

Barthes, Roland, *Camera Lucida*, Vintage, London, 2000

Bate, Jonathan, *The Song of the Earth*, Picador, London, 2001

Berger, John, *Ways of Seeing*, Penguin Books, London, 2008

Berry, Wendell, *The Art of the Commonplace: The Agrarian Essays of Wendell Berry*, Counterpoint Press, Berkeley, California, 2002

Bloemink, Barbara and Beltrá, Daniel, *Spill*, GOST Books, London, 2013

Catsadorakis, Giorgos, *Prespa: A Story for Man and Nature*, Society for the Protection of Prespa, Prespa, Greece, 1999

D'Agata, John, *About a Mountain*, W.W. Norton & Company Ltd., London, 2011

D'Agata, John, *The Lost Origins of the Essay*, Gray Wolf Press, Minneapolis, Minnesota, 2009

Franzen, Jonathan, *The End of the End of the Earth*, 4th Estate, HarperCollins, London, 2018

Gere, Charlie, *I Hate the Lake District*, Goldsmiths Press, London, 2019

Ghosh, Amitav, *The Great Derangement: Climate Change and the Unthinkable*, University of Chicago Press, Chicago, Illinois, 2016

Harrison, Robert Pogue, *Forests: The Shadow of Civilization*, University of Chicago Press, Chicago, Illinois, 1993

Hyde, Lewis, *The Gift: How the Creative Spirit Transforms the World*, Canongate Books, Edinburgh, 2012

Hyde, Lewis, *A Primer for Forgetting: Getting Past the Past*, Canongate Books, Edinburgh, 2019

Kimmerer, Robin Wall, *Braiding Sweetgrass: Indigenous Wisdom, Scientific Knowledge, and the Teachings of Plants*, Milkweed Editions, Minneapolis, Minnesota, 2020

Kolbert, Elizabeth, *Field Notes from a Catastrophe: Man, Nature, and Climate Change*, Bloomsbury Publishing, London, 2007

Lawrence, D. H., Pan in America, *Southwest Review*, Vol. 11, No. 2, January 1926, pp 102–115, Southern Methodist University, Dallas, Texas, 1926

Lewis, C. S., *Surprised by Joy: The Shape of My Early Life*, HarperCollins, London, 2012

Magnason, Andri Snær, *On time and Water*, translated by Lytton Smith, Serpent's Tail, Profile Books, London, 2020

Maitland, Sarah, *Gossip from the Forest: The Tangled Roots of Our Forests and Fairytales*, Granta, London, 2012

McNeil, Jean, *The Ice Diaries: An Antarctic Memoir*, ECW Press, Toronto, Ontario, 2016

Morton, Timothy, *Hyperobjects: Philosophy and Ecology after the End of the World* Illustrated edition, University of Minnesota Press, Minneapolis, Minnesota, 2013

Nelson, Maggie, *Bluets*, Jonathan Cape, Penguin Books, London, 2009

Odell, Jenny, *How to Do Nothing: Resisting the Attention Economy*, Melville House, Brooklyn, New York, 2019

Packer, William and Newcomb, Tessa, *Mary Newcomb: Drawing from Observation*, Crane Kalman Gallery, London, 2018

Pliny the Elder, *Natural History: A Selection* translated by John Healey, Penguin Classics, London, 1991

Purdy, Jedediah, *After Nature: A Politics for the Anthropocene,* Harvard University Press, Cambridge, Massachusetts, 2015

Ritvo, Harriet, *The Dawn of Green: Manchester, Thirlmere, and Modern Environmentalism*, University of Chicago Press, Chicago, Illinois, 2009

Solnit, Rebecca, *Hope in the Dark: Untold Histories, Wild Possibilities*, Canongate Canons, Canongate Books, Edinburgh, 2016

Thoreau, Henry David, *Walden*, Macmillan Collector's Library, Pan Macmillan, London, 2016

West, Thomas, *A Guide to the Lakes: Dedicated to the Lovers of Landscape Studies, and to All Who Have Visited, or Intend to Visit, the Lakes in Cumberland, Westmorland, and Lancashire*, Forgotten Books, London, 2019

White, Gilbert, *The Natural History of Selborne*, Wordsworth Classics, Wordsworth Editions, Ware, Hertfordshire, 1989

Whitlock, Ralph, *Rare and Extinct Birds of Britain*, Phoenix House, London, 1953

Williams, Terry Tempest, *Leap*, Vintage, Penguin Books, London, 2001

Films

Kiss the Ground, directed by Rebecca Tickell and Josh Tickell, Big Picture Ranch, 2020

Honeyland, directed by Tamara Kotevska and Ljubomir Stefanov, Trice Films and Apolo Media, 2019

I am Greta, directed by Nathan Grossman, B-Reel Films, 2020

Index